Praise for

ROLL BACK THE WORLD

"Poignant and filled with unrelenting dedication to her sister's plight, the author sensitively narrates a family's search for alternative mental health care, the physical and emotional price it pays, and the sheer goodness of caring professionals and neighbors. Peppered with poetry and letters, this is an important memoir."

—RABBI DR. TIRZAH FIRESTONE, author of *Wounds into Wisdom: Healing Intergenerational Jewish Trauma*, 2020 Nautilus Book Award: Gold in Psychology

". . . a riveting, courageous and highly personal account of a descent into madness and the mental health system's sorely misguided response. . . By training her sharp eye not only on her sister's sad struggle but also on the complexity of the surrounding family situation, Deborah Kasdan opens a window to a time when psychiatry was emboldened by the advent of new drugs that turned out way more harmful than expected."

—PETER STASTNY, psychiatrist, filmmaker, and a co-author of *The Lives They Left Behind: Suitcases from a State Hospital Attic*

"This raw, real and loving memoir spotlights the loss and responsibility felt by one family when serious mental illness strikes. It is told through the eyes of a sister who struggles to understand and help, but also live her own life while her sister, a gifted poet, disappears behind the symptoms of schizophrenia. Read it also for a glimpse into the decades of shifting attitudes and theories toward mental illness as well as the heartbreaking effects on the author and her family, whose enduring love keeps them struggling to help against devastating odds and stigma."

—RANDYE KAYE, author of *Ben Behind His Voices: One Family's Journey from the Chaos of Schizophrenia to Hope*

ROLL BACK
THE WORLD

ROLL BACK
THE WORLD

A Sister's Memoir

DEBORAH KASDAN

SHE WRITES PRESS

Published 2023
Printed in the United States of America
Print ISBN: 978-1-64742-571-5
E-ISBN: 978-1-64742-572-2
Library of Congress Control Number: 2023908005

For information, address:
She Writes Press
1569 Solano Ave #546
Berkeley, CA 94707

Interior design by Stacey Aaronson

She Writes Press is a division of SparkPoint Studio, LLC.

To Barry, Anita and Diana

Stranger, if you passing meet me and desire to speak to me,
why should you not speak to me?
And why should I not speak to you?

—WALT WHITMAN

AUTHOR'S NOTE

For narrative purposes I have recreated scenes and dialogue in a way that convey what I understand to be the underlying truth of my story. Where possible I have cross-checked memories with friends and siblings to fill in gaps and mitigate the effects of time and subjectivity. Mostly I have depended on family documents and letters, which I quote in italics.

I have changed the names of a few people to respect their privacy.

TABLE OF CONTENTS

PART I

Beginnings

PROLOGUE

I will never forget Rachel's return from Israel.

She walked into our house with her blazing blue eyes set off by newly bronzed skin. She was nineteen then, her limbs sculpted by ten months planting and harvesting potatoes, cotton, citrus, and melons. Her striped sleeveless dress with its white rope belt looped lightly around her newly slender waist. Her face, glowing with the light of the desert sun, dazzled friends who came by to welcome her home. Her worldliness, her talk of Walt Whitman and Henry Miller created indelible charisma and maybe, I hoped, even reflected on me, her younger sister. All that beauty and sophistication. And, oh, her poetry:

> In delicate aroma
> I walked the beach at night
> Where the moon
> Joined sand into sea
> And the waves rolled back the world.

Rachel wrote those lines soon after she came back from her kibbutz just a mile from the shores of the Mediterranean. In the northwest of Israel, in the Galilee, she found romance and adventure even while she dug deep within herself to understand what she wanted from life and art and love, the themes she explored in her poems.

Within three years of her return, everything changed. A friend realized that Rachel was hearing frightening voices as they boarded a plane to Montreal. She called our parents, who picked Rachel up and brought her to the emergency room.

The diagnosis, I learned some months later, was schizophrenia. I couldn't absorb the shock of losing my brilliant big sister to this terrifying disease. Then came the aftershocks and the pain of loving a sister who couldn't find a place to live in this world. How I wanted to see her on that shore where the moonbeams and waves of her poetry held her safe. How I wanted to roll back all the indignities she endured because nobody was able to understand her disease.

Rachel died thirty-six years—and many hospitalizations— after that first psychotic break. She was fifty-nine. I felt some consolation knowing that during her final years she lived on her own terms. She was able to live free at last. But so much was lost. Her health and beauty, huge swaths of intelligence and creative power. And worst of all, the joy of family life.

I once saw a crater out West. The guide told us a meteor collision deposited lithium in the ground, and it leeched into the town's water system. Happily, the effects were beneficial; according to him, the townspeople had unusually low rates of depression. The meteor that hit us, the Goodman family, had the opposite effect. No healing powers at all. Just destruction. Guilt and estrangement. Hopelessness and depression. Stigma and blame.

Rachel was twenty-two when she was first hospitalized. She lived for decades separated from her family, friends, and the mainstream of society. She hardly understood what happened to her, or why people locked her up, abandoned, and rejected her. She tried to hold on to her dreams; delusions were her refuge. God, how I hope they comforted her. I never knew how to explain to her what happened. How could I? I didn't understand either. Even now, I'm still trying to figure out where in the universe this disaster came from.

What I do know after living in Rachel's poetry and in her journals: she loved life, she loved me. I know now that Rachel never blamed me for my inability to help her or for leaving her behind. She would have understood my starts and stops and been glad I found a way through them. Now when I sit down to write, I still hear the clatter of her typewriter ringing across the bedroom of our youth.

Within weeks of Rachel's funeral, I felt an urge to tell her story—how illness deprived her of the life she set out to lead and how she survived the ignorance of those who had no way to help her. Not professionals. Not her family. Not me.

That spring, after her death, I couldn't concentrate. The memory of her tugged at me. As the crocus buds pushed through the borders of my backyard, a new feeling pulsed in me. Rachel had always been our family's writer, our poet. Did I dare to take that space? How could I claim her role, her one great power that even severe illness could not take from her? Did I really want to? I hesitated. I started and stopped. After what happened to Rachel, creativity felt like a dangerous place for me to be.

But the desire stayed. I still wanted to shine a light on Rachel's life, both the horror and the wonder of it. For fifteen more years I struggled to tell Rachel's story, off and on. My life was so full already. My corporate job required daily attention. And then a flood of joys—four grandchildren in seven years—tumbled into my life. But it wasn't as though I didn't have time to write. I did. I tried. I got facts down, but not the heart of my story about Rachel.

I studied cartons of family letters, photos, and documents. I sorted and skimmed them. I scrutinized and scanned those that surprised or moved me. Always, I wanted to know more. I sent off for twelve years of Rachel's hospital records. Now I had two more heavy cartons, thousands of pages copied front and back. After a few months poring through the suffering they documented, I realized they didn't get me closer to the heart of what I needed to write—how Rachel lived in me.

Through all of this, I talked to a therapist about the guilt and shame I felt at not being able to save my sister. It wasn't fair, I told her, that I had an abundance of choices in my life while Rachel had none. Couldn't I have done something to mitigate Rachel's situation and ease her pain? She reminded me many times that—as poorly as schizophrenia is understood today—people hardly knew anything at all when Rachel was diagnosed in 1965. Experts had no clue as to what caused it. Doctors didn't know how to treat it without bringing on symptoms as terrible as the disease. No matter how many books and articles I read, there was no way I could have known what to do. Nobody did.

Finally, I not only heard what my therapist said, I felt it. One day, in a flash, I saw how the guilt I carried inside me, uncomfortable as it was, served only to keep my pain at a distance. Now that I could identify those feelings and face them, I could let them go.

In the summer of 2012, when my brother and I moved our mother out of her St. Louis home, we dug up boxes of family letters and documents from her basement and shipped them to my house in Connecticut. There my mother would live out her life—five more years— with my husband and me. Occasionally I heard her on the phone telling friends I was writing about our family. She sounded proud of me, though she never asked to see my work. She knew that what I wrote was painful, so I appreciated the space she gave me and the approval she sent my way. When my mother died, I renewed my commitment to finish. Her death freed me to write my most disturbing memories. Not that I would have shared them with her, but they would have clung to me, and she would have sensed a distance between us.

Finally, my story took shape.

PARADISE LOST

My father made the desk for me when I started high school. He set an eight-foot length of plywood atop two stands of wooden drawers. The surface ran along the wall, tapering to an angle at the window with the air conditioner. I liked its unusual shape, and even more its colors. The plywood stain matched the green painted cabinet case. The drawers were yellow and orange. I picked the colors myself before my father went to pick up supplies at Central Hardware. When he came back with the paint I requested, I told him exactly how I wanted the sunny accent colors to alternate on the drawers and knobs. I was glad nobody else got involved in the design. Rachel, with whom I shared a room, happened to be away at the time. Michael and Julie, my younger siblings, had their own rooms. My mother was happy to delegate. "If you like it, I like it," she said. I did like it. It was just what I wanted. Jazzy. Unique.

One night I sat at the desk with my textbook open to *Paradise Lost*. Next to it was a spiral notebook with the draft of an essay due in two days. I wanted Mrs. Gottlieb, my world literature teacher, to like it. Augusta Gottlieb. Everything about her name fit. Her first name and her last. August as in distinguished and venerable. She was wise and gentle, with reassuring wrinkles around her eyes and impish cheeks.

In my paper, I was struggling to explain the meaning of Lucifer's rebellion. I wanted to say how noble he was, despite his evil aims; how Milton admired his villain and thought the world was better off because both sides battled so hard, regardless of who won or lost. Ugh. Really? It occurred to me I sounded like a gym coach. A grown-up. Way too conciliatory for my age. Not the rebel I aspired to be. I certainly dressed the part. I wore my hair straight down my back, beatnik style, and shopped at the Army-Navy store for denim work shirts and cotton turtlenecks. But I didn't indulge in sex and drugs. I didn't drop out of school. I wanted to study hard and have my papers come back marked with As in red teacher ink.

Although I had been working on it for a while and now had only two days to figure out where the essay was headed, I still wasn't sure what to say. As I sat there trying so hard to understand Milton's universe, I didn't expect to see cracks of chaos opening in my own. But suddenly I heard bed springs squeal and turned to look. Rachel had flopped on her bed, right behind me. I folded my notebook and pushed it to the back of the desk, glad for the interruption. I needed a break. She greeted me abruptly, with a question. "Debby, did you see my notebook? The blue one?" Rachel did her writing on prepunched, loose-leaf pages that snapped into a small two-ring binder. Its blue cover felt like linen, nubby and intriguing. Rachel never let me read the journal pages, but she sometimes showed me poems. They came from her soul. Lyrical. Anguished.

Rachel was the real rebel. But she didn't bother to cultivate the look. She kept her hair cut shoulder length. She didn't shop for denim work shirts or hoop earrings. She made bold plans and sudden moves, which resulted in big arguments with our parents. What she did was exciting, but scary sometimes, too.

I pointed to the suitcase on the floor at the foot of her bed. "Rachel, the notebook must be in your suitcase. It's not on the desk. I didn't move it."

"Excuse me for asking," she responded. "I wasn't blaming you." She leaned over and rummaged through the suitcase. She picked up the notebook buried at the bottom and took out some blank sheets.

"Do you have any new poems," I asked her. "Are you still writing?"

"Don't worry about it!" She sat on the side of her bed, with her notebook in her lap. Okay, I thought. I get it. Don't pry. Don't pressure her. I waited, hanging on to any opportunity to talk with her.

Rachel lit a cigarette and sat on her bed next to the ashtray on the end table. She was twenty and had travelled to the other side of the world. I was just seventeen and still in high school. Now, two years after her return from Israel, Rachel was not happy about being home. She was no longer bronze and thin, and I could no longer see the muscles that had hauled fruit and potatoes from the fields. After moves to New York, San Francisco, and back again to St. Louis, she looked pale and lumpy. Stocky. Her eyes, once so round and luminous, narrowed when she talked.

Rachel had something other than poetry on her mind. She suddenly launched into an explanation of her reasons for going to California. "Carl told me there was more going on in San Francisco than New York." So that's why she went, I realized. For a boy. She had met Carl in her building on the Lower East Side in New York City. Clearly she was infatuated, since she followed him across the country. Rachel didn't share the details of her relationship with Carl, and I didn't expect her to. She was always circumspect with me about her love life, as though to honor my innocence. I was happy to hear anything she had to say, especially now, when she tended to be so withdrawn, so quiet most of the time. Why did she have to be so damned distant? I didn't take her silence personally. I knew she withdrew to avoid uncomfortable conversations, especially with our parents. She got angry when they asked her to explain her plans.

"A bunch of us lived in this house," she told me now. "The people were okay but the guys there were doing this obnoxious thing—they call it mind-fucking." She tapped her cigarette, dusting the end table. I understood mind-fucking to be emotionally hurtful one-upmanship, similar to what our parents did when they "analyzed" our behavior using the jargon of social work (my father's profession) or psychoanalytic concepts (which my mother seemed to have picked up from reading a biography of Freud). Not the usual criticism you get from your parents. More like what friends tell you so you can become a more enlightened person in a shitty world.

Funny that Rachel should complain about mind invasions, I thought. She's the one who got in trouble for putting kids into trances during recess when she was ten years old and for the next couple of years tried to get everybody she knew to let her hypnotize them. She even gave them post-hypnotic suggestions. I let her dangle her watch in front of my face, but I made sure it didn't work on me. You have to believe in hypnosis to fall into a trance. I didn't believe. I didn't want her to have occult powers over me.

"Everybody did mescaline," she said, flicking her cigarette

toward the ash tray. I imagined Rachel and her friends in a candle-lit room in a Victorian house in Haight-Ashbury. Chipped ceramic mugs with coffee, or straw-clad chianti, resting on stacks of books. Arms and legs strewn across mattresses laid out on the floor. Intensely colored visions beaming through the room as they talked about the meaning of life and the states of each others' minds.

I wanted to know what mescaline was like, but Rachel clammed up when I asked. Is she protecting herself? Or is she protecting me? Does she think I'm afraid to know more? Maybe I am. Finally, I heard her voice again, low and throaty. She had something urgent to tell me. "In the park near my office, I saw two men. They followed me from New York." The words made no sense, just a terrible noise. They hurt. Like cymbals clashing close to my ears. The sound kept ringing, and I realized Rachel wasn't kidding. She was really upset. She was convinced that two men trailed her from New York to California.

"But why would they do that?" I asked her. "Why would two men follow you all that way?" I saw in her flashing eyes, which had locked onto mine, that she was really frightened. I was terrified too. For the first time I was afraid that my parents were right when they talked about Rachel's problems.

Rachel looked away and I was glad she had broken off eye contact. It was too painful to hold. I pulled my pillow to my chest to still my racing heart. My sister was disappearing. Would she ever again send letters from overseas? Soak her oboe reeds in glasses of water? Write her poetry? I needed to know she'd come back, her mind intact. I couldn't let her leave me now.

"Why would the men follow you all that way?" The question hung between us before landing with a sickening thud in the narrow space between our beds. "Never mind," she said, snapping the conversation shut, like the sides of her blue suitcase. She waved my question away, the glow of her cigarette making figure eights in our dimly lit room. I said nothing, helpless to contradict her. I felt her flailing, unmoored from reality. I didn't know how to haul her home. Rachel, I wanted to say, you're my big sister. You fought battles that made it easier for me. The first child is for practice, my mother used to tell me, and she wasn't entirely joking. Don't leave me, Rachel. Don't disappear into being crazy.

For the past two years, my parents had tried to find out what was wrong with Rachel. My mother told me a psychiatrist said she had a mental illness that occurred more often in young men than women. What does that mean? I'd wondered. Rebellion? Wanderlust? Why is that a disease? But my mother didn't see it that way and insisted that there was something wrong with Rachel, even though she couldn't give me any good answers about what it was. "The doctor said Rachel doesn't fit into any of the usual categories." That's all I could get out of her, and I wondered what she wasn't telling me. Now at last I knew. She didn't have a name for it, but it was clearly something bad.

Rachel had no trouble getting a job as a legal secretary when she had moved to San Francisco. That wasn't surprising. I had seen her fingers flying across her typewriter. She typed a hundred words and more per minute, without mistakes. I imagined she even made up poetry in her head while she typed legal documents.

But then one day the lawyer she worked for called my parents to tell them to bring Rachel home. As usual, my parents didn't tell me the details. Why did he have to call our parents? I figured he'd overreacted to her behavior or disapproved of her lifestyle. If he had just fired her, she could have gotten another job in San Francisco. Why did she have to come back to St. Louis and be miserable and make everybody else miserable too? I shouldn't have to worry about her, shouldn't have to try to understand why her boss wanted her to go home to her parents. I was enjoying my senior year in high school. I loved my classes, my teachers, my two best girlfriends and the offbeat social scene at folk dancing. It was my turn now to take off. But my parents were too busy trying to figure out what to do with my older sister to help me decide where I should apply to college.

For months I had argued on my sister's behalf, urging my parents to cut her some slack so she could choose her own way of life. I knew all the counterculture arguments—that people can't be considered insane in an insane world (the arms race and nuclear testing)—and I had thought they might be right. But now, seeing the fear and conviction in Rachel's eyes, I understood why everyone was so worried about her. I saw the reality of how paranoid and delusional she had become. Insanity so real and palpable I could touch it. My resistance to pinning her with a label collapsed, like a pile of children's pickup sticks.

I was tired and wondered what I could say to Rachel that would make a difference but could think of nothing. Finally, Rachel broke the silence and blurted out her demand. "Don't tell Mom and Dad what I said." She caught my gaze and held it until I agreed.

"I won't say a thing," I promised. More than ever, I wanted her to trust me.

The streetlamp shone through our half-shaded window, urging me to keep going into the night. But I was too confused to concentrate, too frightened by the sudden abyss between me and Rachel to think any more about my essay. I took out my contact lenses and went to bed.

Rachel left the room and went downstairs. I could hear the refrigerator door squeak and Rachel pacing back and forth in the living room. I needed sleep. When I leaned over to pull the shade to the sill, I saw the pine tree in our front lawn listing toward the roof above our room. My father had pruned it a year ago and taken down its secondary limb, near the front door. When my mother came home and saw what he did, she was furious. Her response seemed all out of proportion to the severity of his crime.

"What's so horrible?" I asked her.

"It's ruined," she wailed. "He cut off a whole limb. It was beautiful. The shade is gone. Just look at it. It's all crooked. It's disgusting." The loss of shade and symmetry was minor to me, but my mother wouldn't back down from her fury. She criticized my father for months. She mourned the loss of that tree limb as though it were her own arm. If only my mother had howled about Rachel and, by her example, showed me it was okay to do so. But the abyss was too dark. Too dangerous. In our family of six, we talked and argued about what to do. We didn't scream. What was the use? We never agreed on who to yell at. I tiptoed around my grief, careful not to step into it and sink. We cried alone. Looking back, I wish I had wailed like my mother mourning the branches of her pine tree. We should have cried our hearts out and shouted together at the demons that seem to have lopped off so much of Rachel's mind.

How Rachel yearned for moonlight and motion. When I think about the freedom she lost, the loneliness she endured, I want to weep. To carry her to another place, another time, where some trusted adult could show her how to protect herself from the fears and delusions that overtook her.

LODESTAR

Both Rachel and I were born in Cleveland, our father's hometown—she in 1943, and I three years later. When I was a year old, we moved to Detroit, leaving our grandparents, aunts, uncles, and cousins behind. My earliest memories of Rachel date to our time in Detroit in 1949.

Here, we lived in an apartment building with a grassy front lawn and a sidewalk where, some time before my third birthday, I learned to ride a big, chain-driven tricycle, my legs just long enough to reach its pedals. Now, however, I was inside, and the house was oddly still except for the sun winking at me through the living room window. My baby brother was sleeping, and my mother was busy. I couldn't go outside until Rachel got home. I waited eagerly for my playmate to return.

"When will Rachel be home?" I asked Mommy. She was folding diapers that she had unpinned from the clothesline in our yard. They were long and flappy and smelled like the wind outside.

"When the big hand points to the six," she answered, pointing to the bottom of the round clock on the wall above the sofa.

I went to the window on the opposite wall and stood on tiptoe to see outside. Tall trees arched over the black cars going down the big street, and bushes made curvy green bulges by the houses.

I looked back at the clock to see the big hand. I didn't know that number. The little one was on the number that says three, three like me. It never moved. I ignored the crayons and newspapers Mommy left for me to draw on. I didn't want to make pictures by myself.

I wanted to play outside. Where was Rachel? I went to the kitchen and looked for Mommy. She took me back to the living room and pointed to the clock again and left me there. I looked at the space between the thick black sticks. Why are they called hands? They don't have fingers. They can't hold anything.

The next time I looked, a group of children were walking together on the sidewalk. I was so happy to see my sister's plaid coat that I jumped into the air. Rachel left the group and turned to the narrow sidewalk in our front yard.

"Mommy," I yelled, "she's here." I ran to the front hall to greet her.

Rachel walked past me but didn't stop. She kept walking ahead, into the kitchen, until she got to Mommy. I went and stood behind my sister while they talked. Rachel shook her head, and her wavy brown hair flew around beneath the barrette on the side.

I watched and waited and listened. I wanted to grab the folds of my sister's pinafore dress with the green butterflies and pull her to me before the baby woke up and she went over to see him. I wanted her to draw on the newspaper with me. To help me cut and paste. I learned how to wait for Rachel by learning to tell time.

A few months later we moved to Boston. Rachel was six. I walked with her down Blue Hill Avenue to the Franklin Park Zoo, where I climbed the pile of flat pink rocks in front of the elephant house. Our mother was way behind us, pushing Michael in his stroller. Before we got to Franklin Avenue, where I expected to turn, Rachel motioned me to follow her into a vacant lot where weeds sprouted from cracks in the asphalt. I didn't think this was the right way to go, but Rachel was firm. This is a shortcut, I reminded myself. We get to the zoo faster if we walk this way. It's the *diagonal*, she explained, as though to make the decision official. Diagonal. I loved the sound of that word. And I loved how a diagonal turns an otherwise useless lot into two triangles with a shortcut between them.

Rachel was my lodestar. She showed me the way through time and space. If only we had had more time and more space to be together. We would have drawn on sketch pads perched on camp stools in the woods and hiked mountain trails with backpacks. We would have plotted tours through urban streets. Played four-handed piano pieces or figured a way to join her oboe to my viola. We would have discussed love and life, traveling to see each other, no matter how widely our paths and lifestyles diverged. But we didn't get to do any of that. Somehow my sister, the guide of my earliest years, fell into a black hole that swallowed her future, and the future we would have had together.

In her thirties, during one of her many hospitalizations, Rachel sent me a slim loose-leaf binder, its laminated cover decorated with swirls of blue. She had typed out stories on a manual typewriter she found at the hospital. She poked out three holes on each page for the circular metal rings. "Keep it for me," she said.

I did keep it because I knew how much it meant to her to make sure her work didn't get lost in the revolving door of her hospitalizations. But it wasn't until many years later that I could bring myself to read it. When I finally did, I found that amid the stories of lost love, despair, and futility, Rachel had included a brief memoir describing the three years we lived in Boston—memories that revealed the precocity and sensitivity of the little girl she had been: *Boston, Massachusetts, where my family moved to when I was six. First impressions: the strange Boston accent, and the strange school—I was a second semester first-grader.* I recalled the William Lloyd Garrison elementary school exactly the way Rachel did. You waited in the courtyard for the opening bell to ring and then marched through halls monitored by older students. The massive doors locked once school started, and if you were late you had to ring the office to get in. We never thought that was for our protection, but only to intimidate and punish us for being late.

Unlike Rachel, I hadn't noticed the broad As and missing Rs of Boston speech. Maybe because I was new to talking when we moved there. Or maybe my persistent ear infections masked the accent. Soon after we moved to Boston, when I was still in nursery school, I had to have my tonsils and adenoids removed. When I woke up in the hospital on the morning of my surgery, the nurse scolded me for wetting the bed, but my mother yelled at her for yelling at me, and then the nurse was nicer. My mother never got mad at me about that. She had been a bedwetter too.

After the operation, my father walked through the door holding a whole container of orange sherbet. "It will make your throat feel better," he told me with a big grin, and my eyes popped at the sight of that Howard Johnson treat. All for me. No big sister or little brother around to share it with. Not the ice cream, not the special attention my parents showered on me.

Rachel and I were best friends with sisters who lived in the duplex across the street. They were the same age as we were. Rachel paired off with Janet and I with Carol. We were a double set of inseparable companions. For me they were the best part of our three years in Boston. In winter when it snowed, Janet and Carol showed us where to take our sleds—to nearby Blue Hill Avenue, the main street in our neighborhood. Drivers stayed home or made room for us—though it seemed to me then that the cars magically disappeared—and the four of us stood at the crest before swooping downhill. School days, Rachel and Janet led Carol and me on the half-mile walk to our school. After school I held hands with Carol when we crossed the street to go back and forth between our houses. I watched her freckled face, round like mine, break into laughter when my baby brother turned his bucket upside down to splash our shoes with water.

I don't remember being upstairs in their house, but Rachel did, and reading what she wrote about the view still stuns me: *Janet pointed out, through a window in her bedroom, Boston Harbor, soon after we met; it must have been a clear day, because I looked for it again, but couldn't get past the trees and rooftops. Another time, from a hill in a farther neighborhood, seeing the golden dome of the city hall, wondering at its distance and intensity.* In her journal Rachel explained how she and Janet developed a secret finger code that was all worked out in their heads but rarely worked in the classroom. And how she maneuvered the cavernous halls of the city art

19

museum on her way to her art class by remembering the locations of statues and paintings and artifacts. Her typewritten words jogged my memory of the plays and talent shows she and Janet produced, the treasure hunts they set up for Carol and me, with clues hidden throughout the neighborhood.

Once a week, after dinner, we went to their house to watch "I Remember Mama." We sat with Carol and Janet on the sofa to watch a family in San Francisco on a fuzzy black-and-white screen. I loved everyone in that TV family, but especially Dagmar, the younger sister. The older sister had to help their parents out of situations; they weren't used to the way things were done in America. My family, the Goodmans, were from the Midwest, not Sweden, but we too were newcomers. Rachel and I were lucky to have Boston natives as our best friends.

Rachel took care to prepare me for first grade. It wasn't going to be like kindergarten, where we got to spend our time coloring. Now, I would sit at a desk not a table. "If you want to talk, you have to raise your hand first and wait for the teacher to call on you," she warned me, her lips tightening. "Even to ask to go to the bathroom," she added. She looked me straight in the eyes when she told me, and I knew it had to be true.

But no sooner had I gotten used to all the rules at school than everything changed again. After three years in Boston, our parents announced we had to move because Dad had taken a new job in Indianapolis. Later I found out he was pushed out for integrating Black teenagers into the Friday night dances at the neighborhood community center; the board of directors told him he had no future with them.

I was sad about leaving Carol. I have a photo of myself in my winter coat and furry hat for the Boston winter, holding on to the lamppost on the corner opposite Carol's house and looking morose. The image brings back the dismal sense of loss that overtook me. I don't remember talking to Rachel about the move, about her having to leave Janet, but, reading her diary now, I can sense the simmering anger that began to define her.

In the fall of 1952, our father went to Indianapolis by himself to start his new job, so I didn't have to leave my best friend right away. I got to finish the first semester of first grade, and Rachel fourth grade. And from his post in the Midwest, he sent letters and gifts. I got a little wooden box to put on my dresser. It had three multi-patterned drawers—two short ones with a tasseled door to a little compartment next to them, and a long one on the bottom. The box was covered in a pattern of delicate bamboo plants and flowers. I didn't care about putting anything inside the drawers. It was enough to pull them open and think about my father.

Dad sent Rachel a book, *Little Rose of the Mesa*, and when she finished it, I picked it up. It had type large enough for me to read, and a black-and-white photograph in every chapter. I studied the photos and, with what I knew from all the Dick and Jane reading posters at school, learned what most of the words in the book meant. I had to figure them out in order to find out what happened: whether Rose would be able to help a lonely man named Earl reunite with the daughter he left back East when he took this lonely job digging in the ground for ancient Navajo treasures. I must have taught myself to read so I could make sure Rose was reunited with her father. That's what I wanted, too.

21

I expected Rachel to get mad at me for taking her book. But she didn't care. It was probably too easy for her anyway. She had others to discover. She and Janet, she wrote, *studied together, shared books . . . almost simultaneously became voracious readers.* Janet's parents wouldn't let her walk by herself (as Rachel was allowed to do) to the library branch near our house. But they took both girls downtown to the main library. Rachel breathed in the sights and sounds that made her long to know the world. She described how it thrilled her: *Seeing Boston, and [being] away from my family, just driving through downtown streets, fascinated.*

Once we joined my father in Indianapolis, multi-page letters flew back and forth between both sets of sister friends. Rachel would stay in touch longer than I and, even in her twenties, around the time her troubles started, planned a visit to Janet. She never forgot the friend who pointed out Boston Harbor from her bedroom window. She never forgot that brilliant view. Despite the future that was taken from her, despite years of confusion and isolation, Rachel never stopped searching for the grandeur and beauty she glimpsed one clear day above the rooftops in Boston. I also see in her journal, amidst her excitement about the golden city on the harbor, hints of something darker: *I was obsessed with the knowledge of the brevity of life. Proud of the thought that I could foresee death, and frightened. Often, my normal activities became shadows, an interruption to my own vast jealously guarded monologue.* Were these visions and shadows signifiers of the illness that descended a dozen years later? Or the musings of a sensitive child writ large in memory by the shock of subsequent events?

I didn't see Rachel shuddering at shadows in Boston. I

was too young. I was always too young to help her, even to understand her. And, because she still jealously guarded her inner monologue, I didn't know how terrified she was. Not then. Not for many years.

I wish I had known what a wonderful gift Rachel gave me when she entrusted her laminated notebook to me and wish I had told her so. I was too confused then by her illness to want to see into her mind, too scared of the chaos I might find there. So I didn't read it then, didn't know what it would reveal to me about her and about us. But now I bask in those words about our lives in Boston, the sun and the shadows. I cherish the shared memories about those three years with our sister friends in Boston. I am able to read them with an open heart, without fear or shame or sense of guilt. I can fly back in time and join her once again.

See It Shimmer

See it shimmer,
Gliding,
Rolling,
Catching light
Amidst the air,
Ever-changing,
Always moving,
Beauty that eludes all grasp.
Carried
By the winds and breezes,
Left
To thrive by chance
And luck,
While any moment
Death may come,
One prick!
The bubble
Is
No more.

—Rachel Goodman

EXILED IN INDIANA

We moved into a brand-new ranch house in a freshly dug subdivision on the outskirts of Indianapolis. Our lawn was nothing but a depressing quarter acre of mud. My father had bought the house while my mother was still in Boston, and when she first saw it, she said she would never have agreed to that location, so far from the center of town, but what could she do, the deed was done.

Speckles of green were starting to show from the grass seed Dad had planted in the mud. On the border with our neighbor, he put in a row of baby willow trees. Lining the front of the ranch house, along the walkway to the carport, was a red brick flower box planter filled with new shrubbery. That's where Rachel, Michael, and I kept the big green turtle we found crossing the road. But even it got bored after a week and crawled out of its new home, deserting us. The house remained tentative and lonely in its corner lot.

Rachel and I were lonely, too. We'd had to leave our best friends, and despite our letters back and forth, a gaping hole had opened in my life. On the playground at my new school, a girl came up to me, and I thought she wanted to be my friend. But then she asked me whether Jewish people had horns on their heads. The question stunned me. A sense of isolation sent me into free fall, as though sledding alone on a hill with no bottom. Nobody, not my mother or father or Rachel, could help me land safely.

Everything seemed flat and boring here in the Midwest. The houses. The fields that hadn't yet been turned into subdivisions. Even the way people talked. I missed the daily walk to school. I missed the trolley and the elephants at Franklin Park Zoo. The swan boats in the park downtown. The beach and ocean waves in the summer.

At least Rachel had made new friends. Every day after school she rode off on her bike to meet them. Michael had friends too. Little tow-headed boys right on our block who knocked on the door to see if he could play. Sometimes Rachel took me and Michael exploring. We rode our bikes to the outskirts of the development and climbed up unfinished staircases in roughly framed houses. But usually I stayed inside after school until my mother made me go outside. "Don't be a stick in the mud," she kept saying to me. She didn't understand how much more exciting life was in the books I read, and only let me take out four of them at a time during our weekly library visits. For one of my eight days of Chanukah presents, she gave me a little figurine: a ceramic book with a smiling worm sticking its head out.

"Nothing exciting ever happens here," complained Rachel while we waited for lunch one winter day.

My mother finished draining water from the macaroni noodles, then came around and stood at the end of the redwood-stained picnic table we used in our kitchen nook. "I have a big surprise," she announced, setting the pot down. I could tell from the smoothness of the skin between her eyes that she wasn't talking about moving again. I hoped that meant she had a surprise that would make us happy.

With the slant of the winter sun coming through the window and lighting up our kitchen nook, we three children sat waiting for our mother's announcement. I glanced up at Rachel, sitting opposite me. Everything about her seemed intensely alive, like colors at the bottom of the lake, or green leaves in the woods after a rain. Her hair was darker and shinier than mine, closer to black than to my medium brown. Her eyes were bluer and more piercing than my greenish ones. She was silent now, staring through the kitchen window toward the row of willow saplings that my father promised would give us shade and privacy someday. She didn't seem interested in Mom's secret.

Michael sat next to me. His hair was cut close, in a "burr" as it was called then. His big brown eyes peered from between long eyelashes. "What's the surprise?" he demanded.

"It's something you can see on me."

"Your eyebrows?" I asked.

"Your nose?" Michael giggled.

This was beginning to sound like the song on our Pete Seeger record: "Put your finger on your ear and leave it there a year."

Rachel sighed. "Nothing exciting ever happens here," she repeated.

"You're wrong. Something exciting *is* going to happen," our mother said, as she smoothed the cotton blouse hanging loosely over her stomach. "It's here."

We stared at her hands. At her stomach.

"We're going to have a baby."

Later she told me, when I was bored and unhappy with my

siblings, "When the baby is born, you won't be in the middle anymore," as though she was having the baby just for me.

Big Eagle Camp was where we spent the next two summers after we moved to Indianapolis. Our father worked there as the director. In June 1953 the five of us headed out together for the first time in our blue Willys sedan. It was stuffed with all the summer clothes and supplies that Dad hadn't yet driven out there. "You'll like camp and you'll like the Wegs," Dad said. He turned his head to talk to me in the back seat.

"Who are they?" I asked. Tired of defending my space on the crowded seat between my two siblings, I was glad for the change of topic.

"Ed Weg is the assistant director," my father answered, still looking at me. He told me they had two children, a girl about my age, and her baby brother, Johnny, who was deaf— a fact I found fascinating. And alarming.

"Mort, will you keep your eyes on the road?" my mother snapped. My father had a habit of turning his head to talk while driving, and becoming so absorbed in what he was saying that he'd forget to watch where he was going. But Mom's driving made Dad yell too. He got distracted, but she took risks. Like the time she hit the railing on an icy bridge where she didn't bother to slow down. Or made U-turns on busy streets. Years later, when I was nineteen, a policeman stopped her while I was in the car with her; she grabbed my pocketbook and showed him my license because she didn't have her wallet with her. She didn't miss a beat, but my heart did.

Driving to Big Eagle, Dad turned his attention back to the

road ahead, and Mom took over the explanation. She said that Johnny was deaf because his mother got sick with German measles while she was pregnant with him. Our mother, seven months pregnant herself, assured us she had already had that illness, and that once you got it you couldn't get it again. I wondered how her body kept track of its diseases, just as I wondered what genes were made of. My mother had told me genes gave Rachel and me blue eyes like Dad, and Michael brown eyes like her. Nobody could tell me what these genes were made of or what color the baby's eyes would be.

Only a few people were at camp when we arrived. We parked in front of the director's cabin not far from the swimming pool. We passed the mess hall, and I could hear the clanging of big metal bins and bowls and voices of the kitchen staff as they set up the kitchen. Earl Beeler, a local farmer who managed the property, came by to help us open up our cabin. "Y'all come on over to my place when you're settled," he said, before he and my father went off to confer on their camp opening plans.

Over the next week, staff and then campers arrived at Big Eagle. Rachel, Michael, and I moved into our separate cabins with counselors and bunkmates. I wasn't even seven, and Michael was just five, which made both of us too young for sleep-away camp. But with our parents close by we were allowed to participate. I went back and forth from my cabin to my parents' at will, especially when I needed dry sheets. My mother let me hang out on the front lawn with her while she folded fresh ones. I was older than when I had my tonsillectomy, but she still didn't get upset when I wet my bed. She was worried about something else. All the grown-ups were. Those first weeks of June, I heard them talking about Julius and Ethel and demonstrations and appeals. As summer heat rolled in, I sat on the grass listening to Mom and Julia Weg, Ed's wife, talking in low, grave voices. I yanked out dandelions from the grass and tied them together. Julia glanced down at me from her lawn chair and then over at my mother, who finally told me what was happening. "The Rosenbergs were executed last night. The government said they were spies." I knew about the electric chair, but only for murderers. I asked for explanations. "The government just wanted someone to blame for the Korean War," said my mother. "And they picked the Rosenbergs because they are communists."

One month later Ed stood at the microphone in the mess hall and announced that fighting had ended in Korea. Everyone cheered. I couldn't forget about the Rosenbergs, who got the blame for the whole war. At some point that summer I learned they had two boys, the same ages as Rachel and me. The thought of those boys haunted me. Several years later I would weep over the book of death row letters the Rosenbergs wrote to their sons. I would try to understand how parents could choose to die for their ideals instead of taking care of their kids.

I didn't talk to Rachel about current events at camp. We stayed in cabins on opposite sides of the creek, and the bonds between us loosened. Like molecules of warm air in a container, we floated free of each other but stayed connected.

Rachel had things on her mind I didn't understand. I sensed it when I met her on the rocks in the creek and she let me hang out for a little while with her and her friends. I saw some of them wore bras when they took off their shirts because no boys came through this part of the woods. One girl told me I could take my shirt off anywhere I wanted because I was little. But next year I wouldn't be able to. I would have to cover up just as the older girls did. I relished this last summer of bare-chested privilege.

For me, Big Eagle Camp almost made up for the misery of leaving Boston. It was a sleepaway camp in Zionsville, a rural town an hour outside of Indianapolis. It had a glow as golden as the painted rocks the counselors hid in the creek bed for campers to find on our special "gold rush" days. I threw myself into camp activities. I marched to breakfast through the woods and afterwards, while dishes were being bussed, learned all the words to "Sixteen Tons," "The Ship Titanic" and the entire repertoire of camp songs. During the wait outside the mess hall for dinner, I tossed intricately carved Lummi sticks back and forth with another camper, in and out, up and around, to the pulse of what we called an "Indian chant." I hiked with my bunkmates along the side of the cornfield to the swinging rope bridge. The vertical climb, the swaying planks under my feet, exhilarated me. It was my favorite adventure, and I suddenly felt fearless. I shed my books. I shed my loneliness.

I hardly ever worried that anything bad could happen, except for the times when my bunkmates went into a huddle to choose someone to pick on, and I feared my turn was next. But it never was. Maybe my special status as the camp director's daughter protected me.

Two summers in a row I had the same counselor, Lynn, in 1953 and '54. Lynn loved Len, the swimming director, and I loved to see them together. Sometimes I fantasized that I was their daughter. A soft web of protection reached from my parents' staff cabin to Len at the swimming pool to Lynn at my bunk on the far side of camp.

That first summer, in the middle of August, Dad took Mom back to Indianapolis to have the baby, leaving Rachel, Michael, and me under the supervision of the Wegs. We weren't allowed to go home for a week because a virus had been going around camp and the doctor said we could infect the baby. Finally, when our quarantine was lifted, Dad picked us up to take us home. Rachel got to sit up front next to Dad; Michael and I sprawled in the back. When we arrived at the house, I sat up for a glimpse of the big surprise. And there she was—my mother standing under the noon sun right in front of the door. Before giving us hugs, she held out the bundle resting in her arms. "Here's your sister Julie." I was so proud. My mother had asked me earlier what girls' names I liked and I said Julie. That was the one my parents gave her.

Julie had only a little bit of hair then, but in the weeks and months that followed, a mass of dark curls soon sprouted around her head. Her soft baby smells and squeals delighted me, and I loved waking her from her naps when my mother said it was time for her to eat. I'd bend my head near hers and inhale her pinkness, then tousle her bountiful curls until her eyes opened and she peered back at me. I even liked helping my mother by folding her diapers while she slept.

Over the following year, Julie's eyes turned a beautiful dark brown, making an even split in our family's eye coloring. Dad, Rachel, and I all had blue or blue-green eyes; Mom, Michael and Julie all brown. But Julie's sprawl of curls was entirely her own—no one else in the family had hair like that. When we were out shopping, women would stare and admire her. Some even asked if she had had a permanent. I was astonished they thought anyone would do that to a baby. Didn't they know about recessive genes?

Rachel, Michael, and I came up with a crawling contest. We pushed the toys on the floor aside and lined ourselves up on one side of the living room. Sitting in front of the foam rubber sofa with the wrought iron frame, we'd lean over to coax Julie to crawl across the room. "Come here. Come to me!" The first sibling Julie came to, the first one whose leg she touched, was the winner, the one she loved the most. Julie's antics, and the games she sparked, helped make my new home less flat and friendless. Even Rachel seemed to find life a little exciting with Julie around.

FELLOW TRAVELERS

We lived in Indianapolis in the 1950s, during the height of the Cold War. "It's the home of the John Birch Society," Mom told me and Rachel soon after we moved there. "And it has a lot of people in the Ku Klux Klan." Her voice was heavy with dire implications, and although I was only six years old and didn't fully grasp what she was saying, I knew those people were bad. "So don't sing Weaver songs except at home and at camp." She was talking about political protest songs like "Die Gedanken Sind Frei," Apparently Big Eagle was the one place in the area where thoughts as well as bodies were able to run free.

I've often been asked whether my father was in the service when I mention all the cities where I lived. The response I always gave was the one I was given as a child: because my father worked at organizations known as Jewish Community Centers, and most cities had only one, he had to keep moving to new cities to get a promotion. At some point that reason stopped making sense to me. Boston had a large Jewish community with many Jewish organizations. Why did he have to limit himself to Jewish Community Centers? Why did we have to go to Indianapolis?

My father was a teenager during the Great Depression, a first-generation American. And while his family lived comfortably in a Cleveland suburb owing to his father's success as an industrial designer, my father became radicalized in college.

"Was he a communist?" I asked my mother, late in her life, when she had little to do but answer my incessant questions.

"He joined the party when he was a student," she admitted. She was talking about the Communist Party of America. "But just for a little while."

Mom wholeheartedly shared her husband's politics, and for many years it seemed to be what kept their marriage together. In response to my repeated questions, my mother explained that in the 1940s and 1950s only the communists fought for integration. And even more relevant to my parents then, only they mobilized resistance to fascism and anti-Semitism. First in Spain, and then Germany. People who were "premature anti-fascists," as they came to be called during the Cold War, were considered un-American.

In Boston, in the early 1950s, my parents subscribed to the *Daily Worker* and were active in groups on the government's list of communist fronts. The FBI started following them, and the surveillance continued until the mid-1960s. Investigators contacted them regularly to ask which of their friends were communists. I doubt even they knew the full extent of the surveillance that was documented in the FBI files I eventually saw.

FBI agents stopped my father in the street near his office. They knocked on the front door of our new house in Indianapolis and tried to interview my mother. But always my parents told them, "I have nothing to say." They knew their rights and, as we became old enough to understand, we learned them too. Rachel, more than three years ahead of me, may have been more aware of the political context of our lives than I was. More aware of the risks and therefore more fearful.

I wanted to know if my parents remained communists while raising a family. "We were fellow travelers," Mom told me. She explained the distinction. "We weren't actually members of the party. But we shared their values." When I asked her about the mysterious, gentle man who joined our family once in a while, sleeping on our living room sofa in Indianapolis, she laughed as she remembered those days. If people in the party needed a place to stay, of course she and Dad were glad to put them up.

And what about the moves from one city to another? Why would my parents have left urbane Boston for the political wilderness of Indianapolis? Did one of their contacts convince them they were needed there? I searched for answers because I wanted to understand the subterranean currents of our lives. I found in writings of the historian Michael Sachar that the Communist Party of America organized a special section to penetrate Jewish community centers, among other Jewish organizations. Was my father persuaded by his professional and political contacts that he would be able to help the cause if he moved to Indianapolis?

Soon after becoming a civil rights attorney, my younger daughter helped me obtain my parents' FBI files through the Freedom of Information Act. The files came in two fat stacks of begrudgingly photocopied forms, one about my mother and the other about my father. Handwritten notes and bureaucratic coding entered at various regional offices dotted the margins. Typewritten on the appropriate places of the form were surveillance tactics and findings—what an agent learned when he called my father's office under the guise of a credit check to confirm his current address, for example, or how he talked with a secretary at a local junior college to check out my mother's enrollment and attendance record. The names of these informants were all redacted. Thick black rectangles jumped from one line to the next like stone-faced security guards shielding their clients. Administrative stamps and marginalia detailed the transfer of investigative responsibility from one field office to another.

Among the field notes and informant reports were a few notable activities. One involved the time my mother ran for PTA president on a platform opposing a split from the national organization, which was then under suspicion of subversive influence. More troubling to the FBI was the fact she collected dues for the local chapter of the American Civil Liberties Union, which was high on the government's list of communist front organizations. Worst of all, my parents' names showed up in the records of Manny Blum, a party organizer in the Midwest who was arrested in 1956 for violating the anti-communist provisions of the Smith Act. The FBI said Blum was seen in our home. Was this the man who slept on our living room couch and was so kind to me? The FBI agents believed Blum's arrest shook my father up and tamped down his involvement—without specifying exactly what involvement he had. Blum's indictment, like those of other party leaders, was dismissed the following year.

Not in those FBI files, but likely to have caused suspicion among our neighbors in that enclave of new ranch houses, were other Goodman behaviors. During those hours when my classmates were released from public school and taken by bus to attend prayer classes elsewhere, I stayed back in the school building, per my parents' instructions. And every morning, when the class got to the "under God" part of the Pledge of Allegiance (inserted by the US Congress in 1953), I closed my lips. I imagine Rachel or I, maybe even our younger brother, Michael, telling classmates it was wrong to talk about religion in school, a heresy that would have made its way to their Republican parents.

Toward the end of her life, I asked my mother who could have "informed" on them, and she told me her suspicions about progressive friends, who were often pressured to "name names." In Indianapolis, before we moved to St. Louis, we had socialized with one family in a part of town where ample lawns surrounded Tudor houses faced with stone. They had a daughter Rachel's age and a son who was mine. The father, a physician, worked at the local hospital. "He was scared," my mother said, conveying her pity for his weakness. "He must have believed he would lose his job if he didn't give the FBI names of people to investigate."

Then, with compassion that obliterated any sense of betrayal, she added, "It's so sad what happened." I tried to stop the flow of recollections I knew would follow because I didn't want to hear the next part of the story again: the part where the son succumbed to a fatal virus his first year away at college. I didn't want to be reminded how even a father who was a doctor, when faced with nature's cruelty, was helpless to save his own child.

I came to see how these FBI files foretold part of Rachel's story. How surreptitious surveillance became a fear that lodged in her psyche. When psychosis struck Rachel, she had a store of Cold War memories to substantiate and shape inchoate fears. (Just to be sure I checked with the FBI. They had no file documenting any surveillance of her.) The FBI surveillance that resulted from my parents' involvement in organizations associated with the Communist Party would have provided a ready template for her paranoia. When Rachel told me, with panic in her eyes, that two men followed her all the way from New York City to San Francisco, there was a certain logic to her delusion.

TRICKS AND TREATS

Like Big Eagle Camp, trick-or-treating was one of the good things about Indianapolis. We didn't have to cross busy streets to cover a lot of ground. We wore homemade costumes. My mother sewed me a witch's cloak, made me a hat, and arranged for me to go out with Paula, another third grader my mother had insisted I play with. Paula lived two blocks away and had brown hair like me. When I met up with her for trick-or-treating, I saw she had fairy wings. That was a costume I would never wear. I wasn't thin enough to look like I could fly. We cut through yards, knocked on doors, and reached for goodies. Once I filled my bag, I was eager to get home.

Michael returned from the expedition with his friends about the same time. I threw my witch's hat on the sofa, and he pulled off his pirate eyepatch. "Rachel said to wait for her before we eat anything," he piped up. I scowled at him. I didn't need him reminding me.

"I want to see how much chocolate you got," I said, reaching for his bag. "Let me look." He pulled it away from me. I didn't want to wait for Rachel. I wanted to know what Michael had because, as much as the houses looked alike, the people in them handed out different treats. Some people gave popcorn balls. Some gave us Hershey bars. You could end up with chewing gum, candy corn, bags of raisins and nuts, and everything between. Michael's friends had lived here a long time. What if they knew better than Paula which houses gave the best treats?

Before full-court bickering broke out between us, I felt a blast of cool air going straight into the living room as the front door opened and then slammed shut. Rachel appeared, a hobo scarf around her neck and charcoal smudges on her face. "All right, just a minute," she said when Michael and I yelled for her to join us on the floor. The three of us dumped our candy out of our bags and began the post-Halloween reckoning.

Fairness was a standard firmly upheld in our family. Our mother always made sure to give us the same number of shrimps from the chop suey, and the same number of cookies she took home for us from grown-up parties. Mashed potatoes weren't a food you could count, so when one of us protested our allotment, my mother would say, "Do you want me to go get a scale?" She said it to show we were being ridiculous. But fairness was so important to me that I still lived with the guilt I felt back in Boston when I snuck into the kitchen before anyone was awake and stole extra cookies from napkin-wrapped treats our parents brought home. Michael was still a toddler then, almost two years younger than me, and I told myself he shouldn't get as many cookies as I did. I knew it was wrong and took them anyway. I didn't worry then about shortchanging Rachel. Maybe because she seemed too old to care—or knew how to get the things she wanted.

This Halloween night in Indianapolis, Rachel took charge of dividing up the treats. She must have invented the distribution method we used, because our mother wouldn't have bothered with anything so methodical. But Rachel had absorbed our parents' socialist values. She emptied her candy into a pile in the middle of the living room rug, then Michael and I did the same. We admired the big shiny pile filled with crinkly wrappers of every color and shape. Then, at Rachel's direction, all three of us began to refill our bags, our eyes glued to each other's hands. One at a time, going in rounds, we picked the treats we wanted, starting of course with the thickest candy bars and ending with the translucent lollipops. Using this redistribution method, each of us ended up with roughly the same number of our favorites. My envy evaporated. Rachel's method seemed right and natural. I was proud we came to this solution without grown-up involvement. We each got the same opportunity to enjoy the best Halloween sweets.

After five years in Indianapolis, my parents sold the ranch house and bought an older one in the central city. Our rambling old house had five bedrooms. Rachel's and mine were on the third-floor attic; Julie's and Michael's, on the second floor, near our parents. In the backyard Julie even had a tree with outspread limbs for climbing. We walked to nearby stores and movie theaters. And, when it came to town, to the State Fair with its 4-H exhibits and carnival rides. Best of all I didn't have to take a bus to school anymore. In the spring, on the walk to School #66, I snagged fat, purple mulberries from gnarly bushes that grew along the sidewalk, sweet and tart when I crushed them in my mouth (and ever since I have savored the grit of berry seeds between my teeth).

Now, in this real-life neighborhood, I quickly made real-life friends. Lee Ann, across the street, was in my sixth-grade class. She didn't take school very seriously. I got to join her Christmas morning and see all the presents under her tree. Sarah, next door to her, was a grade ahead of us. She read a lot and cared about getting good grades, like me. She loaned me the book her older brother smuggled out of Germany, *Lady Chatterley's Lover*, so I could learn about sex from the pages she marked for me.

Important events were happening. For one, I had to close my bedroom door and check my underpants every night until I got my period, which finally arrived shortly after my twelfth birthday. Another event, though, lingers ominously in my memory. One evening Rachel called me from her bedroom across the third-floor landing. I was surprised because we both tended to keep to our own rooms—hers on the right at the top of the stairs and mine on the left. I remember how thrilled I was when, despite our tacit agreement, Rachel let her friend Anita cross the hall to talk with me in my room. Clearly, Anita liked me: she included me in her visit! Anita's relaxed good humor was a revelation to me.

Now, however, my older sister was calling me in a voice ringing with urgency. When I entered her room, I saw her sprawled on her bed, one arm over her forehead, a book by her pillow, closed shut. As she jumped up, the neckerchief and sweater that were dangling from the foot of her bed slipped to the floor. Accustomed to the low burn of Rachel's moods, I sensed a rise in the heat as she kicked her clothing aside and came to stand opposite me.

"What?" I asked her. "What do you want?"

"Whose side are you on—Mom's or Dad's?" she demanded. I still feel my gut churning when I recall how her eyes pinned me down, pressuring me to choose. Rachel hated Mom, who was always trying to make her clean up and help out or refusing to let her do what she wanted. Rachel only loved Dad; I loved Mom and Dad both. I didn't want a family war. But would Rachel ever care about me if I refused to be her ally? I felt as though she expected me to crumple up my love, like a wad of paper, and throw it in the trash. I couldn't give an answer to her question.

Unfair as it seemed to me, my one happy year in Indianapolis was our last in that city. Shortly after I turned twelve, Mom and Dad announced we would be moving. Again! I finally had a neighborhood I loved. So what if Dad had a job in another city? "That's no fair," I wailed and rushed across the street to my friends. I shouldn't have expected Lee Ann to sympathize. She had learned a few weeks earlier she would be moving soon to Hutchinson, Kansas, which was even farther from Indianapolis than St. Louis, where I had to go. Sarah felt horrible, though. Sarah didn't want me to leave.

During those last months in Indianapolis not even Julie played outside. Temperatures fell below zero. The snow was thick and when the cold hit a new low, Mom's car wouldn't start; a neighbor had to give me a ride to school. Dad was already in St. Louis at his new job while Mom stayed home with the rest of us. She had to sell the house.

During winter vacation, Rachel took the Greyhound bus to a camp reunion in Michigan. (After Dad began directing the day camp in town instead of Big Eagle, Rachel, Michael, and I attended Circle Pines in southern Michigan, a cooperative work camp so progressive and permissive that teenagers were able to buy cigarettes from the canteen.) When I went with Mom to the station to pick Rachel up, it was so cold I felt the cement floor burning through my shoes and socks. On the drive home, Mom talked to Rachel about going ahead to St. Louis to start her new high school at the beginning of the upcoming term. Rachel would stay with family friends, not with Dad, because he was living in a rooming house. "You were good friends with Judy when we lived in Boston," Mom reminded her, speaking of her host family's older daughter. "And you'll see Dad there too."

Rachel didn't seem to react. She had a faraway look in her eyes. "Why don't we move to Chicago instead?" she asked. "That's where my friends from camp are." I wasn't sure whether she was kidding. Of course my parents followed their own plan, and Rachel calmly, as it seemed to me then, departed early for the beginning of her high school term in the far-off city. Maybe she was relieved to get away from Mom for a while. Reading Mom's letters to Dad now, I know what a hard time she had managing Rachel. My mother wrote to him after consulting with a psychologist about Rachel's constant defiance. It's just adolescence, Mom was told.

Despite her moods, Rachel continued to use her talents. She knew how to make things, and how to make things happen. She created hot plates and ash trays from mosaics of multi-colored tiles. She played the piano, and later the oboe in band. She typed out articles for her high school newspaper at lightning speed. And when Dad was away in St. Louis, Rachel came up with a project to take our minds off the separation. She got Mom, me, Michael, and even five-year-old Julie to help her make 1959 New Year's cards to send to friends. We cut out gold-leaf paper for the five and nine. We cut out Chinese lanterns and party hats from red tissue paper and detailed them in black ink using our fountain pens. We glued down all the pieces, in a gaily angled composition of Rachel's design, and signed all our names. We sent out almost sixty of them. She proudly sent samples to Dad with a letter explaining her role in the project.

After two months, the house sold and my family reunited in St. Louis, where Rachel finished her three remaining years of high school. The move must have been hard for her. I noticed she started to get that distant look every once in a while, and then more frequently. The fights between her and Mom, between her and Mom and Dad, intensified. We shared a bedroom again, and I heard her on the typewriter at night. Her devotion to her writing consumed so much passion she didn't seem to care whose side I was on anymore. And I began to understand that Rachel had other places to be.

If only opportunities could have divided up like our Halloween candies. If only we could have had shiny nuggets of health and happiness distributed so fairly among us. But we couldn't. We were powerless. Rachel got a bad hand from both nature and nurture. Rogue strands of DNA must have insinuated themselves into her genome, ready to pounce. And the family stress and confusion of her first few years of life may have made it easier for those genes to gum things up while her brain was taking shape. There was nothing fair about the way twenty years later entire pathways of reason gave way. Year after awful year of her adult life, parents and doctors proved helpless in repairing the damage. Nobody understood what went wrong. Rachel spent decades in hospitals before someone found a way for her to live on her own.

But until she got sick, Rachel always made things better for me. When I lost my best friend in the move to Indianapolis, Rachel showed me the difference that writing letters could make. Soon after she got the bicycle she needed for her paper route, I got a bike too, and she took me exploring. She was my advance guard, fighting for privileges so I didn't have to. And on Halloween, when I envied my brother's treats, she showed me a way to make things even.

Rachel accepted me. She rarely teased me. She loved me casually, unobtrusively. We weren't best friends but we were solid as sisters. That's what made it so agonizing that after she became so ill, I couldn't find a way to help her. She had to endure schizophrenia and all its horrors alone. Hospitalizations in open and locked wards. Mind-numbing, tremor-causing medications. Homelessness. Assaults in hospitals and on the streets. Year after year of illness piled into a towering tragedy.

Ten years after Rachel showed us how to divide our Halloween treats, I knew she would never again be my guide through new neighborhoods and experiences. As ill as she became, though, she never stopped being my older sister.

((

A Few Acres of Woods

There were a few acres of woods nearby,
That I always looked at and relished
Inside the vast recesses I kept
Together, and the woods were the
Recesses too, and the woods led
A whole country of mystery and
Depth wonder. So I always
Pondered on the woods, and never
Ventured very far within, not knowing
Or experiencing or even conscious
Of the fact that it could be my woods too.
Not theirs, not his, but just mine
That I could enter and live and vacate
All these woods meant was another enigma,
And the mystery was far away. Or so
Near I couldn't get to it.

This was my childhood,
With me and the other kids, laughing

—Rachel Goodman

PART II

Epigenetics

Epigenetics: changes in organisms caused by modification of gene expression resulting from environmental factors rather than alteration of the genetic code itself.

MY MOTHER'S STORIES

I felt as though my mother's stories were always inside me, a movie whirring behind my eyes from the moment I was born. Snapped into place, ready to roll like film in its projector. Most of the stories, and the best of them, took place at "the Home," the nickname for the Chicago Home for Jewish Orphans in the Hyde Park section of Chicago. That's where my mother lived from 1928 to 1938, from the time she was eight until she was eighteen. Her name was Sophia, but the kids at the Home gave everyone nicknames. Hers was Skits. Sometimes Skippy. Skits was the one that followed her into adulthood.

My grandmother Anna wasn't able to keep her three children home with her because her husband, Sam Gutt, had abandoned her. He left for good when my mother was five years old. My mother never saw her father again except for one brief visit—right after her last child, my sister Julie, was born. That's when Sam decided to see his daughter and meet her family. Two days later he left town promising he would send me a doll. My mother told me not to believe him. She was right. No doll came and I never heard from him again. None of us did.

In Chicago Anna visited her children once a week at the Home, taking time from her work as a domestic responsible for other people's children. She gave my mother day-old pastries and a few coins to divide among her and her brother and sister. She made sure they got music lessons and other enrichment that was available at the orphanage for children who showed talent.

My mother's tales highlighted her spunk and her triumph over adversity, as well as her devotion to her siblings. My mother, being the oldest, made it her job to smooth things over for her siblings on a day-to-day basis. When Mom needed money she bought chewing gum packs three for a dime and sold them for a nickel each. She cut kids' hair for a quarter. She couldn't buy attention but she could earn it being cute and smart and eager to please. She made special friends with nurses and teachers. Especially in math, she earned the highest grades in her classroom. My mother knew how to outsmart any adult who tried to hurt, cheat, or demean her or her siblings. She refused to cry when punished. She sat in the locked cloakroom and laughed until they let her out. When a supervisor tried punishing her where it hurt—by forbidding her to go kiss her sister goodnight, her nightly ritual—she just snuck out. Her sister was already asleep, but she kissed her anyway.

She had more best girlfriends than I would have in a lifetime. More boys to fool around with than I would ever know. Years later when I packed up her home of fifty years to move her into mine, I found a box filled with small black and white photos. Dozens of "Home Kids" pictures. Portraits of them individually and in groups. Human pyramids at the beach (Lake Michigan). Boating at summer camp. Hanging out on the playground, or as teenagers, on the streets of Chicago's South Side. Now at ninety-two, my mother's eyesight was failing. I handed her the magnifying glass; she peered at the faces and told me the names—all of the girls and many of the boys. With just a moment's thought she could come up with the names of their siblings too. "Did you have a camera when you were at the Home?" I asked. No, she said, and she didn't remember how she got the photos either. I imagined her huddled with her friends, reviewing their photos and passing them around like trading cards.

When I was little, I loved my mother without reservation. She made me feel safe when I couldn't breathe from asthma, when it hurt to pee from bladder infections. Mom's larger-than-life childhood seemed mythical, and I believed for a long time that she could do anything. At some point, though, I felt she couldn't give me what I wanted. I was a middle child for five years and didn't have words to explain my need for attention. So I whined. I whined about hunger pangs, boredom, ill-fitting skirts, about my brother hogging the TV. I knew my mother was just trying to be funny when she told me, "You whine so much I'm going to put you in a wine bottle." I thought it was a stupid pun. It wasn't funny. And sometimes I felt she did want to cork me and choke off my words.

As the stories looped in my head, the sprockets holding them in place began to creak. Who was she trying to impress, and why? The neediness in her voice made me cringe. I was the child needing praise now. Not her. I couldn't tell my mother that, though. She would get mad, and that was scarier to me than anything. My mother crumbled under criticism. Being defensive, as my parents called it. Being defensive always meant a fight. In one of them my father told her she should just see what her face looked like right now. "This is the face you married," she shot back. Then she spat at him. She was almost a foot shorter than him, so I don't think the spit reached his face. But the spray of saliva from her mouth horrified me. Why did my mother have to be so defensive? What had happened to the confident girl in all the Home stories?

When I became a teenager, I developed a gnawing need to have the last word. I wanted my mother to believe that I really would do the dishes—but later, after I finished my homework. "Do them now and stop arguing with me," she insisted.

And I shot back in righteous frustration: "It takes two to argue." I understand now that my mother was only anxious about getting the housework done. But at the time I was furious with her because she never seemed to hear what I was saying.

In my grief at Rachel's death, I made the decision to write because I wanted to bring back the talented woman schizophrenia stole from the world and took away from me. During one of my mother's regular visits, three years after Rachel's death, I mentioned the memoir class I was attending at a community college. "Do you want to hear something I wrote about Rachel?" My mother was always ready to talk about Rachel, to share her version of what went wrong. Maybe, I thought, we could have a two-way conversation now. I read her what I had written about Rachel's return from San Francisco, the first time I realized she was delusional.

When I finished, my mother was silent, a frown on her face. I worked up my nerve to ask her what she thought anyway. "It's okay, but it's too sad of a topic," she answered. A topic? No, that's Rachel. My sister. Your daughter. Like reflux, childish disappointment burnt my throat, gagged me.

My mother expected me to listen to her stories, but she still didn't want to hear mine. It was all so difficult anyway. Once that course was over, I stopped writing for a while.

Ten years later, my mother came to live with me. She was ninety years old, and I learned to adjust my expectations. I didn't care about reciprocity. Instead of cringing, I probed for more information. I sat with her, asked questions, and wrote down every word she said. Often, new details emerged with retelling. About the molestation she endured, for example, as a live-in babysitter after she left the Home. She loved the family she worked for, but when the wife discovered blood, a menstrual stain, on her husband's trousers, she knew my mother had been sitting on his lap. They didn't have sex, my mother assured me, but she enjoyed the kissing and fondling. The wife kicked my mother out of her house.

"Did she give you time to find another place to live?" I asked. "No, I had to find a place that very night. I called my friend," Mom explained. But she didn't want to give them up entirely, so she stayed in touch with the family that abused her. "I liked little Blossom. I played the piano when she sang. The mother liked me. She didn't blame me. She said I just couldn't live there anymore. Her husband had acted that way with other girls." I told my mother how horrible the husband was to do that. And the wife for throwing her out. Why didn't she throw out her husband, a serial molester, instead? I wanted my mother to be angry, but she wasn't. She was resigned. I could see she didn't want to think of herself as a victim. That would have undermined her self-image as the spunky, plucky hero of her own stories. Maybe that's why years later, she was so impatient with Rachel. When Rachel got kicked out of homes where she was placed, it seemed hard for my mother to understand why her daughter couldn't be as independent as she had been. But at the same time she was adamant about making sure her daughter was protected.

I discovered another source of trauma. My mother and her younger brother, Paul, were born in New York and moved to Chicago when my mother was four or five. In addition to her colorful stories about the Chicago orphanage were vague mentions of a New York orphanage. "My mother put me in an orphanage when my brother was born," she had told me, and I always understood this placement to be a short-term childcare arrangement, a matter of weeks. A document I found in an envelope of my grandmother's things—papers Mom tucked away in her basement—showed something else entirely.

Every morning while Mom lived with me, she had half a bagel and coffee with milk for breakfast. Then she settled into her high-backed chair to read or watch television. Several days after reading and thinking about the document I found, I decided to tell her about my discovery. Once she seemed comfortable, I brought it up. "Mom, remember that first or-phanage, when you lived in New York? You weren't there only when your brother was born. You were there almost two years. From the time you were two until you were four."

She looked at me dubiously but took the letter. Faded but still legible, it was dated November 4, 1924, and typed on the letterhead of the Israel Orphan Asylum. Under the name Gustave Hartman, who was founder and president, ran a listing of its board of directors. A brief statement, perfectly centered, was signed by Director May Weisser (soon to be May Hartman, wife of Judge Gustave and partner to his extraordinary philanthropic endeavors). It said: *Mrs. Gutt has this day removed her child Sophie from the Israel Orphan Asylum where the child had been an inmate since January 15, 1923.*

Mom read the document and then put down her magnifying glass. "I didn't know I had been there that long," she said quietly. All of 1923. Most of 1924. She didn't appear perturbed. I knew she couldn't afford to get upset about this bit of personal history from ninety years ago. By now she had physical aches and pains to contend with. But she took a deep breath and told me again the one incident she remembered from the New York orphanage: how she was so excited when her mother came to visit her she jumped out of her crib and hit her head on the floor. As she had done many times before, she pulled back her thick white hair to show me the scar on her hairline. I remembered the story about the scar on her chin—when she slipped on a mess of grapes underneath a fruit stand where she played when she was five and her mother was away working. Scars and more scars.

I wanted to cry every time I looked at May Weisser's note and imagined my mother as a toddler—handed over by Anna, her own mother, at such a critical period of development. I remembered how much I had loved my children's preschool years, when I learned about "flutterbys" and "pasghetti." When lisping words snowballed into sentences. When physical sensations transformed into an explosion of new experiences and connections. I pictured my mother as a baby, holding the railing of an orphan crib, bereft of a parent to interpret her chatter. Dependent on caretakers to tuck her into bed every night and sing her the lullaby she loved most over and over. Or not.

Every story Mom told me, every story I pulled out of the basement boxes, helped me understand what happened to Mom, and indirectly to Rachel. Two decades had passed since she jumped out of the crib and landed on the floor of the New York orphanage. But twenty years couldn't obliterate the effects of abandonment because trust in infancy becomes the latitude and longitude for navigating life. What happens when the attachment is broken? Mom liked to show me the scars on her forehead and chin. I shuddered to think about the scars she couldn't point to.

I wanted not to judge her. I didn't want to inflict more pain. I hated the way mothers got blamed for mental illness. My mother had put up with too much finger-pointing—from hospital staff, from friends and relatives. Even from her other three children, including me. We told her we didn't blame her, but she didn't believe us. She was right. In trying to understand why Rachel's illness became so bad, I had secretly held her responsible for being unable to manage the challenges it created. Managed better, Rachel's condition might never have become so severe.

I understand the nature-nurture debate on etiology to be pretty much settled. Instead of a dichotomy, nurture accompanies nature. The new science of epigenetics explores the intricacies of how environment determines which genes turn on and which lay dormant. High levels of stress during a child's early years are believed to be a major factor in expression of rogue genes. It explains why one sibling develops mental illness while the other one doesn't. To me it suggests that something happened around the time Rachel came into the world, something that spent its fury by the time I was born three-and-a-half years later.

A counterfactual story beckons me: The firstborn child of immigrants, my mother grows up poor but secure in the love of her parents. Sometimes her father has to leave to take carpentry jobs in other cities, and her mother has to take domestic jobs with other families. But her mother is always home for Shabbos dinner, and her father is always there for holidays. Sometimes my mother goes to her aunt's house when her parents are both working, and while she's there she gets plenty of hugs and sometimes her favorite treat—sizzling hot gribenes in schmaltz, chicken skin cooked with onion in rendered fat on the chewy heel of rye bread. It's the smallest part of the bread, but my mother prefers it to any other. And even though her parents can't be with her all the time, she knows their hearts hold so much love they have more than enough for her as well as each other. She grows up knowing she is smart and cute, but even more importantly that she is lovable too. So when she gets married and her own husband leaves for the army, she doesn't doubt his love for her. The war years are hard, but when they end my parents reunite and their own little girl, my sister Rachel, feels that same fullness of love surrounding her too. Even when Rachel grows up and starts feeling confused, she knows that both of them want to help her. Sometimes her thoughts scare her, but she knows her parents have gone through hard times before, and they'll help her get through these difficulties. And together they do.

Oh, if only this fantasy version of my family's history were true. If only circumstances had allowed that rogue DNA to stay dormant, its activation halted. If only it had stayed forever folded, locked in its ancestral spiral: quiet, harmless, asleep. If only my mother had experienced the love and security every child needs to grow up better able to manage a parent's cruelest challenge.

WAR BRIDE

After junior college my mother worked full time for the Chicago company that invented skinless casings for hot dogs. She mocked up, proofread, and got approvals to print ingredient labels on the cellulose wrappers. She enjoyed working with the guys in the art department; they were fun and liked to joke around. But she loved math and science and dreamed of working in the research lab. She had known the factory's owner for years; he was on the board of directors of the orphanage and a benefactor to the brightest of the young people who lived there. Successful and philanthropic as he was, he was a man of his times. "He told me I couldn't work in the lab because I was a woman," my mother explained. She was disappointed, but not bitter; she picked her grievances like she picked her battles. She had to. How else could she have enjoyed life the way she did? She played in the outfield on the company's softball team. She joined B'nai B'rith Girls social events with girlfriends from the Home.

My mother certainly had her pick of men to date during her two years as a single working woman. That's when she first met my father, Mort Goodman. Once, she told me, she ended up with him and another suitor at the movies one night—because neither of them would take no for an answer. "There I was between the two of them, and they both had hands on my legs, one on the left one on the right." She giggled every time she told me the story. It's no surprise Mort won. My father was a smart, handsome graduate student with piercing blue eyes.

His parents, from the suburbs of Cleveland, were well-off by Depression-era standards. Abe and Ethel Goodman occupied one side of the two-family house they owned in Cleveland Heights, an eastern suburb of the industrial city where Abe designed decorative metalwork for elevators in the tall new buildings going up all over the world. They doted on "Morty," their third child and only son. After he left rabbinical school, they clucked regrets at the opportunities he spurned: a scholar who could have been a great rabbi like his grandfather in Russia. Instead of staying for ordination, he joined groups speaking out against fascism in Spain and Germany. That frightened his parents; they thought it put him in league with the Soviet Union. They blamed the girl from the orphanage for his lurch to the left. They offered to support him for the remainder of his graduate studies if he put off the marriage. They must have hoped he would eventually find someone more suitable. But my father held his ground, and they dropped their opposition. They graciously offered their home for the wedding.

Sophia Gutt and Mort Goodman took the train to Cleveland, where they married September 18, 1941. They then moved into a boarding house in Chicago; Mom's job covered the rent while my father completed requirements for his master's degree. "It was cozy," my mother said. They had a bedroom with a living area. And no, she didn't mind sharing a bathroom and kitchen with other boarders. It was better than any home she had had before.

The attack on Pearl Harbor came three months after the

wedding, followed, in another few months, by a draft notice. My mother believed—then, and for the rest of her life—that her husband could have received a deferment if he had tried. She talked about it often, citing two reasons. He still had an affiliation with the rabbinical school he attended before he came to Chicago to study. More importantly, she was pregnant. From what I understand, he probably wouldn't have gotten one, as the draft rules were changing. In any case, my father wanted to serve. He was a healthy twenty-five-year-old. He had relatives trapped in Eastern Europe, facing certain slaughter. His parents had given him a postcard from a cousin pleading for someone to come to Lithuania and file papers that would save him—an impossible request to meet. "I ended up supporting Dad's decision," Mom told me, but she got that look she had when she covered up her pain. I knew she was feeling her father's abandonment all over again.

While my father did his basic training, my mother boarded with a couple in Chicago. "We were friends," she told me. "The woman smoked, and that's when I started smoking too," she remembered. The living arrangement was short-lived. After basic training in Alabama, my father applied for a posting in Pennsylvania, just two hours away from Cleveland. Mom agreed to the plan he proposed. She would move in with his parents, making it easier for him to visit on furloughs.

My mother had another good reason to move to Cleveland, though she never straight out admitted it to me. She would need help when the baby came. Her own mother, still working as a domestic, lived in Chicago, but what did she know? Anna still looked and acted like a greenhorn; she'd left her three children for others to feed and shelter. Ethel, on the other hand, managed a family. She brought up three children and made her home the gathering place for her aunts and uncles and cousins on her side and her husband's. Her daughters visited daily. I suspect my mother hoped to learn firsthand what a real mother was like.

Then came the fence Abe and Ethel put up. It made my mother furious. "That spiteful bitch," she hissed under her breath. On the other side of the fence were friends she had made for her and baby Rachel. Good thing Rachel wasn't talking yet or she might have repeated her curse word in front of the in-laws. I can imagine my mother's rage roiling inside her until she just had to write her husband and tell him about his middle sister's latest attack on her. My mother had no doubt that Abe and Ethel put up the fence at Florence's insistence. My mother had become friendly with the neighbors and her sister-in-law didn't like them. They weren't "her sort." Florence didn't want their children cutting across the lawn to play with Rachel. How mean. How embarrassing. And how was she supposed to explain this fence to her friends? Would she have to tell them how much Florence resented her, that she couldn't stand the fact that her new sister-in-law and her baby were living under the same roof as Abe and Ethel?

I wonder if my mother tried to refrain from writing her husband about this latest incident. He was in a real war after all. But who else could she tell? Hadn't it been his idea for her to live here? One way or another he heard about it and wrote back reminding my mother that Florence was the middle child, younger than pretty, talented Essie and older than her handsome, academic brother. "She can't help it," he counseled. "Just be patient. It won't be much longer." Be patient. What else could she do? Florence would keep being sarcastic and self-centered. She was quick to ask for little favors like using my mother's ration card for cigarettes. Or having her walk her home after gin rummy at Abe and Ethel's because she didn't like walking home in the dark. "She didn't mind that I had to walk back from her place alone," my mother said, still irate decades later at the way her husband's sister treated her.

Behind the Goodman house in Cleveland Heights was a lush garden with winding paths and fruit trees. During the war years some of the flowers may have made way for a victory garden. In the front lawn, though, to the side of the steps, was the glider swing, with tricycles and a lawn big enough for games.

"Amy, come take Rachel outside with you," my mother, standing at the back door would have said. I imagine Mom catching Florence's daughter by the hand and asking her to take her younger cousin outside to play. The early summer sun beamed gently outside, perfect weather for cousins to enjoy the Goodman lawn. If she were still in Chicago, my mother would have taken Rachel to the beach on a Saturday like this. She would have asked her sister to come with them or arranged to meet up with one of her girlfriends from the Home.

Still, suburban Cleveland was lovely in early summer. Outside on this June day, Essie's older boy was kicking a new football, his little brother running behind him. My mother called out to them from the door, "Here come the girls. Help Rachel get up on the swing." She watched as the four of them tumbled onto the glider. The two older cousins gave the younger ones a boost. They were good kids. Kids at the Home always looked out for each other too. The cousins sat two by two, holding the poles and pushing with their legs. Now she could take a few minutes for herself and keep an eye on the kids from her upstairs window. She would write to her husband, fighting somewhere in Italy. The Po Valley, she thought, though the censors made it hard to know exactly where. He was on the move, but the army would get the letter to him.

Sitting down at the desk, she untucked three sheets of paper from the stationery box. She filled the first two pages with reports on Rachel's progress. A burst of air startled her. Florence never bothered to knock. "I'm going out," she announced, without so much as a hello. "Be sure to give Amy a cheese sandwich when you feed Rachel." Just then, in the middle of her instructions, Florence let out a scream. She was standing in front of the dresser, staring at a card sitting next to the photo of Mort in his uniform. My mother saw her sister-in-law's long face transformed by horror, her full lips twisted into a jeering accusation. "Good lord, what is this? Are you trying to get us all in trouble? Communist! This is a communist card."

"I don't know what you're talking about," my mother answered. I can imagine how her ice-cold response fanned her rival's fear.

"The Progressive Club?" Florence shouted. "That's the place you go with those awful people next door. Everyone knows they're all communists!"

"You don't know anything," Mom retorted. "Go meet your friends already. I'll get Amy her lunch." As a foster child, before the orphanage and after, Mom had lived with families who didn't love her. She knew how to make the best of a bad situation. She would ignore her sister-in-law's jibes. She could do it if she tried. While she was here, she would watch and learn from Ethel's cooking. Eat her roast chicken with quartered potatoes. Her kugel and flanken. Noodle pudding and slow-cooked meat. As soon as Rachel went down for her nap, she would go help Ethel make cabbage rolls for dinner. She would place small mounds of ground beef and rice in the leaves of cabbage, roll them up, and cover them with raisin-dotted tomato sauce. She chuckled at the thought of Florence seeing her in the kitchen with Ethel. It would drive her nuts.

Later that day, my mother handed the mailman her letter. She had decided not to mention her sister-in-law's latest transgression but she told her husband about the newspaper ad she saw for low-cost apartments now available for wives and children of soldiers. She told him it looked like a good deal but she'd decided to stay put and wait for him to get home before she made a move. She didn't tell him what his mother said about the idea. "It wouldn't be good for the children," Ethel had insisted. "It's not in a good neighborhood," she said, using a Yiddish slur to refer to the Black people living there. Why upset him? She knew he would be unhappy at his mother's prejudice and derogatory language. He had real battles to fight. He told her the war would be over before too long. France was almost liberated, and the Soviets would help defeat the Germans. She knew her husband would come home. He had to.

My mother decided to put up with her in-laws for a while longer. She appreciated the way her father-in-law showered Rachel with love, the way he sang Al Jolson songs in his British-Yiddish accent, the way he bent down and swept Rachel into a twirl when he walked in the door after work, the way he held out his arms to catch her when she took her first steps. She loved seeing them together even though she knew it should have been her husband. Little girls need their fathers to love them. She held on to the memory of her own father holding her on his knee. That one day, after he moved out, when her mother took her to see him and they walked a little while and her mother pointed to a house and said, "That's where your papa is." Little Sophie couldn't wait another minute. She let go of Anna's hand and dashed into traffic, only to be grazed by a moving car. She was too excited to care. She wasn't hurt. When she got to her father's lodgings at long last, she sat in his lap and felt his eyes on her. Then her father left town and left her for good. Why did he do that? Didn't he know she loved him?

Another counterfactual: If my father had stayed put at Camp Reynolds, the big army personnel replacement depot in northwestern Pennsylvania, he would have been able to complete his service stateside. He wouldn't have been digging foxholes to duck enemy fire in 1944 and '45. He wouldn't have crossed the Po River at night. He wouldn't have marched in mountain battles to capture strategic peaks in the Apennines.

Instead, he would have continued his home visits to his wife and daughter, taken a bus or hitched a ride the seventy miles to Cleveland whenever he snagged a furlough. He would have heard Rachel's first words and celebrated her second birthday. But he left Camp Reynolds and his job in personnel. Instead of interviewing and classifying GIs based on their job potential, he shipped out as an infantryman just a month after Rachel's first birthday.

I grew up hearing that my father volunteered for active duty because he wanted to fight the Nazis. At some point, when I was an adult, my mother told me a more nuanced version. I never knew how much of her story to believe, because she sometimes left out important context or shaded the facts for reasons of her own. Unfortunately, hers was the only interpretation I had. As a child, and a young woman, I never pressed my father for his own account. If he had lived to old age, I could have done that. By then I would have had the confidence to poke the embers of his memory, and I suspect he would have been willing to reminisce.

My mother's version of Dad's combat service was perplexing. He and some of his pals at Camp Reynolds, she said, protested segregation of the dining room, and the brass wanted to break up the troublemakers. As "payback," one member of the group would have to go overseas, and my father agreed to be the one. That's all she could tell me. He often told me how upset he was by the racism and anti-Semitism he encountered in the army. But what did he actually do in the Pennsylvania protest? What happened to the other guys? And why did my father never mention any of this to me?

My generation has so admired the army for its leadership in racial integration that it's difficult to grasp that it wasn't until 1948 that President Truman issued an executive order abolishing segregation in the armed forces. Before that, Jim Crow prevailed everywhere, even at bases in the Northern states. Only in the course of researching this chapter did I learn that race-based conflicts were breaking out in camps all over the country—including in Camp Reynolds just two months before my father's posting there. Official army history records one Black soldier killed by military police (who were both Black and White) and five others wounded at Camp Reynolds. Accounts gathered years later by eyewitnesses and investigators claim up to twenty dead.

Camp Reynolds was a multi-million-dollar base which had theaters and gyms and full rosters of USO shows. But not for the Black soldiers. The camp's weekly newspaper, in an issue published just after my father arrived, displayed a five-column banner headline: "Prettiest Girl on Post to Be Selected at Halloween Party." Underneath, the lead story was an article about upcoming pay raises. Allowances for servicemen with a wife and one child were increasing from $60 to $80 monthly. There was nothing on efforts to improve conditions for Black soldiers or about race relations. My father must have been incensed at the ongoing coverup. My best guess is that his protest took the form of letters he wrote and got his buddies to sign. Maybe he tried to get them published in the camp newspaper, or on some other forum or bulletin board.

Among the family documents were my father's letters from wartime friends. One, in March 1945, came from Leo Oxman. Leo begins his letter urging my father to avoid unnecessary risks. *Damn it, Mort, be careful, will you.* He cryptically alludes to what went down in Pennsylvania, *Well, Mort, our 'deal' is working out pretty well.* Leo, still in personnel, admits his is not a taxing job but he finds great satisfaction helping GIs get the breaks they deserve. He wants to know if my father feels the same way about his work. *What is your feeling about your big step, Mort. . . . How do you feel? Are you disappointed or not? I think you always knew what it was all about up there. Here's one GI who respects you . . . regardless of how the decision came about. I've always felt you quite purposely steered right for it because your convictions were there directing you that way. . . . You were the first man I met who seemed to know the story about all this mess and had firm, sound convictions.*

As a young mother, my mother had her own opinion about her husband's moral leadership and courage. She took pains to say she supported his decision, which was a noble position for a new wife and mother. Eventually, though, her emotions slipped out and she told me that getting sent overseas was a "stupid" thing for him to do. I wouldn't be surprised if my father also thought he made a bad decision.

Or he may have believed he didn't do enough to fight fascism and segregation. I asked him once what combat was like. "We were too far away from the Germans to see if we hit anyone," he told me. His downward glance made him look defensive or embarrassed. He said he dug foxholes, but I couldn't picture them. Were foxholes for shooting or for hiding? When I asked more questions, he reminded me he was a pacifist now. I understood that to mean the discussion was closed.

Mainly, my father told me things he thought I should know about—like North Africa's modern skyscrapers and how Italian people loved Americans more than their fascist leader, Mussolini. My father did have one genuine war story to share. How he found a German hiding in a farmer's barn and turned him in at the point of his rifle as a prisoner of war. I found the letter he wrote to my mother with the news. The encounter took place on April 22 *in honor of Rachel's second birthday* that very day. Reading those words now I sense a dash of humor, even irony. He was too self-effacing, too much the intellectual or former rabbinical student, to brag about even a bloodless act of aggression.

The German surrender came a week after Italy's. Like all the GIs in his division, my father expected to be redeployed. If he had to go to the Pacific, though, he'd at least get to have a nice long stay at home. As it turned out, Japan surrendered and the division stayed put. Instead of furloughs, everyone would get to go home for good. But the waiting lists were long. It took months for available ships to convey a million plus troops. Everyone chafed under the army's strict point system. Even with ten months in combat and three bronze stars, my father had to wait five months for his number to come up. He landed a clerical assignment in the meantime but hated being in an office. The people there were "stiffs," like the Camp Reynolds brass. He missed his combat buddies; it was spring and he longed to be outside. Travel passes became plentiful and my father took to the road. He sketched statues in the plazas and museums, farm scenes in Po Valley villages that he had come to love. He got to move around on his own terms and sent illustrated letters home.

Rachel was two-and-a-half when she saw her father for the first time after earliest infancy. It must have been confusing to a toddler who couldn't help but think of her grandpa as her daddy. Grandpa Abe loved her and played with her every day. But Rachel knew what to say when her mother pointed to the soldier in the photograph: "That's daddy." Reports of the new words his daughter learned cheered him during his months of waiting. He longed to see, hear, and cuddle her—just as his wife longed to hug and hold the man she had married three years earlier.

My mother had been in foster homes before and knew how difficult other people's families could be. Though she never figured out how to manage life with her in-laws, my mother had superb survival skills. The relief she felt when she was able to put the in-law years behind her was worth any trade-offs she had to make to find a home of her own.

Rachel was conceived about the time her father was agitating for social justice at Camp Reynolds. She was one year old when he captured the German soldier in an Italian farmer's barn. Not surprisingly, Rachel would become an activist too. In high school she gained notoriety among classmates for protesting a blackface portrayal of Aunt Jemima in a school assembly. With her friend Judy she joined a civil rights group and picketed a segregated lunch counter in downtown St. Louis: after the morning newspaper reported Rachel's name among the arrests, a bottle filled with eggs crashed through our hallway window. Someone burst open a watermelon against Mom's new car—a VW bug she had just purchased with money she received after fighting for her share of her long-absent father's estate.

In a journal she once sent me for safekeeping while she was confined to a psychiatric hospital—the same journal where she recorded her memories of Boston—Rachel wrote a few lines about my birth in Cleveland: *My family moved for a third time—to a housing project . . . For a year we lived there. My sister was born. My friends and I watched her, awed, when she came home from the hospital. Who could have known a baby is that small? And helpless.*

How those words thrilled me. To think she was awed by me! I took those words as an amulet signifying her love for me. But then I gasped when I read the brutal words about our mother that followed: *My mother and I parted ways early. I found out she was unpredictable and unsatiable; I couldn't forgive her cruelty; I learned from her sharp tongue and quick temper.*

I know that time and experience can alter memories, coloring them with emotions that weren't actually felt until later. But Rachel's memories of childhood ring as true to me as anything I know about our family's history. The sounds of anger turn like a long-playing record in my own memory: Mom shrilly demanding that Rachel wash dishes and put away her clothes before letting her go out; Rachel's scowling refusals followed by instant escalations and accusations of hostility and betrayal. Shouts and slammed doors. Even a sling around Rachel's arm from a fight with Mom that I hadn't witnessed and wasn't supposed to talk about.

Curious by nature, I never held back on questions—at school, at work or at home. Driven as I was to understand my family's history, I kept asking Mom to tell me more. I hoped another glimpse of the past would slip through her framing of events (which often pointed to the people she could blame for unpleasant incidents). But once I began getting the stories down in my own writing, I was able to see a picture that made sense to me. Something about what Mom, Dad, and Rachel went through those first few years in Cleveland put up a wall of eternal resistance. A wall built from shards of love and abandonment, missing fathers and husbands, displaced bitterness and accusations. Somehow, Rachel's anger took root next to that wall and, like weeds clawing deep, rich loam, choked off other growth. I filled in the outlines of the history I got from my mother by circling back, again and again, to family letters, my grandfather's Cleveland photographs, my father's neatly captioned wartime photo album, the fragments of journals carelessly closeted in boxes—Rachel's and my own.

IN A CHILDREN'S HOME, AGAIN

"Oh, you'll see Bubbe and Grandpa all the time," I imagine my mother saying to Rachel as she packed up her dresses and dolls and toys. "They'll come to see you in your new home, and you'll come back here to play with your cousins. We're not moving far."

I can imagine Rachel's face. Confused. Crestfallen. I can see it clearly because I remember how my four-year-old granddaughter's face crumpled when her mother, my elder daughter, told her they were moving out of the house they shared with me and my husband. It had been my granddaughter's home her entire life. Now my daughter was moving into a condo across the street. "Why do we have to move?" my granddaughter kept asking me, and I said that her mother wanted to have her own kitchen. It was the only answer I could come up with. I too felt forlorn.

Two generations earlier my own mother, in Cleveland, had a particular reason for wanting her own kitchen: she wanted to be able to bring her husband his food. A wife, she told me emphatically, should do that, not his mother. And with Bubbe Ethel in charge of the kitchen, my mother was never allowed to serve, let alone cook, any meals.

Housing was in short supply after the war, but through my father's social work contacts my parents found an unusual way to get out of my father's childhood home. My parents worked out an arrangement at Bellefaire, a residential treatment facility for teenage boys. My mother took a job as a house mother caring for thirteen- and fourteen-year-old boys there. In exchange she and her husband were given a cottage to live in.

Everything about Rachel's life changed with that move. During the day, while my mother was caring for the boys, Rachel went to a nursery school for the children of staff parents. She no longer stayed home with her grandparents or played with her cousins. Her mommy fed her in the kitchenette and the daddy she had previously known only from photos left every morning for work and returned every night. When this new daddy opened the door, he didn't sing like her grandpa did. Sometimes he frowned. He and Mommy talked talked talked. Sometimes Daddy yelled and Mommy cried. The playground in the nursery school had swings, but not the kind she could sit in with big cousins who sat facing her and pushed her back and forth with their feet.

Bellefaire had once been an orphanage like the one in Chicago where my mother grew up. But by the 1940s orphanages in most major cities were being phased out, replaced by foster care programs or cash assistance to needy parents who would otherwise be unable to keep their families together. Bellefaire was repurposed to serve children with behavioral problems. My mother didn't see them as all that disturbed; they reminded her of the boys she knew at the Home. They adored Rachel, she said; sometimes they watched her when she and Dad went out at night.

Fritz Mayer, a German refugee, was the director of Bellefaire. He applied his psychoanalytic background to the new field of residential treatment for disturbed children. Among his contributions to the field were publications in which he formulated the challenging role of house parents, and ways the administrators could best support them. My mother was one of those paraprofessionals charged with bringing a sense of order along with commitment and compassion to the lives of her charges.

For many years, my mother wanted me to write a memoir for her. I told her if she wrote her stories down herself, I would help her. And that's what we did. She e-mailed me her memories. I read, copyedited, and formatted them. I posted them online to share with family. In writing my own memoir two decades later, I went back to read her Bellefaire story with particular interest. Maybe it could explain Rachel's confusing behavior decades later.

Despite the physical differences, the atmosphere at the residential center felt similar to the orphanage where she grew up: instead of a large building with dormitories and a community dining room, there were several cottages with the kids arranged by age and gender. Each one had cottage parents who were responsible for the daily routine and activities.

Mayer, she said, hired her because of all the years she'd spent in the Chicago orphanage. It was the perfect background for this job. Compared to other parental figures in the children's lives, caretakers had limited authority. To be effective, he said, they needed to make a personal investment in the children based on their own values. My mother, he saw, could do that.

Mayer also gave her the approval she always sought. She described the relationship in her memoir. *Fritz backed me up when I needed help with any problem. Once I had a skirmish with a kid who would not cooperate and was pretty hostile. When I tried to get him to comply, he angrily pushed me off balance and I caught myself. He tried again but I stopped him and gave him a good fight back. I actually hit him and that brought him to his senses.* My mother felt bad about hitting the boy. It reminded her of her own experience at the Home: *I was whipped for not complying, only then I was not the one who hit first! I can see a connection in terms of adolescent behavior on my part and the boy's feelings which I sensed.*

She reported the incident to Mayer and apologized. She was surprised by his reaction. According to her, the director agreed that she did what the kid needed. He told her she identified with the boy because of her background, and thus intuitively sensed his need for both care and control. I suspect he also gave her advice on how to meet those needs without resorting to force. What mattered so much to my mother, though, was the validation of her position. She no longer felt like an outsider, as she did among her in-laws. Quite the contrary. At Bellefaire she had the inside track.

Many years later, a psychiatrist would ask my sister Julie if Rachel had ever been molested as a child. The question arose during one of Julie's visits to Rachel in an Oregon hospital. Now a middle-aged woman, Rachel's behavior, the doctor said, was consistent with victims of childhood sexual abuse. Rachel was climbing into women's beds at night, demanding sex. Julie immediately thought of Mom's Bellefaire story—how she and my father would go out at night and leave Rachel with the boys. Why, Julie and I both wondered, would our parents have entrusted their toddler to troubled teenagers? Maybe those boys went too far with their attentions. I wondered if my mother was in denial. She had endured molestation herself, in foster homes and the orphanage. She was able, even at the age of five, to ward off these advances. But she buried her anger and fears to survive. She chose not to see certain things. That's life, she would say. What're you going to do?

When I was young, I admired my mother's fearlessness. Her pluck and bravery. Gradually, I came to see how much of her manner was bravado and understand why it must have been hard for her to sympathize with Rachel when her life first fell apart. Mom had faced terrible adversity and coped with it. How it must have pained her to see her daughter unable to care for herself.

And where was my father during these Bellefaire years? I think he wasn't connecting somehow. His mind was elsewhere. In the trenches with soldiers. With his buddies who had died. In the mountain villages he had roamed. From his war letters, I know how excited he was by the Soviet role in defeating Hitler, and by the opportunity to advance ideals he associated with the Communist Party. After the war, when relations between the USA and the Soviets headed for a deep freeze, I think my father grieved for that lost alliance. Even more, about establishing his social work career. He wasn't happy at his first postwar job as a case worker at Jewish Family Services. When he left Bellefaire every morning to go to work there, he had to deal with needy clients and bossy women—as in the family he grew up with—telling him what to do.

I can imagine the forces bearing down on this new family. Now that her husband was back, Mom needed to make sure he would never leave her again. She wanted to hug and hold the man she'd met a few years earlier. But now he seemed colder, more remote. She sensed he regretted the marriage, and from words he dropped over the years, I think that was sometimes true. He was twenty-four when they met, rebelling against his conservative family. (He liked to call himself the "black sheep.") He married the sexy girl from the orphanage and then he joined the army. When he returned home he faced an instant family—a toddler who didn't know him and a wife who needed endless reassurance. He had married over his parents' objections; now, no matter what the cost to his happiness, he had to stick to his decision.

I wonder if Rachel's lifelong anger started at Bellefaire. The competition for my father's flagging attention must have been fierce. In Rachel's toddler mind, her mother took her away from her adoring grandpa, and then went off with her daddy when he came home, leaving her in the care of those teenage boys. If one of them had violated her, my sister would have had no words. Feeling abandoned and unprotected, she would have burned with rage and despair. I can't know for sure what happened there. I do know how irrational Rachel's anger always seemed. For decades I felt and absorbed it, crackling like lightning between my mother and her firstborn. I couldn't understand it. Eventually, the senselessness and sadness of it just left me numb.

When my mother became pregnant with me, Fritz Mayer told her she would be too involved with the new baby to continue supervising the boys in her cottage. She was disappointed. *I wanted to correct the inequities I saw as a child*, she wrote. With the loss of this job, she lost the opportunity for a redo of her childhood experience, this time from the other side of the authority line. Because family living quarters were part of the job, she also lost her home.

So my parents moved on. They rented a unit in a housing project, which had been converted from temporary housing for workers in a factory that produced war materials. My mother hardly minded its shortcomings. She wrote: *It was a small four-room shack with a Franklin stove for heating, coal bin outside, and a deep tub in the kitchen for bathing the babies. It took a year to get a private phone, but we were lucky to be located near a public telephone a few steps away. Between the ground and wood floor there was plenty of space for mice— once I caught eleven of them in one night. I kept resetting the trap every time it snapped. It didn't bother me at all, though Mort would have nothing to do with it.*

I wasn't surprised my mother dispensed with the mice so fearlessly. I knew the orphanage stories. How a supervisor sent her to the broom closet and how my mother refused to cry. How she was fully prepared to pick up any worms and mice hiding in the dark. "None of these things ever scared me," she told me proudly.

Her in-laws of course disapproved of this downscale rental, but Mom would never go back to their suburban home. And her decision did have the blessings of at least one respected authority. When Dr. Weidenthal, her pediatrician, made a house call to see Rachel one day, he put his arm around my mother and said, "I admire you." He knew the in-laws in Cleveland Heights; he was their pediatrician too. My mother understood his words to mean that yes she was right to get away from them and have her own home no matter how poor the neighbors were, or how few the amenities.

Then I joined the family. I arrived in those four rooms with the coal bin outside and mice underneath the flooring. My mother often told me that Rachel used to climb into my crib, and that she had to pull her away to protect me. When she talked to Dr. Weidenthal about Rachel's behavior, he dismissed it as typical sibling rivalry: "How would you like it," he asked her, "if your husband said he had another wife but loved you just the same?"

Wise as the doctor was, I wonder if it was something more than jealousy that impelled my older sister into my crib. I wonder if Rachel crawled into my crib to experience with her own skin my pink newness, my newborn innocence. Maybe she even wanted to cuddle me or take care of me. I say this because all the time we were growing up together I don't remember Rachel ever getting angry with me or expressing jealousy. I do remember her giving me big sister tips. Cheering me on when I went away to college even while she was floundering. No, she never seemed to feel rivalry toward me. The person she resented was our mother.

CHECKLIST

The double helix discovery came in 1953, the year Julie was born. I remember looking at an article, probably in *Life* magazine, that showed the elegant spirals connected by molecular ladders that could zip or unzip as needed to start a new life. I saw how tiny ladders of scaffolding can duplicate and mix proteins to make complete instructions for creating a person. Instructions for making Rachel, Rachel and me, me. For making Michael, Michael and Julie, Julie. For making our eyes blue or brown. For making a mix of straight hair, curly hair, and bald heads in our family.

Ten years later my high school biology book carried detailed diagrams showing how A, C, G, and T proteins formed the building blocks of life. It was so beautiful I dreamed of becoming a biochemist. My best friend's father was one, and I couldn't imagine why she hated working in his lab. Then I got to college and spent six hours a week staring into microscopes with cross-sections of chick embryos. I was supposed to be able to identify their developmental stages. I learned a smattering of developmental embryology, but mainly I learned that doing science is a lot harder than reading and dreaming about it.

While I was grappling with that biology course, Rachel was putting together poems for publication. She was also struggling to retain her sanity and independence.

I never really expected a specific gene to be discovered that could explain what happened to Rachel. Not even several of them working in combination. I was never convinced that such a complex illness was entirely genetic. No, there's no gene therapy for severe mental illness, no prenatal test that identifies damaged DNA lurking on a chromosome. There is no neonatal procedure, no pinprick that will show a newborn's risk for schizophrenia. So how could DNA explain, let alone alleviate, the darkness of my sister's life?

Crick and Watson couldn't explain all the mysteries. Why one cell becomes liver and another becomes skin. One becomes blood, another bone. Over the years, mental health specialists have come to believe that schizophrenia (or the multiple ailments that fit into that broad category) results from a combination of genetic and environmental factors. And during that time I've thought about as many of these factors as I can tease out of our family's history. I know I'll never fully understand what happened to Rachel, why it happened to her and not me. Still, I can't help chasing the twists and turns of the mystery. I go through risk factors and check them off in my mind:

*Bad genes. Epidemiologists know the odds, based on whether or not you have an immediate family member with schizophrenia. If a sibling or parent does, you have a one in ten chance of suffering too. If the afflicted relative is more distant, your chances are lower, much lower. My mother had a half-brother who was institutionalized his entire adult life. She said it was shell shock; his death certificate from the veteran's hospital says he was paranoid schizophrenic. My father had an uncle who needed to be cared for by his sister during his entire life. *Bad genes. Check.*

Paternal stress. With all the sperm in a single ejaculation, why did the sperm that resulted in Rachel's conception have to be faulty? From a psychiatric epidemiologist I learned that paternal stress could churn out the very sperm most likely to be defective. I think about my father starting his family right after basic training and all his conflicting commitments. He was a scholar and a social worker. A pacifist and a suspiciously early anti-fascist. A son whose wife was in conflict with his family. A first-time father at twenty-five years old, who voluntarily left a stateside desk job for combat duty overseas. *Paternal stress. Check.*

Viral impact on developing fetus. I remembered little Johnny Weg, born deaf because his mother contracted German measles while she was pregnant with him. With springtime births proven to have a significant correlation with schizophrenia, researchers point to influenza and viruses contracted during fall and winter months. Rachel was born in April. *Viral impact on developing fetus. Check.*

Hallucinogenic drugs. For some individuals, recreational drugs can kick off brain circuits that don't return to their normal state. Rachel told me about the mescaline she took in San Francisco. Later, her New York City friend told me Rachel went off with friends who were into pot and LSD. It was the early 1960s. Rachel didn't do drugs a lot. But maybe just enough. *Hallucinogenic drugs. Check.*

Maternal stress during early embryonic development. Emotional stress changes a pregnant woman's cortisol levels, which, especially in the early stages, can hurt fetal development. The placenta, that blood-filled, throw-away organ, brings the fetus hormones as well as food from its mother. A bride of only one year, my mother became pregnant when my father finished basic training. She hated living with his family, the temporary arrangement she had reluctantly agreed to because it would be easier for him to visit her when he was on leave. Mom believed her in-laws looked down on her because she came from a poor family. Every time she talked to me about her life there, I would see her as a little girl left to be raised by strangers. My mother was primed to feel unloved. *Maternal stress during early embryonic development. Check.*

Imagining what it was like for Rachel during her first three years, I can almost feel the tumult she experienced as she moved from one Cleveland home to another: first in the heart of my father's family, living with a mother who was experiencing a deep sense of rejection and abandonment; then, after our father removed his dog tags and packed his uniform away, at Bellefaire where she was surrounded by troubled adolescent boys; and finally at the housing project where I was born, at a time when our father was unhappy with his job, and perhaps with his wife as well.

Rachel's first years came when my father had to jumpstart both a career and a marriage. Separated as newlyweds by the draft, my parents never got to enjoy the bliss of coupledom that our mother must have craved. How desperately she must have longed to rekindle the love and passion of their dating days. To fill the gaping hole left by a father who abandoned her when she wasn't much older than her firstborn was when her husband returned from the war.

When Rachel was two, she too had to leave her birth home, a home where she had grandparents who adored her, cousins to play with, and an extended family that often crowded around the dining room table for holidays. Where a grandfather, whom she believed to be her father for two years, sang and painted and took photographs and showered her with attention when he came home from work. What longing did that first separation create in her?

And what must it have been like to have to compete with her own mother for the love of the new man in her life? I can still taste the toxic triangle, so obvious even to me as a child, that endured until my father died. I still tremble at the way it pushed Mom and Rachel apart for so long, like misaligned magnets, while it pulled Dad back and forth between the two of them.

In the years after the war, my father forged a career he loved and threw himself into it. He dedicated himself to the Jewish Community Center field. He organized projects to make the communities where we lived more inclusive and accepting of those who were marginalized—the developmentally disabled and the elderly. Cruelly, he wasn't able to do the same for Rachel when she needed our acceptance. Nobody understood schizophrenia at all, and the stigma was immense.

Even as new research piles up in journals and conferences, schizophrenia and related disorders remain mysterious. I think about Rachel's illness in terms of a fatal misalignment of genetics and her environment. I look at environmental factors that may have caused problematic genes to be expressed instead of lying dormant. I look at Mom's history and Dad's, and what they brought into Rachel's infant years. My theories aren't scientific like Crick and Watson's double helix. But I hold on to them. For me, they are better than the darkness of total incomprehension.

My Life Between Two Childhoods

my life between two childhoods, each one
nasty but to be endured, the first, a waif
swaddled in the skins of animals
and meant to be raced around, or throttled or
tousled, but just to be daring,

then I entered a neat contrite home, and then
they jumped upon me, naming me damned,
but I got used to them, got to like the acid
attention I got, and barely knowing who or where
I was, came to terms with my soul,
and hating with acid bitterness the whole world
found a place in the hazy outside.

this home, troubled and relentless drove me on
to many feats of adventure and worldliness
so I became responsible to no ends of beings
that I still liked people,
and remained proud.

I manage my own personal life now, and have no end
of work and bad times as well as good,
am appreciated by nobody,
but my plain, personal self is adjusted to these times,
and no new will come.

—Rachel Goodman

PART III

Horizons

FBI AT THE DOOR

In the St. Louis area, our parents first rented an apartment in Clayton, a suburb on the south side of the Washington University campus, while they looked for a house to buy in University City, the suburb on the north side. Unlike the rest of Clayton, with its spacious single-family homes, our neighborhood was in the rental area. Our whole street, like the one behind it, was lined with nearly identical brick apartment buildings, three stories each, in varying shades of red. Black metal fire escapes terraced the backs of the buildings leading to an alley where matching garages held cars, bicycles, and neatly capped garbage cans.

After moving from Indianapolis, we weren't in hostile territory anymore. The university area in St. Louis was filled with liberals. It seemed like everyone wanted the Cold War to be over. Nobody asked me about horns on my head, but the girls in Clayton did have very specific rules. I was in seventh grade when a few girls came up to me after school. "Oh, we don't wear lipstick here until eighth grade," they told me. "We just thought you'd want to know." I was mortified.

Rachel knew both towns. She had received special permission to enroll at U City High when she moved early with our father. She assured me I would be happier in U City because all kinds of kids were there, not just a bunch of kids looking all the same in Villager outfits and making all the rules. Meanwhile I decided to lay low in Clayton and stay home after school, even when that same anti-lipstick brigade knocked on my door to ask me to play kickball on the playground across the street. I declined. I didn't want to worry about their rules. I just wanted to do my homework and read, listening to the whir of my mother mixing instant chocolate pudding, or Rachel practicing scales up and down the keyboard.

In October 1959 I heard a lot of talk about Soviet Premier Khrushchev coming to the United Nations. One evening my mother called out to me to come in the living room to see him speaking on television. Dad was working that night at one of his Jewish Center programs. Julie was playing with her friend in the apartment just below us on the ground floor. I didn't really want to leave my book, but I turned it upside down on my bed anyway, pages split at the spine, to join the others in the living room. Because when did my mother ever before ask me to watch TV with her? In the living room I took the end of the couch opposite Rachel.

"Mommy, the news is starting now," Michael called, as he stood in front of the television fiddling with the rabbit ears. The gray-and-white faces stopped scrolling down the screen. Then he looked back at the sofa. "Hey, I was sitting there," he yelled when he saw me. "I just got up for a minute to fix the TV." I could see his long dark eyelashes crinkling for a cry.

"Never mind," Rachel said to Michael. "You can have my place." She got up and flopped into the butterfly chair, leaving her end of the sofa for him. It was fun to sit there, and it was one of the reasons I was glad we still had our furniture from Indianapolis. After leaving my friends in Indianapolis, I savored the shape and feel and smell of the familiar.

I knew our parents were eager for Khrushchev and President Eisenhower to agree to a nuclear arms treaty. Earlier that year, the *Post-Dispatch* had been filled with headlines about the U2 plane shot down over Russia. At first the US denied that Gary Powers, the pilot, was spying, but then the Russians showed evidence he was. "It's embarrassing to America," my father had said. Now Khrushchev had come to New York. My family hoped he would talk about ending the arms race.

When Khrushchev began talking, I couldn't make out what the translator was saying, so I reached over to turn up the volume knob. That's when I heard the knocking. I opened the door, assuming one of our downstairs neighbors was dropping by to watch TV with us. Instead, two strange men stood shoulder to shoulder in the hallway. They had dark blue suits and matching crewcuts, and I realized right away this couldn't be a sales call: the Fuller Brush man always came alone, and always held a small suitcase with samples. Except for the hat one man was holding by his side, these men's hands were empty.

Mom jumped up from her chair before I could open the door further. She stepped outside and closed the door behind her. Michael, Rachel, and I all stared at the door spellbound.

"Turn the volume back down, Debby," Rachel hissed. "I want to hear what they're saying." It didn't take us long to find out because my mother reappeared in just a few minutes. "They're gone," she said, clicking the door shut with a lock of her jaw and a look of satisfaction.

"What did those men want?" Rachel asked. "Are they FBI?" I wasn't surprised by my sister's question. After the first seconds of confusion about door-to-door salesmen, I had

the same suspicion. And I knew this encounter would end
before it began because we were never, ever, supposed to talk
with the FBI. I knew that from life in Indianapolis, where
some songs were too dangerous to sing in public.

We kids had seen FBI men on television, but this was the
first time in real life. It was exciting and maybe just a little bit
scary. Mom reminded us now, once again, after closing the
door. "We don't talk to the FBI." The look on her face was
serious and righteous. It was the look you would expect of a
woman with her hair pulled back in a bun, not a pixie haircut.
"They're just trying to get information about people we
know. We don't have to tell them anything." I believed Mom
when she said they couldn't harm us. But Rachel was already
in high school. She may have been more aware of FBI political
realities than I was.

"But why did they come tonight?" Michael wanted to
know. "Did they want to see if we were watching Khrushchev
on TV?" Rachel and I laughed at him, and Mom explained that
the timing was probably a coincidence. Julie was downstairs
playing with her friend. It was just as well. She was only six,
too young to understand. We would have to explain things to
her later.

"They're just letting us know that even when we move,
they can find us," my mother said. "They follow us, but they
can't do anything to hurt us."

I glanced at Rachel. She was nibbling her fingernails, as
though stifling an argument. Michael was making goofy faces,
jumping up and down from the sofa to the floor. "Dum de dum
dum . . ," he sang to the tune of the *Dragnet* song. I started to
giggle, and he sang it again, delighted to get a reaction from
me. Of course everyone knew the television show about FBI

crime-fighters. After the first four notes of the theme came a long pause, followed by a crash of tympani. Dum de dum dum . . . DUM. Michael, Rachel, and I shouted out the climactic finale, and then we all burst out laughing.

"We must be horrible criminals," I intoned, catching my breath. I tried to imitate the raspy voice of Jack Webb on *Dragnet*. "We're watching the communist enemy speak at the United Nations!" Our whoops and hollers cracked the tension, releasing sprays of silliness.

Mom tried to shush us so she could hear the rest of the speech. But Michael and I danced around the living room until even Rachel started grinning. It was so funny, we told each other, how those FBI men towered over our mother, all of five feet and one-half inch tall, without scaring her. Michael and I collapsed with laughter on either side of the butterfly chair, right on top of Rachel.

When at last we exhausted our giggles, I went back to my room and picked up the book on my bed. I would read until sleep overtook me, or until my mother came in and made me turn off the light. It was the same routine every night, no matter where we lived. I never went to sleep fearing that anybody could hurt us. Not the kids at a new school. Not the Russians. Not the FBI.

I didn't get to see Khrushchev bang his shoe on the table later that night, shouting that the Soviets would bury us. And now, because nobody has been able to find a news clip verifying such a performance, historians say maybe he never really did pound the General Assembly furniture with his footwear. They do know, however, that the Soviet premier got pretty riled up about US imperialism in his speech. But I must have been asleep by the time that happened.

Eighteen months later we moved to University City. The house was perfect. Four bedrooms on a tree-lined street, with parks and schools and shops in walking distance. Every house had unique architectural details. We had a Mediterranean roof of red, curved tiles. Wrought iron balconies. Stucco walls with arches. This turned out to be the last family move for the Goodmans. This is where the egg-filled bottle crashed through our window after Rachel got arrested. Where Michael and I had parties while Rachel was in Israel, where Rachel lived when she was first hospitalized. It's the house where I got married, where my father died, and where my mother stayed into her nineties, even after the rest of us had moved away. It's the house I see when I remember the joys and sorrows of my family.

AEROGRAMMES FROM ISRAEL

A black mailbox hung right outside our front door. A flat metal rectangle, it was fastened to the red brick exterior of our University City house. The box was there when we moved in and still hung there, askew on one remaining bolt, when my mother moved out fifty years later. Of all the mail dropped into that box over the years none was more exhilarating, more hopeful, more promising than the wispy blue aerogrammes Rachel sent from Israel. Hold on to them, she had said, I'm writing these instead of keeping a journal.

In high school Rachel joined a Zionist youth organization, a departure from the civil rights and peace groups she was involved in previously. Our parents, while supportive of the new Israeli state, did not join the organizations promoting aliyah—emigration to Israel by United States Jews. Rachel, however, was looking for an alternative to college. She loved learning, but not in classrooms. Through the Zionist group she learned about the Habonim Workshop, a post–high school program that featured a ten-month stint working on a kibbutz, along with study and travel.

Rachel decided to join, even though it would mean putting in extra time to catch up with the others and learn basic Hebrew. In September after graduation, when all her friends were going off to college, Rachel went to New York City to join the Workshop group on a ship headed to Israel.

Once there, Rachel wrote at least every week. My heart leaped when I got home and saw, peeking through the day's batch of paper, a blue aerogramme. I loved getting home first so I could read and relish it without interruption. Rachel was happy now. She was open and communicative. The letters seemed proof that our shaky family life was righting itself. Her happiness signaled an end to the incessant, angry fights with our parents. She was doing what she wanted most: getting away from home, working out of doors, and meeting people from all over the world. I was happy also. Now in my first year of high school, I had found two new best friends.

Aerogrammes were smart and efficient. Practically weightless, the light blue writing sheet transformed to an envelope when folded with tabs along the edges that had to be carefully slit when opening. Sometimes Rachel packed the letter with miniaturized, but always readable, script. Sometimes she used a typewriter, turning the aerogramme upside down near the end of the sheet to squeeze in one or two last lines that the machine's platen otherwise obscured. Sometimes she had so much to say that she used two aerogrammes, marking them clearly outside, Part 1 or Part 2. She made sure we got the full story in the right order.

Rachel's sentences radiated light and energy and thoughtful reflection. Her paragraphs were peppered with transliterations, along with context to help you understand what the Hebrew word meant—"camping trip," "work schedule," or "holiday." Most of the letters were written to the entire family, and we passed them around, marveling at her travel descriptions and commentary. Mom and Dad thought them worthy of publication in a local newsletter, but Rachel, when asked permission, said no. Her thoughts

were private, she said, and she preferred circulation be limited to close family and friends. Mom made blue-tinged
copies to share on her office mimeograph machine.

Toward the end of her time abroad, Rachel vacillated about
what to do next. She talked about applying to Washington
University, less than two miles from our house. But then, despite her newfound passion for the poetry of Rimbaud and
the philosophy of Schopenhauer, she would say she was not
cut out for formal schooling, at least not at this time. While I
loved the rigorous academics I was being exposed to in our
high school, I admired Rachel for taking a stand that she felt
strongly about. She still had worlds to explore.

Rachel's letters prepared me for a big change. But not the
one I saw when she came home. Even though she had written
frequently about her manual labor and cross-country hikes, I
was flabbergasted by her stunning appearance. How wonderful
it would have been if the magic of her nineteenth year had
presaged an unfolding of long-term happiness. If the startling
clarity of her letters had marked the beginning of a rising star,
a mind ready to unfold its singular, glorious strength to the
world.

As it turned out, despite her physical grace, despite the
best efforts of a mind and soul yearning to encounter the
world more deeply, the invisible pathways of Rachel's brain
were surreptitiously rearranging themselves, ready to send
phantom perceptions on a collision course with reality. We
Goodmans, having survived so many changes together, would
soon float away from each other, adrift in mutual incomprehension. Our family would never feel the same again.

Rachel returned from Israel in September of 1962. When
she walked in the door for the first time after ten months, I

had to catch my breath and avert my eyes to keep from staring. The angles of her face and body were new, re-sculpted. Her sleeveless knit dress with pencil-thin stripes circled her torso from shoulders to knees and exposed the full length of her tanned, muscular arms. The corded belt caught her waist, as though to pause her body's headlong motion. The calves of her legs, always prominent, bulged larger. She must have shed twenty-five pounds since she'd left.

Soon after, we talked in the living room at night. The stippled white walls, with just a hint of green, reached over the arches to the hallway and dining room. Two French doors that faced our front yard gave onto faux balconies with wrought iron railings. Never opened, the doors were a decorative accent, a foil to the roof that made our house instantly recognizable near the end of the long block of midwestern brick. Rachel sat smoking, her back to the French door closest to the fireplace and bookshelves. I took a chair closer to her so I could soak up every word.

"Who was your favorite roommate?" I wanted to know. How much Hebrew did she speak? How many boyfriends did she have? What did she eat, since meat was so scarce in Israel? It was hard to take in her answers. The strangeness of her heightened beauty, like a vision or a dream, eclipsed the words emerging from her sun-kissed lips. More than answers, I wanted to breathe her back inside me. Inside the family.

"Okay Debby? I need to do some things," she told me, gently disengaging for the evening. "I'll still be here tomorrow."

We Goodman kids had gone away, individually and sometimes together, to summer camps, but never for this long. Rachel had celebrated her nineteenth birthday not with us, but with her friends in the kibbutz. Now, enclosed by the cool stucco of our living room, she made our family complete again. During the following week her friends, the ones who were still in town, dropped by to greet her and visit. I took breaks from my homework to join them. Rachel leaned against the square orange cushions of the high-backed teak chair. She waved her right hand while she talked, swiping the air with a cigarette and staccato flick of ashes.

I already knew a lot about her adventures from letters that overflowed with joy and confidence. But they were so rich with detail I couldn't absorb everything she said. Now I wanted to hear the stories firsthand. About her study groups on a heaving ocean ship. Work assignments at the kibbutz. The poisonous snake she killed. The melons she hauled. The tractor she rode to seed potatoes. The hikes across the Galilee hills. The Arab villages. The digs with ancient ruins. And oh, the romance of dances on the beach with young men from South Africa about to join the Israeli army. And what happened to her boyfriend Glen?

I was proud to see my older sister the center of attention among her St. Louis friends. They were smart. Sophisticated. Scouts from the future, they seemed to me. They knew what was happening in New York, Chicago, Boston, and brought new trends back to our corner of the Midwest. Even before her return, Rachel had already helped me gain entrée to the most interesting crowd in University City. Their younger siblings knew and admired Rachel, which helped me to feel at ease with them. Now Rachel had taken worldliness to a whole other level. Clearly she had found herself and would shine wherever she went. Where that would be, she hadn't yet decided, she explained. For the moment she was just checking in at home, but she'd be leaving soon.

As the excitement of her return subsided, I sensed her voice lacked some of the fervor of her letters. She became preoccupied deciding on that next step. "I can go to school part-time in New York," she would say at dinner. "I have friends to live with in San Francisco." Mom and Dad would push back on her ever-shifting plans and encourage her to stay in St. Louis for work and school. In the kibbutz, she had daily work schedules to follow. Weekend trips deferred until work hours were fulfilled. With no structure to contain her, she bounced back and forth between an infinity of possibilities. She sometimes seemed to be throwing them against the wall, one after another, to see what would stick. I realize now that without the structure that had worked so well for her in Israel she was in freefall. Maybe the arguments she provoked with our parents was her way of asking for some limits. But I was sixteen then and rooted for independence. I had every hope that Rachel would make it on her own, and her years of discontent were ended.

For a little while, at least, with her taut limbs and flashing eyes, Rachel glittered like an Egyptian jewel in a golden pendant.

The Front Porch

The front porch
Is where people congregate
In the hot summer.
Dressed in clinging shorts
And limpid halters
With the blazing sun
Oppressing their spirits
They whimper about the heat
And watch the hose sprinkle on the grass.

—Rachel Goodman

THE PRODROME
YOU CANNOT SEE

There was more going on with Rachel than she let on in her letters. I know now how she was able to cover up the cracks in her life, and looking back, I can find subtle evidence of them even in her wondrous Israel aerogrammes. In March, five months into her Israel experience, she wrote, *I'm beginning to see a purpose to my life. Undefined, almost a nothing, but the germ of an understanding that I must follow to its ultimate end.* Out of the confused thoughts and feelings of her childhood a *clear pattern* was emerging that put everything in startling relief. She felt she was developing a foundation of thought processes that were changing her thinking. But this wasn't a kind of purpose that could be put in cubbyholes or into action. Her sense of direction, she said, was coming from literature she admired: *Leaves of Grass* and *Tropic of Cancer*. That sounded romantic when I read it, though I felt queasy when she said a friend told her that her ideas sounded like Henry Miller's. As far as I understood, Miller was mainly interested in unfettered sexual expression. Was she? I wondered. There must be more to him I don't understand. I don't think my parents took any of this talk very seriously. I suspect they did become concerned when she wrote two months later that she planned to live in San Francisco and support herself. *Don't expect me to have a college degree in four years*, she told them.

Back in the States, the gap between what she did and what she said widened. After stopping off in St. Louis for two months at most, she went to New York City, not San Francisco, to live with her Workshop friends. Her letters home still made sense. Perfect spelling, calm sentences and cogent paragraphs about her activities and plans. To me they were the letters of a sister who knew her own mind.

After she died I contacted people who knew Rachel to interview them for this book. Judy, Rachel's best friend from high school, spoke with me at length about her stay with Rachel in New York. She told me how frightening my sister's life there really was. Rachel lived on the Lower East Side, two levels underground, in a room with a dirt floor and a bathtub under a countertop in the kitchen. She shared a toilet down the hall with drunks and addicts. Rachel had written home about the oboe she rented for lessons she was taking. She didn't tell us that she turned off the bulb in her room to practice because, as she told Judy, "I could hear myself better." Rachel played the oboe in a pitch-black room, stark naked, surrounded by the poetry she had written on her walls—her own translations of Rimbaud and Baudelaire.

Rachel wrote a chatty letter home about the trip she and Judy took to the seashore at Cape May on the Jersey shore. Of course she didn't tell us about the men she went off with for sex, her face, according to Judy, devoid of visible emotion. Or the policemen who picked them up and drove them to the bus station with a warning about hitchhiking. When I went back and reread Rachel's letters during that period, I was amazed at how convincingly she covered her condition up. I even felt angry at being fooled (as though she could help doing what she did).

Even so, we all knew Rachel was floundering. She kept moving around. Switching roommates. Changing plans and schools and jobs. She came back to St. Louis for a while and took courses at Washington University. Mom was working as a volunteer coordinator at the Baby Tooth Survey, an anti-nuclear-testing project (scientists analyzed teeth donated by kids for radioactive isotopes of strontium 90), and got Rachel a job in the campus office of one of its founders, the ecology activist Barry Commoner. But Rachel couldn't keep it. She decided to go to San Francisco. After her boss there called my parents to tell them something was very wrong, she came home again. It became increasingly obvious that Rachel was disintegrating. But I didn't want to judge her and talk about her with my parents. I wanted to give her the benefit of the doubt.

Finally I had to admit something was broken inside Rachel once she told me about the two men who'd followed her to San Francisco all the way from New York City. I could only imagine how the bland, furrowed faces of two random businessmen standing together in dark suits, white collars, and narrow ties might have triggered in Rachel memories of pursuit. Memories of the FBI visit and talk of surveillance. Maybe the two men she saw near the lawyer's office where she worked were bankers or sales managers taking a walk during their lunch hour. There was little about her life in San Francisco that made sense to her, but surveillance was a scenario she knew. Maybe its very familiarity comforted her.

I hadn't understood then why Rachel thought she was being followed, but I knew she was losing touch with reality. I didn't know about the theory that mutations in DNA, inherited or acquired, can cause brain circuits to go awry. That the damaged circuits then have trouble locating the source of perceptions, so that sounds and images generated by memory and emotional circuits appear to be coming from the external world.

There's also a theory based on neuronal or synaptic pruning in the brain. It seems counterintuitive, but the fact is we're all born with far too many neural connections. Starting in childhood, immune cells engulf and eliminate the excess; this normal developmental process picks up again in adolescence, until finally an efficient organization for thinking emerges. In people with schizophrenia, however, the process runs amok. And oh, the horror of it! I ponder this cruel twist of nature. I can practically hear the synapses succumbing in Rachel's brain: Someone is following me! Threatening me! The signals went to the wrong parts of the brain and her senses deceived her. Stop, I want to scream. Don't take away so many neurons; don't destroy that extraordinary brain!

I try to imagine how psychosis raced through Rachel's mind, shearing off limbs tangled with neural branches trying to hang whole. I suspect that even when all seemed lost, Rachel's memories of childhood love and laughter occasionally glowed like embers remaining in dark beds of coal. I like to believe that she was able to warm herself once in a while with those bright memories.

Experts now say it's possible to recognize early symptoms

of schizophrenia. They call the signs during that period—such as disconnected language and manic behavior—the prodrome. Like the aura before the migraine, the prodrome predicts. It points the way.

But you only see what it's telling you in retrospect. You don't know anything when you're looking ahead. Not until all hell breaks loose and the doctors give a diagnosis—complete with categories and sub-categories. Paranoid schizophrenia. For some, especially the family, it's a relief to have a label, no matter how horrible, and no matter how much anger, confusion, anxiety, depression, or some combination of all they feel as a result. For others, especially the sufferer, it's a violation, the reduction of a mind and a soul to a crude, dehumanizing classification scheme.

At first when you hear the label you don't know what to believe. After all, people, especially young people in their teens and twenties, can talk strangely and behave erratically without being crazy. If their behavior returns to normal, what you thought was mental illness turns out to have been a passing phase. "That's just how adolescents behave," friends tell your parents when your sister drops out of school, can't keep a job, and stays up till dawn writing, pacing, smoking. They say, "Let her be. Let her do her thing."

So I understand why people minimized those behaviors. And why I did, too. You need to be supportive; you don't want to overreact. Everybody wants time to work its magic.

However, against the odds, just one in a hundred, your sister's neural circuits get crossed. In the bedroom you share, she tells you her fears and you know she's experiencing a delusion. A judge declares her incompetent despite legal arguments from her court-appointed lawyers about alternative lifestyles. And then you wonder whether her incessant writing, her constant need for adventure and fierce independence weren't so awesome. Maybe they were signs of something awful.

Your sister gets a diagnosis, but you can't believe it. You're not sure of anything at all. You spend a lifetime trying to understand what happened to her. You wonder if parents or doctors or even if you yourself, young as you were, might have been able to head off the worst effects of the disease if only you had seen it coming. If you had made out the shape of that predatory prodrome circling below the surface, below the murky waters of adolescent rebellion.

In later years, as I came to learn about the prodrome, I began to wonder whether Rachel's downfall came as suddenly as it seemed at the time. Was there something wrong with all those things that seemed so special about her? The way she wrote, for example, was remarkable. For three years, when she was in high school, the sounds of her writing put me to sleep: the rapid-fire clicks of steel keys, the clang of the carriage return. Then when she went off to Israel and sent home those letters filled with vivid descriptions—her experiences, thoughts and doubts filling all the blue spaces right up to the edges of the paper.

I expected the bright flares of talent her letters contained to light her way to a career of creative fulfillment. Now, looking back, I wondered how much her frenetic writing was a sign of the oncoming storm. Were the leaps and turns of her poems really a symptom of disordered thought? Or were they what poetry *is*? In Rachel's case, perhaps they were both.

Experts now study ways to head off full-blown schizo-phrenia through early intervention. But Rachel's symptoms came before anyone knew about prevention.

She didn't seem to understand anything was wrong with her. At least not for a long time—eventually she wrote about her "schizophrenic eyes" in her poetry and journals. It took me some time to accept her illness too. I just thought she was too proud. Too stubborn. Maybe even a little heroic, like the Beat poets who couldn't be bothered with conformity.

Perhaps today's medications can subdue voices, lower levels of suspicion and improve thinking ability with less severe side effects than Rachel suffered. Hers were terrible: tardive dyskinesia; fog-filled brain; bad teeth from dry mouth; meta-bolic issues including a big, slack belly.

Rachel had a psychotic break when she was twenty-three, following several years of erratic behavior after she returned from her year in Israel. And here's my quandary. If my parents had seen her behavior as part of a prodrome, could they have averted the crises that followed? Rachel excelled in the physical labor on the kibbutz. She loved the vigorous hikes across the country. Could another version of that experience have been replicated and helped return her to health? Parents today send vulnerable adolescents to wilderness camps for that very reason. Could Rachel have been kept away from marijuana and mescaline, potent trig-gers for psychosis?

Maybe not. Rachel was too hard to contain. She knew how to get away and she knew how to get *her* way. But once she slipped from prodrome to syndrome, did her condition have to become so cataclysmic? Others with severe mental illness stabilized, even got better. Rachel didn't. I don't know why but I can't help suspecting that the medications she was given early on damaged her terribly. And that being locked in psych wards against her will severely traumatized her.

Time and again, I replayed in my mind the plans we made— Rachel's parents, her two sisters, and brother—and those we didn't make. Failures and disappointments separated us for years at a time rather than bringing us together. I regretted the compromises we felt we had to make, individually and as a family, for the sake of our own sanity and well-being because they came at such a cost to Rachel. I know there were no good answers. But still, I wish I could have been more helpful to my big sister.

BALLAD OF BAGNELL DAM

They say when catastrophe happens, neural centers deep in the brain take a snapshot, fixing the image into permanent memory. That makes sense to me because I do know exactly where I was and what I was doing at historic, world-shattering moments: when I heard that President Kennedy was shot, when the Challenger exploded, when the Twin Towers were attacked.

Maybe family catastrophe is different. There are no loudspeakers or radios. No neighbors or colleagues huddling in front of televisions and bonding over shared memories. There was none of that for the news that shattered so much of my family's world. I don't know how it came to me or what exactly I was doing when I first learned that Rachel had lost her freedom and tumbled into what seemed a living death.

Camp Hawthorn was nestled in a rustic state park by the Lake of the Ozarks. In the summer of 1965, following my first year of college, I was a counselor there. Private resorts and other summer camps dotted an endless shoreline on the immense waterway created by the Bagnell Dam, a hydroelectric facility built thirty years earlier across the Osage River.

I was glad to be away from the heat and humidity of St.

Louis County. I loved climbing down the vine-covered hill to the waterfront, jumping off the dock for a swim, or grabbing a canoe from the boat house to paddle among the hundreds of secret coves. I had already spent two summers here as a camper after we moved from Indianapolis to St. Louis. For me the highlights of each summer were the outings when we paddled three straight days on the lake and set up campsites at night on remote wooded shores.

Now more than anything I was happy to be outside, even in Central Missouri, in the middle of nowhere. And I was relieved to be away from all the arguments about Rachel and her behavior. I looked forward to letting family tensions slide off me as easily as water from the lake.

Among the boxes of old letters I found were a few of mine from the first weeks of that summer. I described the thrill of flying across the lake on water skis for the first time. I joked about the drudgery of cleaning out oversize pots to help get the mess hall ready for the first session of campers. And, as though warning them of possible communication gaps, I took pains to inform my parents that our phone calls were plagued by terrible static.

During the previous months, my freshman year at University of Michigan, both my parents had written me at least weekly. They made only occasional references to Rachel, her plans and activities. I knew they didn't want me to worry. Rachel herself, living at home with them, wrote me long letters, encouraging me to enjoy campus life even though she herself had decided that formal, full-time study was not for her.

Rachel was a steadfast correspondent who chatted about local gossip, books she read, and plans she was making. Soon after I arrived in Ann Arbor, Rachel wrote me to say our parents were sending her to a psychiatrist. She was hopeful: the doctor was tall, dark, and handsome, and the visits might be some fun. She soon changed her mind: *September 9, 1964. I'm afraid my doom is foretold. When a headshrinker sets to work, all-encompassing knowledge must vanish. I guess vague genius cannot survive in a "real" world. And how I did love my ghostly terrain.* I wasn't sure what she meant, but it sounded ominous.

After I confided my concerns about fitting in to campus life, she tried to fulfill her role as older sister: *November 3, 1964. Your letter sounds confused and I guess you are, which is, of course, a healthy state in a "normal-thinking-young-person-out-in-the-world-on-her-own-for-the-first-time-in-her-life" . . . The best advice I can give of course is "don't do anything I wouldn't do," which, however, won't help too much I'm afraid.*

On subsequent pages her words became even darker: *Remember that the anarchist is supreme. . . . Life is never easy but one has to use a little intelligence even in the midst of violent despair and suffering. . . . Perhaps if you put this letter in some safe drawer, you can refer to my bits of wisdom in some future need.* I did put her letter away, but not for the reason she suggested. I couldn't bear to think further about Rachel's troubling words or where her life was heading.

In July of that summer, I learned that Rachel had been committed to St. Louis State Hospital, a psychiatric facility with locked wards. I never found a letter informing me of the commitment—so my parents probably told me on a phone call. But I don't remember it. I simply don't recall the moment I received this bombshell news. Was there static on the line? Long silences or angry cries?

Whenever I've searched my memory, all I've been able to hear is "The Ballad of Bagnell Dam" burrowing in my head like an ear worm. That's what the whole camp sang after dinner in the mess hall, recounting the fate of the people living in the town of Zebra, on the Osage River. We sang about what they lost when the engineers opened the floodgates of the dam. How the release of water from the bloated river obliterated their town and the residents had to move on. The song taught me what it cost for the rest of the region to enjoy abundant hydropower, along with a new manmade lake for swimming, boating, and water-skiing.

Even without a snapshot in my brain, I have always felt the shockwaves of that summer. Recalling them has been like canoeing with a missing paddle. Still, I've been able to pull from memory—my own and my sister Julie's— some of what we did and said after we learned how Rachel lost her freedom.

The air conditioner in the window groaned. I would have been glad for the relief it blew my way if I were inside the camp office for any reason other than this call home.

"Rachel will be safe in State Hospital," my mother explained. "They'll be able to help her." She told me the doctors worked with the psychiatrists at Washington University medical school.

"But what will they do?" I asked. My mother seemed so sure of what she was saying, but I teemed with doubt. I even doubted my doubt. Now she kept talking, and I struggled to keep listening. I rubbed my fingers on the old oak desk where the telephone sat, as though the right words for me to say would magically appear there.

"They're doing research on new medications," my mother continued. "Once they get her settled down, Rachel can talk to a therapist and work through her problems."

My tongue felt thick. I asked if Dad was still on the line. He wasn't. He had dashed off to Central Hardware on an errand. Of course. My mother never let him get a word in edgewise after his initial hello. I would have liked to hear what he thought, though I had no reason to think he disagreed with Mom on this decision.

A few months earlier my parents had received the phone call from Lola, one of the friends Rachel made in the kibbutz two years earlier. Rachel had gone to New York and met up with her and was going with her to Montreal, Lola's hometown. When they boarded the plane, Rachel had some type of frightening episode, and Lola could tell she was hearing voices. Lola got her on a flight to St. Louis, where my parents met her at the airport and took her to an emergency room. She was released to their care, and then they brought her to yet another private psychiatrist. They tried settling her into an apartment and a job. But Rachel's erratic behavior remained a problem and she couldn't seem to care for herself. She must have had another episode because now she was in State Hospital. Just for a while, they said.

I'd gotten glimpses of this drama, as though skimming through pages in a Gothic novel too scary to absorb, when the Montreal trip was aborted, and in the months that followed, when Rachel went in and out of emergency rooms. But they were glimpses from afar because I was away being a college freshman. In December, however, I'd gone home for my long winter break and seen the drama firsthand. This was when Rachel was still living in an apartment, and I went with my mother to visit her there. All her belongings lay in tangled mounds like an archipelago of garbage arisen from the ocean floor. I could see a look of revulsion on Mom's face. I tried to convince her it wasn't the end of the world if Rachel chose to live like that. My mother didn't agree. I could tell she wasn't interested in an argument from me.

I knew my parents wanted me to enjoy my life free of worries about Rachel. Maybe that's why my father was so emphatic in his suggestion that I work for the summer at a residential camp, rather than stay in St. Louis and do typing at Mom's office, where I could make more money. I'd been only too happy to follow his suggestion.

And now I was away when they made their decision. In July, while I was working in the sun and swimming in the lake, my parents had Rachel judged incompetent, gained guardianship, and had her committed. I didn't know what they said to get her in the car and drive her over to the hospital. I didn't hear whether Rachel yelled at them or resisted. But I imagined the sounds of despair and anger bouncing from the stucco walls of our living room. I pictured Rachel, startled and panicked, like a bird bursting from the chimney and beating its wings against the windows.

They said she needed to be protected. With the way she lived, she could get robbed, beaten up, raped. But a locked psych ward? Wasn't there another way to protect her? Something less harsh, less demeaning? I didn't argue with my mother on the phone that summer. I didn't have any answers to Rachel's problems and felt, as always, that Mom would fall apart, just melt into the ground if I pushed back too hard. But what about Rachel's life? She was twenty-two and just starting out on her own. Shouldn't she have freedom to make choices? I didn't argue. I was torn between loyalties and that paralyzed me.

So my objections stayed at the bottom of my throat and I let my mother change the subject. I let her tell me about the sandals she discovered in my hard-to-find size at our favorite department store and that she would send out on the camp truck the prescription sunglasses I had ordered. She wanted me not to worry and just have a good time. She warned me not to get overheated. To write soon. I wasn't angry but I was perplexed and troubled. Part of me wanted to accept my mother's gift—releasing me from worry—but something about it didn't feel right. Shouldn't I do something? But what?

I hung up the phone and walked back to my cabin in Bluebird Village, where six little girls were waiting to pepper me with questions about missing beach shoes and bossy bunkmates. They always needed my attention.

In the woods that evening, far from St. Louis, I listened to the campers' shouts. I heard the crickets sing. I was three hours from home. I couldn't hear whether Rachel cried or fought, or whether she succumbed silently to her fate.

Julie was also at camp, in Indian Mound, the older girls' unit, placed there so she wouldn't be in my group of younger girls. I didn't normally see a lot of her—just at flag-raising and then maybe a glimpse later at dinner. I was surprised when the camp director approached me the next day and said how sorry he was to hear about Rachel. He asked me if I would talk to Julie. She was complaining of stomach aches.

Julie was a month shy of twelve, and I knew she was having a difficult time. You only had to look at the other kids in the group to see the problem. Julie was tiny and wiry. She had the body of a nine-year-old. All the other girls in her bunk were on the other side of puberty, with hips and breasts. Somehow Julie was always the littlest. Just like at home, Julie could never keep up. At dinner, when Mom would catch Julie sneaking under the table and running out the door, even before dessert, she would yell at Rachel, Michael, and me to include her in our conversation.

I needed to talk to Julie about Rachel. It was my job to tell her it was somehow okay that our older sister was being sent away to a hospital. And now she was in the infirmary with stomach pain. Mitzi, the camp director's wife, met me at the front door of the infirmary. "I just talked to your sister," she said. "She's upset. I told her I understood and she calmed down a little. She'll be glad to see you."

I felt the blast of cool air when I entered the cabin. The office and infirmary were the only cabins with AC. The central area held a desk for the doctor and the room on the side had three beds for campers. Julie was the only one there. She lay on her side, her knees drawn up, the sheet pulled up to her shoulders. She looked so alone. So vulnerable.

When I reached over to kiss her, she turned her head away. "My stomach hurts," she moaned, her thin shoulders pulled up to her ears. I understood why her eyes and cheeks were so dry. Her sobs, like mine, were stunned into silence.

"Julie, you know Rachel has been sick. That's why she's staying in the hospital for a while," I said. Julie still wouldn't look at me. "Are you sad about that?" I asked. No answer. Julie kicked her legs free of the top sheet. I tried to hug her, but she wriggled out of my grasp.

Only when I compared memories with Julie decades later did we discuss our inability to connect with each other. Julie told me how she had been pulled out of her camp group by a junior counselor who sat her on a bench outside and told her about Rachel's hospitalization. Julie was mortified. Terrified. She barely knew this counselor. Why wasn't I the one to tell her? And then when I came to her in the infirmary my words sounded stiff and distant. I was the grownup in the room, but I couldn't help her make sense of what was happening. My feelings were in lockdown, like Rachel in that psychiatric ward. Looking back, I wish that Mitzi had stayed with Julie and me. We both needed her compassion and understanding. We needed help keeping our family together.

I knew enough then to say I was sad about Rachel. But not in a way that got through to Julie. "I'm sad because everybody in my cabin hates me," she answered. She averted her big brown eyes with their long upcurved eyelashes, and I wished I could kiss away the hurt in them. "Oh, Julie, that's not true," I answered. "They're just interested in different things right now—clothes and boys and make-up. Just have fun doing what you like to do. And you know what, Rachel will get better soon." I had no idea if this was so.

A tray from the mess hall was sitting on a side table. I brought it over to Julie. "Try to eat your lunch," I said. "Maybe your stomach will stop hurting." I hugged her and dipped my fingers into her thick curls.

"Everybody says my hair is kinky," she said. "I'm ugly."

"Don't listen to them; you look cute." I wished she would believe me. I told her I had to leave now but would be back after dinner. Maybe tomorrow she would be able to go back to her cabin, I suggested hopefully. I hugged her and went to my cabin to change for swimming duty. It was a relief to get back to work, where I knew how to do my job.

Afternoon sun pounded my bare shoulders as I walked to
the lake. I didn't worry. After summer's first burn, I turned
bronze and stayed that way. I took a shortcut down the steep
brambly hill. My toes found the viney footholds. I walked
across the narrow beach and onto the swimming dock, where
I took my position by the deep water. My job was to stand
there with a pole to extend if a swimmer got into trouble. I
never had to use it. I never had anything to do there but day-
dream. I tried not to think about Rachel locked up in a hospital
ward. I wanted to remember the blue aerogrammes she sent
three years ago, describing how she scrambled up and down
the hills of Galilee.

I leaned down for a splash of water on my face. I wondered what was happening in St. Louis now. I wondered
what Lola saw, and what words she used when she called
my parents. I wondered what I should have said to Julie. I
wouldn't be nineteen for another month. I had to fake being
a grown-up. Nothing I thought about being a sister made
sense anymore.

Luke and I sprawled across the lumpy couch on the rec hall
porch, his arm around my shoulder. I heard the hurt in his
voice when he told me how he felt about the injustice done to
my sister. I didn't know how to respond.

Evenings and days off, we hung out. He was a boy I
knew, but not well, at high school. He had wiry good looks
and a dry sense of humor. He was one of the popular guys,
and I was surprised when he came looking for me evenings,
after campers' lights out time. I remember the evening we ran
into the lake, held our breaths to submerge, and entwined our

limbs. When we kissed I felt bubbles rising above us to the surface, a release as airy as our flirtation, an escape from the pressure of college and all my worries about what was happening at home while I was away.

But now I felt horrible and lost interest in socializing. I couldn't do anything about Rachel, and wished I knew how to make Julie feel better. I managed to get through my days supervising the girls, but by nighttime, after they were all in bed, I just wanted to cry. I met up with Luke less frequently. When I agreed to meet him outside the rec hall one night, I blurted out my news. He listened, shook his head, his dark brown curls bouncing in protest, "She doesn't belong in a mental hospital," he insisted. He reminded me he had met Rachel at a party eight months earlier, during Thanksgiving vacation. He thought she was fine just the way she was. I hadn't come home for Thanksgiving and couldn't say for sure whether she was fine then or not. But I knew how well she could fool people into thinking she was.

Although Luke couldn't have known Rachel very well, I cared what he thought. I felt ashamed of what my parents had done, and of Rachel for pushing them into it. I wished I could explain to him how troubling her behavior had been the last three years. How she couldn't stay put, dashing off from one city to another, how she stayed up all night just pacing and smoking and eating. I wished I could explain how so much more was at stake than a bohemian lifestyle, as her court-appointed lawyer argued, and as so many friends—and now Luke—were saying.

But there wasn't much I could say to him. We knew nothing of each other's fears or dreams; the complexities of my family life would have been far more of a weight than our casual summer fling could bear. I opened my mouth and I stopped mid-sentence, falling into silence, a knot of shame bursting through my entire body.

After camp ended there were only a few days before I would return to Ann Arbor. But first, I had to visit Rachel in the hospital. I tried to block out the thud of the double door locking behind me when I entered. I tried to ignore the stiff glances from nurses at their massive desk, the blaring television in the dayroom where Rachel, who I had rarely seen watch TV, came out to meet me. I looked straight ahead. I didn't greet the other patients, not those collapsed into themselves on couches and chairs, nor those who wandered into the conversation space between me and my sister. I was too frightened, not of who they were or what they suffered, but of Rachel's association with them, what it meant about us, what it would do to her. I saw only one thing: that Rachel was angry and conversation with her was futile. As I pushed away my terror all I could feel was a tight, hard knot of confusion.

"How was she?" my mother asked that evening, as I was packing my suitcase for the trip back to school the next day. I pressed the magnetic latch to open the folding doors that covered the drawers in the bureau Rachel and I shared. I heard the ping of its release. And then inside I saw Rachel's cotton turtlenecks. I picked up the wine-colored one and another one, in dark hunter green, underneath. I had sent them to Rachel the previous fall when she was living at home. Before St. Louis State Hospital. She didn't usually care too much about clothes, but when I wrote her about what I had found at a campus store, she implored me to send her two. I couldn't find her size in black, her preferred color, but I did send her these.

"Rachel? You know, angry," I muttered in answer to my mother's question. What else was there to say? "Mom, tell Dad to bring these to Rachel," I said, handing her the turtlenecks. Rachel didn't allow Mom, only Dad, to visit her. Rachel told him what she needed, or wanted, in the way of clothing, books, and supplies. Then my mother would gather everything together and pack a bundle for him to deliver on his next visit.

"When the weather gets cooler, I will," she said, patting the shirts back down in the drawer. "She doesn't have much space in the hospital to store things."

"Will she be home in the winter?"

"Maybe. We have to see how she responds to the treatment. The medication and the therapy." I still didn't know what to say. I had to focus on getting back to school. And besides, Mom and Dad knew what they were doing. Didn't they?

I didn't talk with anybody about what I saw in the hospital. I may have said a few words to Dad when he drove me to the airport the next day. But I didn't discuss my feelings about Rachel with my brother or, since that first conversation at camp, with Julie. Only when I started this long project of reconstructing Rachel's life did I share emotions with my siblings. "I thought they were going to lock me up in a hospital too," my brother finally told me.

Julie told me how she defied our parents by going to the State Hospital to see Rachel. "They wouldn't let me visit her. But I went anyway." She hadn't wanted to be protected; she'd wanted to see her sister and what was happening to her.

Today, when a child or adolescent is diagnosed with serious mental illness, programs are available to help siblings understand what seems so horribly inexplicable. They learn what can be expected from treatments, how to talk about mental illness, and how to share feelings within the family. The National Alliance on Mental Illness (NAMI), a peer-to-peer support organization—which in fact my father was involved in founding—offers this type of "psychoeducation" in its Family to Family workshops, and others. Sadly, only a small portion of families who need this support know about it, or care to use it. We didn't and I know what can happen without it. Trying to control family grief, parents hold back. Blame festers, siblings flee. Like fingers from the flame, we pull away.

When from the Tree a Bluebird Sings

When from the tree a bluebird sings
Skipping stones bumping down the spine
I rush my eyes toward
The stars of my dreams that play among the moon.

A lullaby in a spider's web
Catches the magic dust
As the harp plays its sonorous notes
Lolling full as a mournful bell.

Numerous suns tease my sockets' eyes
With half-torturing secrets
While the warbling sounds
Are skipping black through chill.

—Rachel Goodman

HOT PROTESTS
AND COLLEGE COOL

Back in Ann Arbor I told my roommate, Barbara, about Rachel. Not a lot, because although she knew how to listen, I didn't feel like saying very much. It was just too hard to explain what happened. The shame and guilt were too overwhelming. I much preferred to gossip about the people in our housing co-op and their endless display of curious behaviors than think about the grim reality of my sister's life.

The co-op I had joined with my two friends from the dorm was known for its political activism. Two years earlier it had been the gathering place where buses came to pick up students headed south for the civil rights marches. Now, it was headquarters for anti-war organizers and its phone lines were believed to be bugged. The boys from SDS, Students for a Democratic Society, sprawled across our living room floor during their weekly meetings. My girlfriends and I marched downtown to support them when they burnt their draft cards. But we laughed them off when they suggested we voluntarily suppress our grades to lower the curve and make it easier for them to keep their student deferments.

The anti-war movement heated up during the three semesters I lived in the co-op, and culminated in the country's first teach-in, with speakers and seminars lasting until dawn.

Even with coffee, I couldn't make it all the way through. I had early classes to get to in the morning.

I look now at the letters I wrote home that year and see a wall of adolescent cool between my hand and my heart. In a five-page handwritten letter on yellow lined paper I find only three lines asking about Rachel amid pages covered with chatter about the anti-war demonstration I went to in Detroit, my procrastination tactics, my social life, and my smoking habit. There's nothing about the aftershock of Rachel's commitment, or how I felt. Was I afraid my pain would collide with my parents' and make all of it worse? Did I fear a flood behind the dam? I couldn't ask them what I really wanted to know. What was happening to Rachel? What did that mean for me? Instead, my inquiries about Rachel were brief and formal. I had no way to be open about my fears with my parents, or with my brother and younger sister. I wasn't open with myself.

Not that I didn't write to Rachel directly. I did. Dutifully. But I heard nothing back. As it happened, Miriam, the daughter of friends of my parents who were part of the same pro-communist crowd, was also a student at the University of Michigan and was also writing letters to Rachel that didn't get answered. She had asked me if Rachel was allowed to receive mail. "Does all Rachel's mail go through?" In October 1965, three months after Rachel was put in the hospital, I wrote my parents saying neither of us had heard back from Rachel: *Miriam especially is anxious and concerned about her. Ask her if she got Miriam's letters so I can let her know.* Miriam especially is anxious and concerned? What about my worries? Clearly, it was easier for me to write about Miriam's feelings than my own.

Michael wasn't answering letters either. That bugged me. It bugged me even more when my parents urged me to write him: *I'm not going to have a one-sided correspondence with him*, I wrote back, using an uncharacteristically snappy tone with them.

I'm not sure how I decided to break Michael's silence, but I imagine I told Barbara, my roommate, how unreasonable my parents were being. She would have understood my frustration. She was the type of person who listened all the way through instead of bouncing off to her own topics. "Do you have your brother's phone number?" I imagine her asking. "Just call him up." She would have pulled the telephone into our room from its stand on the second-floor hallway, closed the door against its stretched-out cord and told me, before going downstairs, "I've got dinner prep now." Phone calls then seemed so extravagant, especially all the way to Seattle, where Michael was in his first year of college. (Long distance rates were based on geographic zones.) But I called, left a message at Michael's dorm, and he called back later that night.

"What do you want to talk about?" he asked impatiently. When I asked him why he wasn't writing, he railed against Mom and Dad. He was bitter. His rage encompassed the totality of their lives, not just their treatment of Rachel. I tried to defend them, but my words seemed useless. He was adamant in his refusal to speak with them and by extension with me because I defended them. I hung up the phone desolate. Why did I have to lose my brother as well as my sister?

Decades later Michael told me how tortured he was by his sexual feelings when he was young, and then I understood it wasn't only Rachel's treatment he was angry about during those first college years. As I thought about what he told me I began to wonder whether our parents could have addressed his needs if they hadn't been so preoccupied with Rachel and her problems. Maybe not; boys didn't talk with their parents about sexual molestation or same-sex romances then.

But couldn't I have supported him? He and I were buddies in high school; others in our crowd were close friends with the older boy he became involved with. If I hadn't felt such a need to be the good daughter and protect my parents from more conflict, could I have befriended Michael? Drawn him out about what was going on in his life? Made him feel less isolated? Or even just noticed that he was troubled. Eventually I learned to stop indulging the fantasy that I had any control over the situation. I was only nineteen. Practically a child myself. How could I have seen then what was troubling him?

Rachel came home from the hospital on weekend leaves while I was home for the month-long break between fall and winter terms. To survive those visits I depended on my parents. I followed their lead in dealing with her withdrawn and erratic behavior. While my father drove my sister back and forth to the hospital, I listened to my mother pour out her frustrations about what she was going through. My father never said anything when he returned. Nothing about what Rachel said during the drive, or how he felt about leaving her once again at the hospital. I never asked. Only now do I dare to imagine the starts and stops of their conversation. Halting. Pleading. Insistent. Twenty minutes inside Dad's used Dodge, as he drove that six-mile route of city streets, stopping at one light after another. I can feel her anger and desperation. His lifelong sense of duty and guilt.

It felt so strange being home those cold winter weeks. Inside the house, everything felt different. Even the living room sofa where I listened to music and the chairs piled with books by the fireplace. But it wasn't that the furniture was rearranged. We were. I struggled to engage with the new Goodman configuration when I arrived home. And to disengage when I left to go back to school.

"How is Rachel doing?" family friends asked during those first years of her illness. I knew the questions were well-meaning, but still I couldn't help recoiling from them. Did they really want to know? How much could they take? I wished I could say, "Oh, she's getting better, thanks for asking." Then came the follow-up questions and they were even harder: "Were there any signs beforehand, indications of mental illness, when she was growing up?" I heard a note of fear in the question. Could this have been prevented if something were done earlier? Is there something I might be missing in my children, or those of my friends and family? There did have to be a way of preventing this, didn't there?

I disliked dealing with other people's fears then, but I came to be more sympathetic. When I hear of someone with a rare and horrible disease, I too want to know the early signs. I care about the person who has been afflicted. Of course. But I also want to cross that person's disease off my list of things to worry about happening to myself or my loved ones. I'm so sorry, I too say, while thinking that's your disease, your family's heartbreak, not mine.

"What was Rachel like growing up?" people asked. Well, she was angry, I answered. She was rebellious. But then I have to add the obvious: lots of children grow up angry, without ever receiving a diagnosis of schizophrenia.

I tried not to show my discomfort (or was it shame?). I always explained that schizophrenia typically would begin in late adolescence or young adulthood. It was an easy answer; neutral and factual. I didn't tell them about the fear and terror I felt when an alien force took possession of my sister.

TRANSFER STUDENT

I returned to Camp Hawthorn after my sophomore year. Julie was a camper there again. Rachel was still in the hospital, refusing to see Mom, but tolerating visits from Dad. Michael had gone to Seattle for college and stayed there over the summer.

I stood on the dock with my friends from last summer while everyone took tests to determine their swimming level. We watched as someone I had never seen before took his dive into the lake and did his laps. "Perfect form," said the waterfront director, "I'm giving him a ten." I took a second look at the newcomer. I was curious about this highly rated swimmer. I soon learned he was Barry Kasdan, the supervisor of the older boys' unit, and he had come all the way from New York to work here. I also heard he was hanging out with Nancy, the tall blonde woman who was my supervisor that year, when I was assigned to Indian Mound, the older girls' unit. The previous summer my supervisor had been my friend and mentor, and now I missed her. Nancy and I kept our distance.

In the mess hall the next few days, I watched the new guy surreptitiously. I glimpsed something odd about his thumb as he held his fork, and I kept glancing back to figure out what it was. I couldn't keep my eyes off the rest of him either. His deep brown eyes. His ready smile. Everything about him intrigued me. People said he looked like Peter Sellers. Or Peter from Peter, Paul, and Mary. High forehead. Curved nose. I could see his staff liked being around him. He made them laugh. I was definitely interested in him. But he was going out with Nancy.

The campers came and I was assigned to teach "Minnows," beginner swimmers. I held a young boy under his back encouraging him to float. He loosened up and thrashed off doing the dog paddle. His father, who was the camp doctor for the session, made a point of thanking me. And at the staff lounge one evening, he gave his ping pong paddle to Barry and told him to play a round with me. Barry and I volleyed. We played for points. And then he asked if I wanted to ride into town when we both had time off later that week. "I'm going in to do my wash. Want to come with me?"

We drove the pitted country roads to town in the gray VW bug he had driven out from New York. We picked up Dr. Peppers and sat on the hard chairs of Brown's Laundromat, our eyes on wads of twisted clothes being tossed up and down in the big dryers. The hum of the revolving drums and the washing machine blades created a hypnotic soundtrack.

Barry told me how he took the job at Camp Hawthorn because the St. Louis Jewish Community Center was paying for his tuition at graduate school. In return, he agreed to work for them once he graduated with his master's degree in social work. He didn't mind moving to St. Louis to work, but with one more year of school to go, he had been disappointed to find out that his two-year deal included a summer stint at camp before he graduated. That meant giving up his position as a waterfront director at a camp in Westchester County. The owners there treated him like a son and gave him a hard time about leaving. But he had to give up the job he loved. He drove his VW from the Bronx to central Missouri.

I asked him about Nancy. No, he wasn't dating her. "She just wanted to talk with me," he said. "We compared notes about staff. She said she wasn't sure how to relate to you." I prodded him for more. "She thought you seemed stand-off-ish," he finally told me. But he quickly made it a compliment. "It's just her insecurity. You have more experience at camp than she does, and she heard about the way you handled a difficult group last year." I smiled with pride. I hadn't known my reputation preceded me.

This second summer as a counselor turned out to be much easier. The Indian Mound girls didn't need nearly as much supervision as the younger ones. But July brought a midwestern heat wave so severe that people were dying in St. Louis and Chicago. For three weeks, temperatures were over one hundred degrees. Few homes had air conditioning, and at camp only the office and infirmary did. After lunch in the mess hall, we made sure that campers all took the salt pills needed to replenish electrolytes shed during those sweat-soaked days. Everyone seemed to move in slow motion and spend a lot of time cooling off in the lake. I didn't mind the languor of those hot days at all.

And for the first time in my life, I had a boyfriend who wanted to make me happy. When it was my turn to stay in the unit at night, after the kids had bunked down, Barry drove to Howard Johnson's to bring me back ice cream. "What flavor do you like?" I asked for orange sherbet. That's what my father had brought me from Howard Johnson's in Boston, when I was three years old and had to stay overnight in the hospital for a tonsillectomy.

Barry and I became inseparable during our free hours. My heart raced when our paths crossed during group activities. I remember seeing him with a group of campers at the trampoline and feeling like I would burst with longing. I wanted to run from my group and hug him. How could I wait until evening? I couldn't stand our time apart. When I went off with my campers for a three-day canoe trip on the lake, Barry put his class ring on a string so I could wear it around my neck.

Barry had boundless energy and optimism. I had never known anyone quite like him. His thumb, I learned, was the result of a joint that failed to develop before birth. It didn't make a dent in his confidence. "It's easy to compensate for a missing joint," he told me. For him, almost any challenge could be overcome, with ingenuity and optimism. His belief became my life raft.

Four years older than I, Barry seemed more grounded, more mature than my friends at home or at school. He had no interest in pot or LSD. "There are so many things to do in life," he said, "And that's enough of a high for me." His favorite seemed to be outrageous pranks. He got his friends to move the camp trampoline in the middle of the night to the area in front of my cabin just to say good morning to me. Another morning everyone went to flag raising only to find his VW sitting on the porch of the camp's office building. He got away with these stunts because he was so good at what he did. He kept his staff loyal and motivated, his campers enthusiastic about taking on challenges. Counselors on probation were assigned to Barry because he was always able to turn them around.

Once our campers were bunked down for the night, Barry

and I looked for places to be alone. We held each other close behind the arts and crafts cabin, surrounded by the dark woods. Only the occasional mosquito landing on an arm interrupted our enchantment. We kissed goodnight by the Indian Mound tree that guarded the unit. We scrambled down the hill to our cove on the lake, which went on for miles twisting through the Ozark foothills. As we lay on the beach, our conversations rolled through the night and whispered against the thick tree-lined coves.

But in the midst of all this happiness, I felt overwhelmed by what was happening to my sister and my family. Rachel was angry and distant, and nobody had any answers. At any moment terror could overtake me, like strong, gnarled fingers grabbing my throat in a chokehold, causing the ball of confusion to lurch painfully inside me.

When I confided to Barry my sister was in a mental hospital, I had to overcome the feeling that I was making a bid for sympathy. Or at least that it would appear that way. The stigma of mental illness was bad enough. I felt even worse being pitied. And because it was all so overwhelming, I didn't want a lot of questions. After a week or so with Barry, my reluctance melted away. Barry didn't feel sorry for me; he empathized. He told me how his father, five years earlier, was fatally hit by a truck crossing a Manhattan street, and how sad he felt that his siblings—an older brother and twin sister—had drifted away from each other after their father's death. Barry seemed to have come through his family's tragedy whole and strong. He comforted me. The tenderness of his words in my ears and his hands on my body pushed back the fright. He didn't judge, he didn't burden me with opinions or probing questions. He soaked up my grief.

Some nights Barry and I took a canoe out and paddled to a hidden cove, where we wrapped ourselves in the night. No motorboats buzzing, no waves lapping the shore. The only sounds were the cicadas in the trees and the murmur of our own voices. Every night we parted longing for more of each other.

He wore a brown pullover on cool nights. I loved to touch it. I loved its feel. Like velvet but heavier. He told me it was velour. I had never touched velour before.

I took Barry home with me during the break between first and second sessions. When he met my dad, he laughed in sudden recognition. "Mort, you picked me up from the airport when I had my job interview at the JCCA." My father hadn't remembered. He was always a little distracted. Taking care of things with Rachel in the hospital must have made it worse. My mother told me Barry was just the kind of guy she would go for.

The fall term started early at the University of Michigan, and I had to leave camp before the others, in mid-August. Barry and I wrapped ourselves around each other in a tent that had been pitched on the lawn in front of the office. Barry told me he wanted to marry me. I laughed. Or maybe it was a nervous giggle. I wasn't twenty yet and wasn't thinking about marriage. I had vague notions, without any what's, where's, or who's, of starting a career and having a string of lovers before settling down. Of taking more road trips with my girlfriends, like the one I had made in the spring with my housemate from school, finding people we knew in East Coast colleges and crashing in their dorms.

Now Barry was talking about marriage, and I was reacting like a silly girl. I saw he was hurt when I didn't take him seriously. "I mean it, Debby, I want to get married. After you graduate." I went back to him the next night, and I said yes. He gave me his brown velour pullover to take with me.

Back in Ann Arbor for my junior year, I grew despondent at the thought of waiting two more years to be with Barry. Even though he drove from New York to visit me at every opportunity. Vacations. Long weekends. We wrote almost every day. But it was his voice that sustained me when we were apart.

"We don't need to wait until I graduate," I said between tears of loneliness and longing. We talked long-distance almost every night, an extravagance in 1966. It seemed to me that the wires between Ann Arbor and New York City were spliced together just for us, to hold our long-distance engagement together.

"I'll transfer to Washington U. Then when you start your job in St. Louis, we can get married."

Barry wasn't so sure about my new timeline. "I don't want you to jeopardize your education," he said. "You love your courses at Michigan; you just got into the honors program. That's a lot to give up. We'll be able to visit more when I'm in St. Louis."

But he was already doing all-nighters driving his VW bug between Ann Arbor and New York, and I knew it was a strain. Ann Arbor to St. Louis wouldn't be that much shorter. With his full-time job, they certainly wouldn't be more frequent. Most of all, I didn't know who else could absorb the grief that still overwhelmed me at times. With Barry I was able to share feelings I couldn't with my parents. When

Rachel sent me a mimeographed booklet of poems written before her hospitalization, the contrast between the poems and the letter accompanying them broke my heart. I felt safe telling Barry about my grief and confusion over Rachel:

October 27, 1966. She doesn't write [poetry] now; she doesn't fight the world anymore. Instead . . . she is making a purse in occupational therapy, which she says is something nice to do. The Rachel I knew before would never say such a thing. . . . I don't understand what they've done to her, Barry. I realize that the almost grotesque kind of rebellion which formed the basis of her behavior and thought before could only lead to self-destruction. Now there's none of the old behavior . . . but nothing has replaced it. She is tractable and docile, expresses only the blandest of feeling. . . . My parents want her to stay hospitalized—they say that since she hasn't really faced and coped with those old emotions, they will lead to the old behavior if she is on her own. And if they allow her to be released, they have no way of keeping tabs on her or controlling her since she's over twenty-one. I know there's a lot of truth in that reasoning, yet the alternative of keeping her hospitalized seems so unreasonable and even inhuman.

I trust my parents about this, but sometimes I don't. I have told them that I didn't see why she should be hospitalized, but yet I could give no feasible alternative. I can't stand it, I find it unbearable to think that her life, potentially such a rich one, is being dried up and shriveled away there so that she is happy making purses in occupational therapy. I've been so caught up in my own problems and worries that I've hardly thought of Rachel's dilemma. And now, for the first time— perhaps since the summer of '65 when they committed her—

I'm crying for her. I have this nagging guilty feeling that I should try to persuade my parents to do something else with Rachel, but I have no idea of what to suggest.

Finally, I raised the floodgates enough to let through emotions I could no longer hold back.

The need to do something must have contributed to my decision to transfer in the middle of my junior year—even while I told family and friends it was because I wanted to be in St. Louis when Barry arrived there. I left the honors program and the co-op house filled with protestors and sit-in organizers. I went to live at home, just a mile from campus, while Barry finished up graduate school in New York. I had to put up with my parents and their arguing but at least I felt involved now. I could see firsthand what was happening even if I couldn't change anything.

Rachel was often on home visits scheduled by the hospital so instead of roommates I adored, I lived with two sisters, each difficult in her own way. Julie was thirteen and behaving like a teenager. Rachel was twenty-three, a psychiatric patient who acted like an adolescent too—but much, much worse. Ferociously stubborn. Resistant to the simplest request. Always ready to run off. Any hopes I may have had of helping were dashed. I couldn't relate to her. I couldn't understand her. I dreaded her endless pacing at night. Circling, cigarette glowing between her fingers, from living room to dining room to kitchen and back around again. Over and over. Like a caged lioness yearning for exotic lands. Living with my family and commuting to college was unbearable. I needed Barry to get me out.

Barry agreed to shorten our engagement. We set a date for September before my senior year. I had just the wedding I wanted. Small and intimate—a couple dozen friends and relatives in my parents' home. Julie played the piano as my father walked me down the steps to the living room. Rachel stood next to me under the chuppah wearing a cornflower blue dress that matched her eyes, her face flattened by medication, but beautiful still. Barry's brother stood next to him. He passed him the rings and surprised us with champagne at the hotel suite he had booked for the night. Our honeymoon began in Kentucky Lake State Park, with a furnished rustic cabin. It ended at Mammoth Cave, where mysterious underground passageways enchanted us with their dark and silent solemnity. Then we moved into a one-bedroom apartment in Clayton, on the same block where I lived when my family first moved to the St. Louis area and the FBI knocked on our door.

Not too long ago, I asked Barry to look for our ketubah in the attic. He found our traditional wedding contract somewhere amidst our fifty-year accumulations and had it framed to set off the gold-leafed swirls of its intricate design. The certificate now hangs at the bottom of our stairway. Over the landing. On the bottom line are two witness signatures side by side. Rachel Goodman. Stuart Kasdan. What irony. Our older siblings, our witnesses, both died at fifty-nine years of age, their lives cut short by treatable physical illnesses they ignored too long because of the damage to their minds. My brother-in-law, who lived with us for several months, also spent time living on the streets, though he was never hospitalized. Before he deteriorated, he achieved a measure of professional success as a physicist but never the recognition he craved. Both our siblings were shadowed by unfulfilled promise and talent. And both endured years of self-inflicted punishment because of roiling thoughts they couldn't control. They suffered; Barry and I were lucky. We hold their memories in our marriage and in our hearts. In the life we have made together.

I Remember You, Chuck

I remember
you, Chuck.
It was a game we played
that dawn; though neither won
I gained a treasure.
for as you lay there sleeping
all else eluded me
but ecstasy.
Hair, eyes, nose, arms,
mouth, legs, and breathing,
made a solid imprint
on my mind.
And I will always remember.

—Rachel Goodman

ROCKY LANDINGS

I didn't understand what was happening to me when I started having crying jags out of the blue. It was 1968. I was a newly-wed in my last year of college, so why did I burst into tears walking across the grassy quad on my way to Renaissance history class? Why did I cry when I gazed at the graceful gingko tree in the library atrium? And always when I drove past a cemetery? Somehow, I didn't connect my outbursts to losing the sister I had always known and seeing a zombie instead when I visited her in the hospital. Three years had passed since she was diagnosed with schizophrenia, and now I felt there was nothing I could say or do to help her. I didn't understand, but I was shaken enough by these outbreaks of emotion to get myself to the student health center. I talked for a while and the doctor offered medication. Antidepressants. I was horrified. My sister was mentally ill, not me!

That evening, in an apartment so compact I had to climb over our bed to get to the bathroom, I told Barry, "I'm not going back to that shrink."

"Washington U psychiatrists use the medical model," he sighed. "They're big into medication. At least go back and tell the doctor in person," Barry urged, concerned about closure, but I don't remember if I did. I knew I just needed to finish college, enjoy married life, and get away from all the Goodman hurt and confusion.

Over the years, I still cried for no apparent reason. I became unreasonably angry at people I loved, even banged my head on kitchen cabinets in front of my children when I felt I couldn't cope. Fortunately, by the time our second daughter went away to college, the new generation of antidepressants were widely used, and I didn't need to worry about the stigma of mental illness. I was just glad there was a pill to even out my mood swings.

After I graduated college and Barry finished the first year of his new job, we took a road trip west. We drove from St. Louis in our new little red Renault, an R10, and camped en route to Yellowstone National Park and the Grand Tetons. I left my birth control pills at home—despite the Zero Population Growth movement, despite the specter of the Vietnam War and the apocalypse to come, despite what I knew about the risks from nuclear tests and radiation fallout, despite my youth. One thing I never worried about was the possibility of transmitting to a child whatever it was that Rachel had. Barry and I were fine, and I was confident our children would be too. I worried more about my children having normal fingers and toes than inheriting mental illness.

We pitched tents outside of Salt Lake City and floated in the lake. We camped in the Rocky Mountains during an August snowstorm. We fended off an invasion of flying bugs that smothered us in Dinosaur National Park. We watched the Yellowstone geyser spout, then hiked around Jenny Lake and up the Grand Teton trails.

When I got pregnant a few months later, I told my friends our decision to have a baby was a leap of faith. "There's no reason to give in to despair," I said, quoting Barry. His optimism was my life raft. Ostensibly, I was talking about the terrible things happening in the world. In truth, the battles between my parents, fueled by the stress and uncertainties of Rachel's situation, caused me much deeper despair. They were frequently at odds with State Hospital. They were frequently at odds with each other as well.

But Rachel did seem better for a while. She was able to live at home and keep a job, according to my father's notes for the lawsuit he later filed: *Took care of her own things. Attended night classes. Participated in a young adult club at the JCCA. Saved money. Decided to go to back to Israel. Interviewed by an official at the Hillel Foundation, was accepted. Left in October, 1968. Wrote several letters but suddenly stopped writing in January, 1969.* Worried about Rachel, my father contacted the embassy and friends in Israel and finally got word in March that she was in a psychiatric hospital in Tel Aviv. Israeli officials demanded that she be taken home to the States. They wrote Dad saying that the Law of Return, granting every Jew in the world the right to live in Israel, did not apply to people like Rachel, who were a burden on the state. My father did not take the next flight over to get her. He asked an Israeli social worker he knew to visit her and let him know how she was doing. Hearing that she was stabilized and was receiving treatment as adequate as she would get in St. Louis, he and my mother must have decided the Israeli demand could wait a few months more. Maybe they felt her work on the kibbutz seven years earlier had earned her the right to treatment in Israel. Maybe they felt she was getting better treatment in Israel than at State Hospital and wanted to use that time as a respite. Maybe, too, Rachel felt abandoned after sending them letters saying she was ready to come home and finding out they weren't ready to come get her.

I didn't know about any of these letters at the time. I

didn't have discussions with my parents about Rachel's situation in Israel. My mind was elsewhere. I now had a husband. I had started graduate school. I only remember the tension I felt when Barry and I went to their house for dinner. And the choking cries I let out when we returned to our apartment.

Sandy was one of Rachel's friends in Israel. I talked to her after Rachel died. She shared memories of their happy months together in the Habonim Workshop, and then of another type of life on the Lower East Side of New York City. Sandy told me how much she loved Rachel. She told me stories of their escapades and how Rachel decided to lose her virginity with one of the Machal boys from South Africa who came to volunteer at the kibbutz. Sandy had found Rachel so smart, so beautiful, and such a hard worker. She sent me photos from their 1962 return journey. They had stopped in Greece on their way to the Atlantic. Rachel's profile glows with passion, engagement; she is surrounded by her Workshop friends. "Rachel was the intellectual," Sandy told me. "The rest of us knew all about Zionism, but she knew so much else. Politics. Poetry. Philosophy. And she had endless energy working on the kibbutz. Other girls tried to get out of jobs in the fields. Not Rachel. She would tackle anything. I was in awe of her."

Sandy returned to Israel after the Workshop and New York, and Rachel sought her out there. When she called her from a beach in Haifa, she was incoherent. She had been raped and needed help. Sandy sent her boyfriend out to get her on his motorcycle. "She was psychotic," Sandy said. They got Rachel to the hospital—which is where my father finally located her many weeks later.

Five months pregnant in July 1969, I lay on our lumpy second-hand couch with Julie and Barry to watch scratchy black-and-white television images of astronauts visiting the moon. Julie was staying over at our apartment while Mom and Dad were away. Dad had found a month-long professional conference to attend in Israel. My mother accompanied him and went on tours while he was at his meetings. When the conference ended, they would bring Rachel home with them from the Tel Aviv hospital. None of this seemed real to me. Not the space shot, and certainly not whatever was happening with my parents and sister in Israel.

Rachel's return was a far cry from her triumphant appearance in 1962. Instead of the sinewy, glowing teenager she'd been then, she was now a prematurely aged woman, heavy with defeat. They readmitted her to St. Louis State Hospital. There she would stay through an endless cycle of discharges, crises, and readmissions, again and again, for another ten years.

NASA could put an astronaut on the moon, but where were the breakthroughs that could restore Rachel's balance? Where was the giant leap for mankind that could help her? All that science offered her were tranquilizing medications with terrible side effects, most notably the twitches from tardive dyskinesia, and weight gain. Plus endless, relentless days of apathy. I had no idea of what her future held. Nobody did. Schizophrenia was a hopeless diagnosis. But my attention was turned inward at this time, to the new family I was creating. I had a baby on the way.

It was hard for me to become hopeful, even when Rachel, in a stabilized state, showed signs of improvement. I grieved for the sister who burned to be a poet and explorer. I wanted Rachel to get well but couldn't accept her the way she seemed to me now—bland, defeated, and indecisive. Two years later she would write:

October 25, 1971: Dear Debby, I was home visiting for two days last weekend and the past weekends too, of course. You may know I passed the nurse's aide course, but the only job I could find was babysitting. It's something different to do, and I enjoy it. I read to the baby, change her diapers, take her to the park. Then, there's another child who goes to kindergarten. In the afternoons I type at a job [at the university]. It's hard work, but I've been doing it. The girls in the office are nice. I've been reading and doing a little bit of art. Now I'd like to try macramé work, but don't know that much about it. Maybe I'll get a book or take a course. My plans for the near future are indefinite. . . . Hope to hear from you soon. Love, Rachel.

I didn't allow myself to feel joy at Rachel's steps forward because I didn't understand then how gradually recovery takes place. How expectations need to be calibrated and small successes celebrated. If I had, I might have found patience and hope instead of the despair that sometimes threatened to engulf me.

I was twenty-three. None of my friends had babies. I needed my mother's help with mine, but I was torn between love and resentment of her. She'd come by my apartment on her way home from work and pry the baby off of my soggy shoulder. She fed her, held her, pushed her carriage up and down the street. I was grateful. But when she and Dad visited together, my heart sank. If my father held the baby more than a minute, my mother grabbed her away from him. "Enough already, Mort. Give her back to me." I couldn't stand to be in the same room with the two of them together. I could only love them one at a time.

The tension between my parents wore me down. Made me crazy. One night Barry and I came home from dinner at their house and I burst into tears. I criticized him on trumped-up charges, I yelled at him. Usually he absorbed my pain and confusion. But this time I pummeled him on the chest. He had had enough. He slammed the door behind him and went out for a walk. I knew I was being unfair, even cruel just then, and he had every right to leave the house. I knew we would be better off, just the two of us and the baby, in a calmer place, far away.

My parents' marriage seemed frayed to the breaking point. Rachel came home from the hospital on weekends, and every visit caused drama and recriminations. Mom attempted to set limits with her, make her clean her room, control the all-night eating. All the attempts were futile. Rachel had meds to calm her down, but they didn't help her get along with my mother. If my father tried to resolve an issue his way, she would yell at him. The tension attached itself, like pollen, to every subject they discussed, and it never went away.

Barry finished his two-year commitment with the JCCA, and then stayed one more, the year I was pregnant. After that, he started looking for another job. He wanted to work in a more clinical setting, helping kids directly instead of running social groups for them. He looked for jobs near St. Louis, but the one that best suited him was in Connecticut, not far from New York City. I agreed it would be a good move. His mother lived by the ocean in Queens, his twin sister, Barbara, in Manhattan with her family. Stuart was at Brown University working on a PhD in theoretical physics. I figured the East Coast would be a good place for me to start a career in a few years, though I had no idea what that would be. I urged Barry to take the Connecticut job; it was a great career opportunity for him, and besides, I needed to get away from my parents.

We packed up our clothing, our books, pots and pans, and the Finnish tableware from our wedding registry. The only furniture we took was our platform bed, a card table with a couple folding chairs, the crib, playpen, and highchair. I was happy to strip down to essentials. Not much from our St. Louis apartment seemed worth taking. Not the fuzzy pea-green sofa from the Salvation Army. Not the used dining room set with the scratched mahogany veneer that just got blotchier the more Barry tried refinishing it.

Everything went into the miniature U-Haul, which looked like a toddler's Tonka toy. We hitched it to the R10 we had driven two years earlier to Wyoming. Connecticut was a full two-day ride, and we camped along the highway. On the second day, our little red car huffed up and down the steep mountains of Pennsylvania with an audible groan.

"God, I hope the trailer load isn't burning out the transmission," said Barry, worrying aloud.

"Oh, it'll be okay," I said, as I climbed into the back, next to the buggy seat, keeping the baby calm with bottles of juice. I had no idea what I was talking about, but I knew I couldn't add the long-term health of a car to my list of concerns. I had to trust that everything would work out.

We got to our new home the evening before Barry started his job. With the cumulative stress of packing and driving and camping out along the way, Barry had a bad cold. "Stay home and rest up," I urged, but he felt well enough to show up at work as planned. He left for his fifteen-mile commute. That's when I sat on an unopened cardboard box in the bare living room, tears salting my face, sobs choking my throat. I had been eager to leave St. Louis. I just didn't know how lonely I would be.

Now it begins—after my move from St. Louis—and recurs for years. It isn't exactly a nightmare but descends on me before I go to sleep—when I close my eyes and consciousness begins to fade. I feel a shadow closing in on me as rationality, the faithful guard of my thoughts during the day, grows weary. I hear Rachel knocking. I open the door and see her standing in front of me. Tangled hair. Dirty shirt. Blue eyes staring into mine. "Debby, Debby," she cries, "I need a place to live." I have no answer. I am terrified for her, and for me. I can't let her in and I can't send her away. How can I abandon her? I don't know what to say to her. I am wracked with grief and guilt until Barry holds me and my sobs subside.

PART IV

No Way Home

THE LIBERATORS

The Shady Oak Theater showed the best first-run movies. With tasteful arches and art deco adornments, it stood close to the sidewalk of the main shopping street of Clayton, where I had briefly lived years earlier. The mid-summer sun had begun touching down as we walked out of the theater. I blinked my eyes to adjust to the streetlights. Trembling with rage and pain, I wanted to weep, but the burning I felt stopped my tears. I struggled to gain control.

We'd just seen *One Flew Over the Cuckoo's Nest*; my response to it is seared in my memory. I never watched horror movies, and I hadn't known this would be one. At the end of it, Jack Nicholson's character met a horrifying fate. A shocker, a blow to the gut. Even worse, it left me feeling mauled and manipulated by what seemed to me strong doses of dramatic excess. I was horrified and angry.

I wailed to my husband as we drove home. "How can they romanticize mental illness like that?" Barry looked at me quizzically. "You know, make mental illness so heroic, so fascinating," I explained impatiently.

Barry understood what I meant but didn't share my anger at the production. "You have to admit it was a great flick. Jack Nicholson was really incredible." His response raised my level of anger a notch. I wanted to yell, stay with me, Barry,

don't defect! I needed him to crawl inside my head and under
my skin to feel exactly what I did. He accepted my neediness
and put up with my bouts of hyperpassionate criticism. He
had a sense of humor and a way of putting things into perspective.

We were in St. Louis that week for our annual summer
visit. We had brought our children to the house where I
lived from the age of thirteen until I was married. The house
with the red tile roof and wrought iron balconies. Whenever
we visited, my parents managed to give me and Barry a
mini-vacation. They shopped and cooked for us. They
watched and entertained their grandchildren so we could
have an evening out.

"I hope the kids didn't give Mom and Dad any trouble
going to bed," I said to Barry, switching the subject to something more manageable. I didn't need to worry; our girls
slept soundly in their grandparents' home. But I felt better
worrying about them than Rachel. Right now she was in the
hospital. But I knew she would be discharged soon. Where
would she sleep? Her life was too confusing so I focused on
things I could control. Or things I could argue about. I pushed
away grief by acting like a protective mom. Or a hot shot
movie critic, a wannabe Pauline Kael. As hard as I tried to
expel it, grief always came back. I'd been ambushed by a
Hollywood blockbuster.

I wished that people who cheered the high jinks of a
counterculture figure whose rebellion symbolized resistance
to a repressive, conformist culture could understand that my
mentally ill sister was no metaphor. I wished they knew that
her life in and out of hospitals didn't represent any higher
truth.

Rewatching the movie now, I can see why it snagged the five top trophies from the Academy for 1975. A sweep like that hadn't happened in forty-one years: best director, screenplay, actor, actress, and movie. Jack Nicholson's masterful portrayal of a heroic rebel was comic and tragic. Brilliant and compelling. So was the entire cast, including Louise Fletcher, the actress who played Nurse Ratched of those beautiful and evil blue eyes. Audiences everywhere were glad to salute its 1960s setting and pay tribute to the counterculture that helped, finally, end the Vietnam War and bring down Richard Nixon.

As I learned later, the mid-1970s film was based on a book written ten years earlier by Ken Kesey, one of the Beats in Kerouac's madcap circle of friends. Kesey, who grew up in Springfield, Oregon, based the story on his experiences as a psychiatric aide in California but set it in an unnamed Oregon hospital.

To the film's Czech director, Milos Forman, mental hospitals were political prisons. He had survived the Holocaust only to endure Soviet oppression: dissidents were declared insane and confined to mental hospitals. His gripping story was about power and oppression. It happened to be set in a mental hospital, but it could have taken place in a school, an army base, or a ship at sea—anyplace where the powerful can oppress the weak.

Forman filmed in Oregon State Hospital, where the head of the hospital granted him extensive access to patients, staff, and procedures. The hospital in the movie looked uncannily realistic, not like a Hollywood set. It wasn't all that different from the massive brick building on Arsenal Street, a few miles from the Shady Oak, where Rachel stayed during her inpatient stretches. I had seen the nurses' station guarding the entrance to the locked door. Chipping paint on the walls of the day room. Patients tapping time away. Bored. Medicated. Impassive faces and shuffling feet.

In the *Cuckoo's Nest* Jack Nicholson's manic antics were meant to give heart to the oppressed, his martyrdom to expose the evils of absolute power. The authorities could destroy him by brute force, but the moral victory would be his. Somehow, at that moment in our collective mindset, political and cultural forces had combined to make madness—in the form of poets and artists and geniuses—an act of resistance.

I knew better. Madness was just misery. Rachel didn't need a liberator like Jack Nicholson loping down the halls with a lopsided grin and fire in his belly. At least I didn't think she did. Even then, before I fully understood what Forman brought to it, I felt sure the film incorrectly identified the worst abuses of the mental health system. By 1975 deinstitutionalization had swept the country. Instead of keeping patients locked up, hospitals were turning them out. At St. Louis State, Hilary Sandall, a psychiatrist from England, was hired to run a community care program, which was then a new, if experimental, approach. Her plan sounded good to mental health professionals as well as to state legislators looking for ways to save money. The plan was to make that money available for services in the communities that cared for the hospital patients when they were released there. In practice the money did not move with the patient; it was cut from appropriations bills. Rachel was one of the first caught in the revolving door of hospital discharge and admission so characteristic of deinstitutionalization. As my parents dealt with the chaos it caused in Rachel's life, Dr. Sandall became, whether she deserved it or not, their own Nurse Ratched.

St. Louis State Hospital on Arsenal closed down years ago. When I found its early history memorialized on the website of the state's mental health department, however, I was astounded to read the summary of a study Sandall published in 1975. In it she maintained that patients who showed little potential successfully adjusted to supported housing programs. *Benefits accruing to [them] . . . so outweigh the bad effects of possible failure, it is unwise for programs to be overly cautious in placing patients.* A colleague of hers in those early days lauded this radical approach: *Her idea was to skip all of the unnecessary steps to prepare people to move into the community, but to just help them move to their desired setting along with necessary supports.* What seemed like arbitrary, wrongheaded treatment to my parents was endorsed as a necessary risk. Ready or not (and with or without those highly theoretical support systems), Rachel was expected to go out and make it on her own. This concept of rapid discharge, the website noted, was far ahead of its time and not widely accepted. In the ensuing years, however, wholesale "dumping" of psychiatric patients would become a common practice nationwide. Like Rachel, many would suffer from the dearth of "necessary supports."

My parents kept me informed but didn't burden me with details of their interaction with the hospital. I didn't probe. When Rachel was first committed to State Hospital, I was away at camp. I had just finished my first year of college, Michael had just graduated from high school, and Julie had finished sixth grade. I felt uncomfortable hearing my parents telling me they didn't want Rachel's needs to impinge on ours, our opportunity to go to college. But when I asked if Rachel was getting the best care available, if a private hospital might be preferable, Mom assured me it didn't matter. "Doctor Rubenstein says private hospitals aren't really better for someone like Rachel."

Rubenstein was the private psychiatrist they consulted, the doctor who concurred with Rachel's disastrous return to Israel and whose judgment I came to doubt. But, at the time, I understood my parents' calculus. A private hospital might look nicer, but it would be ruinously expensive, and the actual treatment would be no more effective. Since there was no end in sight to Rachel's illness, it didn't make sense for my parents to mortgage their future. I didn't like this reasoning, but I didn't argue with them. Maybe that's why I was so upset seeing the *Cuckoo's Nest*. Yes, I was angry that it oversimplified complex issues. But it also put me face to face with the tragedy I had tacitly agreed to.

After Rachel got sick, Dad joined up with other parents of chronically mental ill adults to expose the gaping deficiencies in the mental health system. He was a gadfly and an advocate. He talked to reporters. He pleaded with officials. He wrote letters. Made phone calls.

Parents who had adult children with severe mental illness faced steep barriers when they looked for solutions: chaos when they took children home, blame and mistrust when they took them back to the hospital. They still do. But with the formation of grassroots advocacy networks that coalesced into NAMI at the end of the 1970s, parents began to gain a voice in treatments for their adult children. Leveraging its political power as a national constituency, the organization began lobbying for research funding and appropriate services at the state level. My father, ever the community organizer, understood the need for peer support and political action. He cofounded a NAMI chapter in St. Louis and participated in establishing the national one as well.

I didn't know it at the time, but shortly before I saw the *Cuckoo's Nest* in the mid-1970s, my father had penned his own letter of protest. I discovered it years later in a box of old documents. Reading it for the first time after so much time had passed, I could feel the depth of his frustration.

My father wrote directly to the Missouri commissioner in charge of the state's department of mental health, bypassing the hospital administrators he'd been dealing with so unsuccessfully. *October 17, 1974. As a last resort and because of the urgency of our daughter's mental problem and physical safety, we are appealing to you personally*, he wrote. He explained how Rachel had been in and out of the hospital with different doctors and treatments, the most recent being the community placement plan. *The hospital personnel anticipated that she would adjust in the community, but Rachel has in fact deteriorated into a hopeless, defenseless, disoriented person incapable of the minimum amount of self-care.* Dr. Sandall, he explained, encouraged Rachel to go to college, get out and live in a room by herself, get a job—and do all of that at once. He explained how the hospital refused to readmit Rachel after she left a boarding house they chose for her. How she made her way to Columbia, Missouri, where she ended up with a five-week jail sentence for shoplifting. After five or six more (dis)placements, Rachel *burst into the house imploring us to let her have a place to spend the night.* He recounted one telephone call, when Rachel berated them for not helping her and threatened to "destroy" her boyfriend. Even then, he explained incredulously,

Dr. Sandall maintained her belief that Rachel "belonged in the community."

In cri de coeur that breaks my own heart, my father concluded: *My wife and I find the present situation unbearable. At this moment we don't know where Rachel is nor can we be sure that if she returns, things will be any better.*

From the time Rachel got sick, I tried to make sense of what was happening by following the latest theories of mental illness. The anti-psychiatry movement and its spin-off, deinstitutionalization, started in 1960s England and despite its anti-establishment appeal didn't impress me. Yes, it was visionary, with its new paradigms for thinking about mental illness. But it didn't seem to have a lot of practical answers, and it didn't offer a way to work with parents as partners for implementing the new approach. For my parents, the new paradigm of community placement did just the opposite, as my father explained in his letter to the commissioner: *We engaged in many discussions about these moves with Dr. Sandall and her staff at her request as part of Rachel's treatment. We expressed grave doubts about Rachel undertaking these actions at that time in light of past experience, but unfortunately our opinions and concerns were spurned. Rather than open communication, we experienced hostility from them. We feel that these four years were particularly damaging because there was no communication between Dr. Sandall and ourselves. We feel . . . that Rachel was not seen as an individual needing, perhaps, a different kind of treatment, and she suffered gravely as a result.*

My mother spoke to me about Sandall with great bitterness: "She blamed me for Rachel's illness. She believed everything Rachel said about me, even if it made no sense. She told me I gave Rachel a hard time about dating a Black man. She doesn't know a thing about me and she says that." She was insulted to be judged as a bigot. I knew how resentful she could be of authority figures given her own experience growing up in an orphanage. How abrasive she could be. But even my father, a social worker so skilled in community outreach and partnerships, seemed unable to establish any rapport.

Rachel's situation didn't change during most of the 1970s. I accepted what my parents told me: her illness was chronic, and if she couldn't be cured, she at least needed to be maintained and protected. After years of futile meetings and letters, my parents decided to take drastic action. In 1977, with the full support of my mother, my father filed a federal lawsuit against St. Louis State Hospital. Having been admitted as a patient, he argued, Rachel had a right to protection and treatment as long as her medical condition required it. A friend of theirs, a civil rights lawyer prominent in the St. Louis community, took their case.

A district court dismissed their suit. The federal appeals court reinstated it. I listened to the updates whenever I talked on the phone with my mother. I wished her and Dad well with it, but I had more immediate things on my mind. Having determined to start a full-time career by the time I turned thirty, I was now a working mother. My life was full. I trusted that my parents knew what they were doing.

My brother, on the other hand, had an entirely different take on the lawsuit. Michael had his own ideas about what Rachel needed, and he decided to put them into action.

I didn't know what Rachel herself felt about the case until I read her letters to Mom and Dad years later: In March of 1979 she wrote from St. Louis State Hospital, *I suppose you* *are doing well in your court trials. . . . Perhaps you will win, but <u>some people are against you</u>. I do not know if you are doing any good except for a few.* She and Michael had been talking. Were her underscored words a warning?

After years as a remote presence, my brother came lurching back into my life in 1979, not long after the lawsuit was filed. Fresh off a divorce, he had moved from Seattle to New York City. Michael and I talked more in that one year than we had the entire decade. I was cleaning up after dinner when he called me that spring. With the receiver cradled in my shoulder, I felt his anger and urgency pressing into my ear: "They've got her on insulin now. They're poisoning her with narcoleptics; they let her eat refined sugar. They'll turn her into a comatose, corpulescent blob." He was talking about State Hospital, where he had stopped to visit on his trip East.

I rolled my eyes. Like Jack Nicholson in the movie, my brother had a big grin, a mistrust of authority, and a ready supply of verbal antics. "We've got to do something before Mom and Dad settle their lawsuit," he pleaded. "They'll keep her locked up forever."

This conviction of his alarmed me. "No, they won't. They want more state funding for hospital services and more accountability," I told him.

"You have no idea," he retorted. "They want the state to take care of Rachel forever."

Neither of us made much headway convincing the other; we could have talked in circles forever. But Michael had an idea for breaking the stalemate. "We should all go to St. Louis to meet with Rachel and Mom and Dad. You and me and

Julie. I asked a therapist I know in Seattle to consult with us. She'll fly out and meet with us. I think you'll like her—Sherri."

Before I could ask about Sherri's credentials, I heard my daughters yelling at each other upstairs, then Barry running up the steps to check on them. It was a welcome distraction. I was too tired to stay on the phone with Michael. My feet were throbbing and I longed to lay down on the couch, catch the news with Walter Cronkite and hear about other people's problems.

This would be no ordinary trip to St. Louis. Only three months earlier, my parents had taken care of the girls while Barry and I had time alone at Four Seasons, a resort not far from rustic Camp Hawthorn, where we had met. But a return to St. Louis with all my siblings? It would certainly be no vacation. I couldn't even think of a time the six of us had been in the same room at the same time since my wedding twelve years earlier. The timing of Rachel's first hospitalization in 1965 coincided with other forces pulling apart our family. Michael and I had both escaped to distant colleges and early marriages. Somehow our trips to St. Louis had rarely coincided. We never got together to discuss Rachel's care, not with each other, not with Julie, not with our parents. Now, here was Michael insisting we do so. It was hard to imagine what the meeting proposed by my brother would be like.

Corpulescent blob! I could roll my eyes at my brother's silly words, but their emotional freight reverberated. In my heart I knew the lawsuit wouldn't make Rachel's life better anytime soon. I had no idea what the future held for her other than a life in back wards of State Hospital. Involuntary commitments punctuated by an unrelenting cycle of discharge, arrest, and re-admission. I swiped my wet hands on the side of my jeans and leaned back against the counter. "Okay, I'll go, but there's one thing I want you to promise me."

"Anything," he said. "What is it?"

"Just, don't go off on Mom and Dad. We can't go out there and start criticizing everything they've done. I know you don't like the lawsuit, but they've put a lot into it. They mean well and they're trying their best." Michael cleared his throat to protest but I continued. "I'm not sure how this will accomplish anything for Rachel, but it will be good for her to see we all love and care about her. So let's not have a big blowup."

Michael chuckled. "I promise I'll be good. And listen. I've talked to Dad, and I think he's open to new ideas. Mom too. You'll see."

In early July three siblings flew from New York to St. Louis, where we dropped our bags in our old bedrooms. Michael picked up Sherri from the airport. Dad drove the five miles to State Hospital and brought Rachel home. We sat in our parents' dining room, where I saw my brother straining to control his impatience as the meeting proceeded in starts and stops. Dad sat at the table with a puzzled look on his long, serious face. Rachel, sitting opposite him, looked eerily placid, except for the occasional twitch from tardive dyskinesia, the movement disorder caused by her medication that made her tongue roll awkwardly in her mouth. It made her speech slurred, hard to understand, and it was difficult for me to watch her as well.

After initial exchanges with Sherri, Goodmans began moving around the room like chess pieces. Julie stopped jiggling her legs in her chair and scooted forward, sideways, and forward again to the piano bench where she leafed through the music books on the rack. Our mother, taking the queen's prerogative, made a beeline into the kitchen and then back to the dining room with coffee and brownies, insisting that we all partake. I advanced two paces to the window. I saw a small summer garden in the yard and a new sturdy fence on the side, put up by the neighbor with a dog. I made out the section of patched bricks on the side of my parents' garage that had to be rebuilt after the little boy in the house behind released the brakes of his family's car. It had rolled down his driveway and into my parents' garage. I returned to my spot at the table thinking how amazing it was that a freakish, out-of-control accident like that could result in no serious hurt or damage. Just a patch of barely off-color bricks.

I turned my attention back to the room. I watched the movements of Michael's hands and long squared-off fingers. I saw how he held the sides of his head with them, listening to other people talk. How he splayed them against the veneer of the table when he wanted to be understood. His hands had always been so expressive. I remembered him as a teenager holding a calligraphy brush to draw Mandarin characters. I remembered him standing with his double bass, long fingers pressing out the notes of the Koussevitzky concerto on the giant fingerboard, his hands pulling back the bow to draw out the low fervid sounds. Even as a child his hands had moved with passion. When he was in first grade, in a school auditorium overcrowded with baby boomers, he stood up in front of his seat, waving his arms in the air to conduct the visiting orchestra. I sat four or five rows behind him with my own classmates, squirming with embarrassment. But as I grew up, his music and language talents made me proud. Now, despite the painful issue he raised, I was glad Michael had brought us all together. I was glad he wanted to do something to give Rachel back her life.

I waited for weeks to hear Sherri's recommendations. They arrived by mail several weeks after the St. Louis meeting. They seemed to all of us superficial and sadly irrelevant to Rachel's immediate needs. Most frustrating was her recommendation of private hospitals. We knew how prohibitively expensive they were. We had already inquired and quickly learned why middle-class families relied on state hospitals. What alternative was there?

To my amazement Michael had an alternative—one that was both radical and affordable. In the weeks that followed he began explaining it to me and Julie. He wanted to take Rachel back with him to Seattle where he would make a home with her, where he had a network of friends and professionals who would help with her care. I was shocked. I demanded more explanations, which he quickly provided. He was eager to show me how his plan would work better than anything my parents or State Hospital could do. He told me how much he needed my support, both financial and moral. "Mom and Dad won't agree to let Rachel go unless you do." *Of course*, I thought. I was the settled and stable one. I had always defended them against my younger siblings' criticisms. I had always been grateful they made the decisions about Rachel. But now my brother said her siblings should be in charge. I wasn't sure I was ready to make life-altering calls.

In August Michael took the train from the city to see me. It was time to talk face to face, just the two of us. We sat in the screened porch, facing the backyard strewn with children's toys. "We have to help Rachel now," he said, his eyes searching mine. He returned to the point I had refused to concede: that once the lawsuit was settled, Rachel was doomed. "When they make a deal with the hospital, Mom and Dad will win the right to keep her incarcerated forever."

"Incarcerated? Oh, Michael," I said, exasperated once again by what seemed to be hyperbole. "Mom and Dad want her to get appropriate treatment, whether she's in or out of the hospital."

Michael's face clouded over. "You can believe that if you want," he answered. "But they'll never help Rachel. Call it what you want. I call it incarceration."

I thought about Rachel, as I had seen her a month earlier in St. Louis. Placid. Shoulders slack over her protruding belly. Speech slurred. Clearly she was overmedicated. Surely she deserved better. Michael was right in a way. Rachel wasn't incarcerated on criminal charges, but she was the prisoner of an inept, inhumane system. It was time for me to stop arguing about words.

Moving in a haze of uncertainty, I refilled our coffee cups, put out fruit, pastries, and Michael's favorite, pistachio nuts. I watched him crack them open and palm the shells in a plate. I heard the front door open and voices mixing, low and high, trills and Barry's reassuring murmurs. He and the girls were home. Knowing I had only a minute or two before they would want my attention, I turned to Michael and asked him the question that most gnawed at me: "You'll have your own daughter to see when you go back to Seattle. How can you take on responsibility for Rachel?"

"My daughter will be fine. I'll be able to see her too. I have to do this. I know I can make it work—if you help me," he answered. His hands reached for mine. "You and Julie will be part of this. We'll have a plan. I'll tell you about every step I take. Every healer I consult. Every dollar I spend."

Michael's enthusiasm infected me. I appreciated what my parents were trying to do, but I didn't believe any court decision could make an impact on Rachel's life. My hopes for Rachel were simple. Like my parents, I wanted her protected from assaults. "Rachel was raped in one of those places," my mother had told me years ago, her voice tight with fear and shame. "She needs to be protected. Protected and treated."

I too wanted Rachel protected, but safety wasn't enough. I wanted her to live someplace where she could walk out a front door to visit friends, go to the store, bring her sketchbook to a park, make her art and poetry. I no longer cared if she held a job, washed her feet, or put her belongings in drawers instead of in piles on the floor.

My mind raced as I drove Michael to the station. Maybe he was onto something. Maybe it was time to take a risk. To support his plan to bring Rachel to live with him in Seattle.

"Let me think about it," I said when he asked me one more time.

"I'm counting on you, Deb-Deb," he yelled as he bolted up the steps to the platform.

"How's it going with Michael?" Barry asked as we got ready for bed that night. "Is he still talking about taking Rachel to Seattle?"

"Yes, he really wants to do it," I answered. "Maybe it's not such a crazy idea."

"What about her treatment?"

I explained what I understood from the conversations

with my brother. "You know he's into all those alternative approaches. Holistic medicine. Nutrition. But when it comes down to it, he's realistic. He knows Rachel will need conventional medication. He knows doctors who will consider weaning her off the high dosages of insulin and antipsychotics."

Barry nodded. "It's all trial and error," he said, reaching against the wall to flip the light.

"Mainly error," I mumbled.

"What's that?" asked Barry, turning back to me.

I blurted out the words that had been my silent mantra for months: "It couldn't be worse," I explained to Barry. "Nothing could be worse than what she goes through there." State Hospital, I knew, hadn't done a thing for her in fourteen years. I was tired of all the fear and futility. I was tired of hopelessness. Just thinking about Rachel started me sobbing. "You know I'll support you whatever you decide," he said, reaching out to hold me.

I heard the air conditioner groan in the window and pulled the sheet over my shoulders. I would have turned the unit off altogether—I preferred summer heat to the mechanized chill. Barry though would have a hard time sleeping. AC was a minor concession to a husband who provided unlimited amounts of solace and acceptance. I was grateful for his unswerving support and the space he gave me to think things through. I didn't yet know whether I could agree to Michael's proposal, but I sensed hope taking root in me. All the tension that had built up as I struggled to figure out a path for Rachel gave way to a shudder of relief as I crept into my husband's arms.

Over the following weeks, Michael's proposal became more and more detailed. He created budgets with line items of expenses, lists of healthcare professionals. He went over them with me by telephone and in person with Julie during their get-togethers on the Upper West Side, where they both lived. Now, we agreed, the three of us needed to speak face to face to get closer to a resolution.

We met under the tiled arches of the Oyster Bar at Grand Central Station. It was a convenient location, but its opulence was unsettling to me. So was Julie's comment. "I think Michael and Rachel should find a place to live around here," she said. "That way Debby and I can help Michael out when things get difficult. It'll be better for both of them to have family nearby."

I dismissed her idea. "Julie, we can provide plenty of moral support by phone. And it'll be a healthier environment for her out West." It didn't occur to me then that Julie was the only one of us who had lived at home with Rachel after she became ill and experienced firsthand the chaos she created. I just knew I didn't have room in my life to cope with Rachel's crises. Julie didn't press her point. When she saw Michael and me aligned, she went along. Before we left that night, Julie and I had agreed to help our brother with living expenses. She would contribute a lump sum from her savings, I would send a check on a monthly basis.

On my ride home, even the rhythmic motion of the train wheels, usually so relaxing, couldn't quiet my mind. Would our parents agree to the plan? Could Michael make good on his intentions? It was all tentative, I reminded myself. If I felt that it wouldn't work, I still had time to say no.

The next morning I asked Barry what he thought we

should do. He knew my family. He knew mental health. He was clinical director at a child guidance center where parents brought children with behavioral problems identified by schools, doctors, police, or a family's own sense of something being very wrong. But parents, and sometimes siblings, were expected to get involved in the treatment as well. Even though individual therapy could help the child's behavior improve, other problems were likely to crop up in the family. To avoid the whack-a-mole effect, Barry explained to me, therapists worked with the whole family system.

Barry had no immediate answers, but he knew leading practitioners in the field. He gave me the name of one who particularly impressed him: Peggy Papp. She used a therapeutic technique called "sculpting," a kind of role playing to help family members gain insight into family dynamics.

Michael's plan had not been on the table when we consulted with Sherri. Now it was and I needed advice from another professional before I could decide. So much was at stake. Michael wanted to yank Rachel free from a family knot. I wanted to make sure that he didn't pull it apart entirely, leaving a collection of loose ends. I arranged a meeting with the therapist Barry recommended.

Five Goodmans, all of us but Rachel, met with Peggy Papp at her private office, a space as reassuring and gracious as the therapist herself. From my seat on the couch, I could see a wrought iron stairway ascending to the next level of the Upper East Side townhouse. I felt the warm creams and calm blues of the furnishings blend together peacefully. I heard the room whisper a promise of hope and renewal: sit here and rest, you Goodmans, speak softly and you'll find harmony too.

Our first meeting took place without Rachel, as the therapist had requested. Leaning forward from the matching blue chair, she asked how she could help us. Michael laid out his plan. Peggy Papp listened carefully and elicited reactions. My father voiced his reservations but said he would go along if the rest of us were agreed it was the right thing to do. My mother spoke, with great emotion, about how unfair and painful it was that everyone blamed her. She was still furious at St. Louis State Hospital and its community psychiatry program. She repeated her longstanding grievance against Dr. Sandall—that she believed everything bad Rachel said about her. Worse, said Mom, was the blame that came from her own children. "Aunt Florence told Michael that I didn't love Rachel when she was a baby. That's crazy. How could I not love her? Rachel was my daughter. But Michael believed her." I winced seeing the pain and anger in my mother's face. "And he got Debby and Julie to believe it too," she added, to my chagrin.

Quietly, in a series of nonjudgmental questions and observations, Peggy Papp managed to defuse the charged atmosphere of guilt and resentment. It wasn't a matter of blaming anyone, she emphasized. I nodded in agreement. "If we can make a better life for Rachel," I said, "I think we should try. I don't see how anything could be worse than what she has now." Two hours later, we agreed to have a second family session in a few weeks, one that included Rachel. If everyone still agreed, we would move ahead with the Seattle plan.

WESTWARD HO!

When she got back to St. Louis, my mother threw us a curve. She said she would stay home and sit out the second session. I was disappointed by her decision, given how much was riding on the proposed move. But I wasn't surprised. I knew how uncomfortable she was with Rachel, how agitated when they were together—like all those times Mom would eagerly shop for Rachel's clothes but then give them to Dad to bring to her in the hospital. "I already got what I needed out of the first meeting," she told me. "I was so relieved when Peggy Papp said to all of you that it wasn't my fault. I'll be fine with whatever the rest of you decide."

Rachel of course was eager to go to the next meeting, partly, I suspected, because she saw an opportunity to go to New York City. As soon as she heard about a trip East, she talked about visiting friends there. I was wary. I could just imagine the disasters that would befall her if she went off to revisit the grit of her bohemian years on the Lower East Side. "It isn't healthy there for you," I told her on the phone as we made the plans. "Stay and visit me for the week." Rachel quickly agreed.

For years, I had dreaded the day I would find Rachel at my front door, pleading to stay with me. She never did. Now I wanted her to come. I knew it was past time for her to be with me in my home. I couldn't help being nervous, though. Years earlier, while I was home in St. Louis during a college break and Rachel was home on a weekend pass, our parents went out for an evening and told me to make sure that Rachel stayed in the house. I felt like I was watching a melting candle, that its molten wax would sear right through me. I couldn't hold Rachel back. She was bigger and bolder and more decisive than me. I was sure that if she wanted to leave, she would glare, push me away and walk right past me. I never felt that I could contain Rachel.

But I was no longer a college student charged with my sister's safekeeping for a few hours. Rachel now was medicated, and less overtly defiant. I need not have worried about hallucinations or bizarre behavior—the long-term doses of the meds she'd been injected with for this visit took care of that. What I did worry about during the three nights she stayed with us was fire. She was a chain smoker. What if she fell asleep with a cigarette between her fingers and caused a conflagration that engulfed my family and home?

"Just tell her she has to smoke outside," Barry said when I fretted in anticipation of her arrival.

"I will, but I don't know if she'll listen." How often had I seen her in St. Louis, lying on her bed in silent reverie, taking half-hearted aim at the ashtray on the table between us. I never saw her fall asleep with a cigarette, but back then she never seemed to sleep. Did she now? Would her medication make her dangerously drowsy?

"It's okay. She'll go outside," repeated Barry. And she did.

The other thing I worried about was that Rachel might take off. Hitch a ride with a stranger. Take a bus to New York. How often over the years had our father received a call from a policeman to pick her up at a station in Tulsa, or Chicago, or Kansas City?

As it turned out she did go roaming, but not very far. Rachel told me she was taking a walk around the block, a half-mile loop. My stomach in knots, I looked for her outside. I panicked when an hour had passed and she hadn't returned. Finally, she called—from the phone booth at Stew Leonard's dairy store, hardly a mile away.

As soon as I drove up, I saw her. She stood planted at the crowded entrance, looking vague. Clueless. Shoppers wheeled their carts past her as she remained in place, shifting her weight from one leg to the other, the buttons of her shirt pulled tight against her slack Thorazine belly. I got out of the car to give her a hug.

"I didn't know how to get back to your house," Rachel said.

"I know. I'm glad you called me."

If I hadn't been so worked up, I might have thought to take Rachel inside to see one of Stew Leonard's animatronic displays—the ten-foot celery stalk dancing under the rafters with its radish and lettuce partners. She wasn't really clueless, she just looked that way. She would have been amused by those hallucinatory antics above the vegetable bins. Rachel was no stranger to the absurd.

Our daughters were polite and respectful with Rachel. She wasn't a total stranger to them. They had met her during visits to St. Louis. Older now, more aware of social expectations, they seemed to accept my explanation of illness and special needs. Rachel patted the girls on their back, awkwardly but approvingly. She enjoyed being around them. A few years earlier she had written me about adopting children with her boyfriend at the hospital. Whatever feelings she may have had toward me for usurping her position as the eldest and having children before her, she was never resentful. She smiled at the pictures my girls showed her; she looked at their books and toys. She even petted Blacky, the rabbit who lived in the empty space under the back porch. Successful as it was, this was the first and the last time she would visit with me and my family in my home.

Her last night with us I spoke to her about the next day's plans. We would meet Dad, Michael, and Julie in the lobby of the Ackerman Clinic, where Peggy Papp worked in addition to her private practice. I watched Rachel draw long drags of her cigarette, her stained fingers going through their various smoking motions. Every so often she coughed from deep inside her chest. The hospital seemed to put no limits on smoking.

"Tomorrow we'll talk about living in Seattle," I said to Rachel, sounding her out once again.

"Yes, I want to go," Rachel assured me. "Michael has good ideas." She talked slowly. The muscles of her face and tongue were thick from years of medication. It was hard to discern the depth of her feeling until she nodded her head for emphasis.

She really wants this, I thought. What does she have to lose? Nothing could be worse than her life at State Hospital. That's what I told myself again and again. Rachel and I sat lost in our thoughts until the screen door banged open and the girls clamored out to say good night to us—and to aging Blacky parked peacefully under the porch.

The next morning I drove with Rachel to Manhattan. She didn't talk. She exhaled her cigarette smoke out the half-open car window. I navigated the potholes of the Cross Bronx Expressway, the weight of the upcoming family decision tugging at my stomach with every jolt.

Without my mother, we were once again just five Goodmans in the family session. A father and his four adult children sharing our dreams of a better future. My father seemed somber, sad but willing to let Rachel go. He had tried so hard to help Rachel, to make the system work for her, and now his children were telling him his efforts weren't good enough. Did he feel betrayed? Rejected? Relieved? How I wish now that he had shared more of what he was feeling.

Michael reiterated his commitment to Rachel's health and well-being. He talked about the scope of his support system in Seattle—professional and personal. Rachel reaffirmed her wish to go with him. She said she understood he would manage her food, cigarettes, and activities based on the advice of doctors and specialists they would be consulting there.

Rachel was decisive but distant. Her face showed almost no emotion, a flattening that began when she became a psychiatric patient. I said I very much wanted Rachel to have this opportunity for a healthier life outside the hospital. I noticed Julie said very little, which puzzled me, but I didn't ask her why.

Peggy Papp was a facilitator, not a psychiatric advisor. She didn't accept or reject the therapeutic value of the plan; she emphasized the challenge. "What you are setting out to do is very difficult," she said. "You will be taking a boat out in the rough seas. The only way to get to the other side is to row together. Do you think you can do that?" We said we did. We agreed to try.

After the meeting Dad and Rachel went to the airport for the flight back to St. Louis. Dad and Michael, we had all agreed, would begin making arrangements for Rachel's move to Seattle.

Back home that night, I tried to recount the details of the family meeting to Barry. "She didn't do the sculpting technique. She just had each of us talk about what we expected to happen and what we are concerned about. She said this move will be like crossing a channel in a boat. To make it work, we'll all have to row together." It was too hard, too exhausting to remember the specifics of what everyone felt and expected. That was the one bit of information from the meeting I could hold on to. The boat. The paddling.

Barry and I sat in the toy-strewn living room, on the sofa under the front window, facing the wall that separated the living room from the kitchen. It was about to come down so we could build a new kitchen where the porch was now. I had cabinet specs from a catalog and was drawing up the lay-out on graph paper. "It's kind of like remodeling the house," I mused. "We're restructuring the family." When it came to metaphors for this situation, I was more comfortable with a house than a boat. A house couldn't capsize.

And that got me thinking about an issue with our literal house. Before the carpenter could start on the new kitchen, we needed a foundation poured underneath the back porch. I asked Barry once again where he thought Blacky would live. "Not inside. I'm too allergic," I emphasized, lest he forget that rabbits made me as asthmatic as cats did.

"We'll figure out something," he said, drawing from his well of optimism.

Some weeks later, the very day before the mason was to pour the cement, I came home from work to hear a cry from Barry outside. He had just found Blacky cold and stiff underneath the porch. The girls were sobbing. Barry was too.

Later that evening we ended up laughing through our tears. Blacky, we realized, had decided he didn't want to move. "How in the world did he know?" I said to Barry. "That was some weird karma."

I have a photograph of Rachel from that 1979 visit. She is on the Lady Joan, a tourist vessel that chugged out of Cove Marina and around the Norwalk Islands, where migratory birds and boaters go. Rachel is smiling and the photo transports me to this excursion I arranged for her. My two daughters, then ten and seven, sit nearby. The engine is humming. The boat contains us, holding us within the oval arms of its cool railings. We look like a normal young family, enjoying an afternoon on the water with a slightly dowdy but pleasant aunt visiting from out of town. My face catches the kiss of the salt spray. I inhale the cool breeze and the pungent smell of its sea life churning in the currents below. Off to the side, the girls pepper Barry with their curious chatter while Rachel and I sit quietly enjoying the gentle swells against the hull. I like to think the saltwater spraying the deck of the Lady Joan brought Rachel back to the Mediterranean, to that transatlantic ship in the photo her friend Sandy sent me. I like to imagine that Rachel again felt whole and happy leaning on the railing over Long Island Sound.

Shortly after Rachel got back to St. Louis, she sent me a thank-you note, reflecting on her visit and her return home. She was unhappy to be locked up so often in the hospital. She didn't explain what rules she had broken to get her privileges taken away. It must have been difficult going back there after the good time she had at my house in the "country." She complimented my daughters. Told me how much she enjoyed taking walks with us and our family dog. Included with her letter was handwritten sheet music for a song she wrote for me titled, "Running Brook." Ever the older sister, she urged me to try music composition. *It's a good thing to sit down and express your whole being. . ..* Rachel ended her thank-you letter with a fervent wish: *I'm hoping that when I get out of this miserable place, life will look up for us and we'll be able to continue in a different vein. Your loving Sister, Ray.* When I discovered this letter not long ago, I sat at the piano and tried to play her composition, but her scoring was too ambiguous. Then I closed my eyes and remembered other rounds of music. Mom at the piano. Dad moving our song along with his forceful tenor and Rachel standing next to him. The heft of her alto voice still echoes in my ears.

I have often wondered why I supported Rachel's move to Seattle, given the risks of such an unconventional and untested plan. I have to remind myself that nobody—no doctors, no therapists—had come forward with any better ideas. I have to remember the joy I saw in her face on that harbor cruise. The song she sent to thank me. I have to remember how badly I wanted more for my sister than psychiatric wards and chemical strait jackets. How I believed she needed a healing environment where it was possible to "express your whole being." Where she could make music. Write poetry. Paint and draw. Michael seemed able and eager to provide it. And so I agreed to his plan, imperfect as it was.

IT'S COMPLICATED

I don't remember hearing about Michael's lover during our many conversations in the early months of 1979. I learned about him when my brother began looking for a house to rent in Seattle at the end of that year. That's when he made it clear that Keith would be living there with him and Rachel.

I had learned about Michael's affairs with men two years before our conversations about Rachel's future began. His wife had outed him when she called to tell me about their impending divorce. I was surprised, and disappointed that my brother didn't tell me himself. I assumed that a bisexual life-style was the reason for his move to New York. But then, when his focus turned to Rachel, I just put questions about his love life out of my mind. It never occurred to me a boyfriend would factor into his plans for her.

Now I felt blindsided. Angry that Michael hadn't been forthright with me but unsure whether I should make an issue of it. The situation was murkier than before, but I was still hopeful—and glad Rachel was getting a fresh start. I was also happy for my eight-year-old niece: my brother would be able to see her frequently. I just hoped Michael could sustain his relationship with his daughter, build a new one with Keith, and manage Rachel all at the same time. As though anticipating my concerns, my brother wrote that Keith was a wonderful support. He helped shop and cook. He contributed to the rent. Keith even hung out with Rachel—reading, playing Monopoly.

As long as things seemed to be working out, I didn't feel I could voice my concerns in any constructive way. I refrained from roiling the waters. The boat had set out to sea, albeit with one more paddler than I expected.

Rachel arrived in Seattle in December 1979, with no medication or prescriptions. Michael had planned to taper off her medication in consultation with doctors, social workers, naturopaths, nutritionists, and other assorted healers he had lined up. But the doctors in St. Louis weren't responsive to requests for help with the transition. So she made the move cold turkey.

Instead of meds, Rachel arrived with a raging abscess on her leg. Michael got antibiotics for the infection and applied compresses three times a day. Rachel, he wrote, bawled like a baby when he cleaned the wound and changed the dressing. But he persisted and was able to heal the infection. How satisfying it must have been for him to be able to fix that part of her.

Michael doled out her cigarettes—one pack of low tar, low-nicotine cigarettes a day. He began weaning her off of insulin using a macrobiotic diet recommended by a Chinese healer. No chemicals or additives. No Tab sodas. No pretzels or crackers or potato chips.

He recorded these details in letters to the family. I was glad to hear from him, but I did little more than skim what he wrote. I was absorbed in thinking about my own life, specifically my career. After three years of writing about the beer industry for a trade publication, I was restless, determined to find a new job. I put away his letters and trusted that he would find appropriate care.

To Rachel, who had no control over her sexual urges once she became ill, Keith was irresistible. Just days after she arrived in Seattle, Rachel made her moves on Keith. *I had to drag her out of my room*, Michael wrote, *because she hovered around Keith on the bed and drooled over him while he was sleeping.* Michael pulled her downstairs and made her promise she wouldn't come upstairs again. If she needed him in the morning, she should call from the bottom of the steps. She cried and sulked. Michael finally got her to say she would respect his wishes, and his privacy. He told her Keith wasn't interested in sleeping with her and that restraint was part of the deal—along with brewer's yeast and bathing her leg. She said she understood.

For three months Michael believed his cure was working, and that healing for Rachel, though difficult, was on the horizon. Early on, he began the process of getting her into a day treatment program. It would provide socialization for her and respite for him. Michael wrote about the small successes, periods of calm and camaraderie. He described how Rachel wrote and drew in her journal. How she dipped her hands into the bags of clay he brought her and created a sculpture to bring to her new psychiatrist. When she asked for a haircut, Michael recruited his ex-wife. He took Rachel to Portland and visited Aunt Dorothy (our mother's sister), who altered a skirt for her while Rachel did yard work with Uncle Dave.

In a February 17 letter, Michael wrote: *Rachel is fine. Improving daily. Her leg is stronger. Her blood sugar stabilized, her skin clear, and her breathing deeper. We walk every day. We ride the busses, the car. We shop. Ray cooks some, cleans the kitchen and her room. She talks and joins in.* He said Rachel had pinned the valentine card Dad sent her on her wall. The thought of his note on Rachel's wall filled me with joy—his simple gesture of love given and accepted. Our father had always expressed his feelings so much better with drawings and written words than in conversation. I didn't know then how little time he had left.

I was happy to hear about progress, thrilled to have my hopes confirmed.

I never spoke with Keith, though. I can only imagine his bewilderment. How his patience wore thin as weeks passed. It wasn't long before my brother and Keith started counseling to figure out where their relationship was going. The counselor (surprisingly to me) came to meet with them at home. For some reason, Michael expected Rachel to stay out of the way. He was upset that Rachel kept barging in on their session, insisting she should be involved because she had things to discuss with the counselor too. Why wouldn't she, I wondered. Michael's expectation didn't seem realistic. As I knew from family systems theory, every relationship was part of a dynamic structure that included every family member. A change in one affected all: an altered emotional state, a relapse, or a recovery. Certainly a new relationship.

Rachel, with her adolescent heart and rebellious ways, needed a father figure, and Michael was eager to take that role. A stepfather had just stepped into his own daughter's life, and maybe that intensified Michael's eagerness. In any case, Michael's attempt proved courageous, but naive. How could he possibly have been prepared for the lengths Rachel would go to resist him? Grabbing his crotch and talking about incest. Ruining carpets with her cigarettes. Plunging the household into darkness. Literally. Because she wasn't allowed upstairs, she went to the basement and pulled a breaker circuit, cutting off electricity for the entire house.

Yet progress did seem real. In January Rachel's sugar levels came down enough for her physician to take her off insulin. Encouraged, Michael continued his macrobiotic food regimen, along with massive doses of vitamins C and B12. He wrote about his delight at hearing Rachel play Schumann on the piano. How surprised he was that she could sight-read the music so well. And he must have been relieved when Rachel agreed to attend the day treatment program he finally got her into.

Despite the progress Rachel was making, tensions mounted. Reading between the lines of letters both Michael and Rachel wrote, I can now see that quite clearly in this letter from Rachel: *Seattle. February 1980. Dear Mort and Sophie, Now it's about time to write again. Life has been going along fairly smoothly. We've been going outdoors a lot. Recently we took the train to Oregon to visit David and Dorothy and Aaron. They seem to be getting along OK. Now I've [been] getting some psychic therapy and am growing well along in spirit and body. Every bit helps. I hope I won't waste my life in hospital after hospital.* She enjoyed the beauty of the area, the trips to the bustling farmers' market by the harbor. But she found the new family relationships problematic. *Michael seems to wander a bit but is certainly trying to do his best for me and the others. Keith does his best to keep the common life going along but gets moody and serious and withdrawn. It's such a hard life here that we're all involved in it deeply. Your loving son, Rachel*

Your loving son? What the fuck? Well, why not? It's really not that crazy. Why should there be only one Goodman son? Don't sons have power? Becoming a son, Rachel put herself on an equal footing with Michael. And gender confusion was really the least of Rachel's problems. By this time she had been fleeing unnamed persecutors for fifteen years, embodiments of evils that only she could see and hear and feel.

Rachel's desire to be an equal to her brother may have been a sign of what was to come. In retrospect I believe that two power struggles doomed further progress. Michael and Rachel fought each other for control of her food, her sex life, her cigarettes. And at the same time Michael fought to take control of Rachel's finances from our father. He wanted our father to transfer guardianship so that her disability and Medicare payments would go directly to him, and he wouldn't have to ask his father for reimbursements. But our father rejected that part of Michael's plan.

By the middle of March, the boat we launched from Peggy Papp's office had capsized. Keith had broken up with Michael, and Rachel was back in a psychiatric ward. I don't know exactly what happened in the fight between Michael and Rachel that sparked their separation. I do know their struggles became physical as Michael sought to set limits that collided head on with her desires. I also know her admission to Harborview was voluntary. Maybe she was seeking protection. Maybe she craved conventional food again. When they separated, I had no desire to figure out why. It all seemed so far away. So exhausting and futile. More real, and more pressing to me, was the job I had just gotten, which involved editing articles about global agribusiness and campaigns to get advertisers into construction magazines for developing countries. New and obscure as all of this was to me, it was easier to understand than Rachel's behavior.

Michael reported on his visit to Rachel in Harborview. He wanted to see how she was doing and talk about the future. Rachel told him there was no possibility that she would ever live with him again. A few weeks later, he got her on the phone, and she told him not to visit her. After one or two more tries, he took her at her word and left her alone. He wrote on April 1 to our parents and explained: *Rachel is indeed very disturbed. And if she can make any improvement in the future at all, it will be on her own terms. My involvement was fraught with dangers, mistakes, and illusions. Washington State [hospital system] is not too bad for Rachel at this juncture.* My brother had been so brave and hopeful. Now even he had to give up his dream of healing Rachel. When I heard the news, I was angry not with him but with Rachel. I thought she was being stubborn.

We all agreed it was better to leave Rachel out West than bring her home. Rachel would have hospital passes and outings with opportunities to enjoy the outdoors. And for those times she went off on her own, wouldn't life in the great outdoors be better for her wandering lifestyle than the streets of St. Louis? I had never seen the Northwest, but I nursed a hope that its mountains and spaciousness would give Rachel some kind of respite. She would have woods to hike, and inspiration for her poetry. My parents would have a break from their longstanding battles with St. Louis State Hospital. And I would never be faced with the impossible responsibility of finding a therapeutic placement near me.

I wanted my sister to be free, but I wanted my freedom too. It didn't occur to me that she would miss any of us given how often she took off. I didn't think about the family events she would never attend. The Thanksgiving and Passover gatherings. The bat mitzvahs and weddings, recitals and graduations. Rachel did, however, come to St. Louis for our father's funeral about eighteen months later: August 1981. Julie's deft intervention brought that about. But after that, it would be many years until any of us would see Rachel again.

Rachel lived with Michael for only three months before leaving to check into Harborview Hospital for two weeks. She was soon released to a group home. She had never adapted to group living situations in St. Louis and she didn't out West either. She was picked up by the police, committed by the court, and sent to Western State Hospital in Fort Steilacoom, a repurposed military facility south of Tacoma, Washington.

After another round of discharge and arrest, she decided to take off. She crossed the border to Oregon, where she was picked up for shoplifting and arson. She was committed by court order to Dammasch State Hospital, near Portland.

Thus began her Oregon years, where she remained for the rest of her life. Between 1980 and 1992 Rachel would be released, readmitted, and transferred back and forth among three different Oregon hospitals: Dammasch, Oregon State Hospital in Salem, and Eastern Oregon Psychiatric Center in Pendleton. She stayed in hospitals, shelters, halfway houses, and boarding houses. Sometimes she camped outside in the woods. For two of those years, in Salem, she was in the very hospital where Milos Forman's award-winning movie had been filmed seven years earlier. In that drama Randle McMurphy's buddy, the

Chief, yanked a hydrotherapy tank from the floor and threw it through a window. Rachel wouldn't need to eject a water tank to free herself. Miraculously she was able to leverage poetry instead of brute force. She left the hospital system for good and became the hero of my family drama.

The Boy

Always his boyish self
Yet so persevering.
All his life he assumed
Many roles but kept his
Austerity apart.

He learned to live on his own
So when I said I'd join him
It was a very special kind of
Commitment, that soon led to
Chaos but it united so
That I sprang and fled,
And mobilized on my own
With a mob beside me,
Saying goodbye to all his
Worth and unkindly actions.

When he was young
He succeeded in accepting the family,
He worked and played on his own
Away from the girls, and led
A kind of violated life, so that
When he was older he lived to
Maturity, practiced his lessons,
His own family, his
Wife and children,

Who cherished and respected him
On his own merits
And continues to work
That boy has been around the
Scenery of academics and his own
Kind of Oriental flavor,
So that if anyone asks about
His own special calling he spits
Out his kind of advice,
And be futile to the
Rest of the world he calls
His own and anyone else who
Cares to comment.

—Rachel Goodman

"I ENCLOSE MY MISERY"

We didn't make a new plan; we just let things happen. Michael stayed in Seattle, Mom and Dad in St. Louis, Julie in New York, and I in Connecticut. We let Rachel stay out West because why? Because the hospitals there seemed better than St. Louis? So Mom and Dad could finally enjoy their life? Because Rachel would do better amidst woods and mountains than urban squalor? She *would* be better off, wouldn't she? And that's what she wanted, wasn't it? I managed to convince myself she did.

Years later, I learned differently. In the basement of my long-widowed mother's St. Louis home, I found the letters Rachel wrote to my parents during that first year out West. I looked at them and put them away. Took them out and read them again: twenty-two letters in which she pleaded with them to bring her home. She wrote them to Mom and Dad both, but many to Dad alone. My hands trembled when I saw notes marking the date of receipt in Dad's handwriting. Why was he saving all her letters if he didn't plan to take her back? I was overcome with the despair he must have felt. Despair and determination.

Rachel began her campaign for release as soon as she parted ways with Michael: *March 18, 1980. Dear Mort and Sophie, The time has come for me to beg of you to come here*

*to Seattle and bring me safely home to that big barn called St.
Louis. Right now I am at a place called Harborview, which is
another one of those places that are common but hard. . . . After
all the experiences I've been thru, this is one of the worst. So
please come right away and take me home. Could an attendant
do that also? . . . If you could come and arrange for me to
leave, I hope it won't be longer than a month. . . Your daughter,
Rachel*

She was soon transferred to a psychiatric hospital in
Washington and she appealed to Dad again: *May 1980. Now
I'm in Tacoma. It's Western State Hospital. For a while I had
great fun in Seattle. It's a strange town and great too. Now that
I'm here I'm kind of taking it easy. We have a few walks out in
the country environment just as I used to do back in the big
city. Please can I return home soon to St. Louis? Now I'm getting anxious for the old Southern home. Try to get in contact
with someone and send someone to get me. [Michael] has
called and Julie may visit but that is all. Your son and loving
friend, Rachel.* She sent four letters in June alone. She wrote
with bravado, fear, and contrition. *Could she go back to Israel?*
she wondered. *Or could she live with Debby?* she asked. *And
where are the books you said she would send? How long will I
stay locked up in this mental ward. . . . They say I'm a "long-
term case." How does that sound?*

Rachel didn't wait to be rescued. She slipped through an
open gate at Western State and took off. I was told she was
on her way to San Francisco when she got herself arrested in
Oregon, and I believed this story for many years. When I
pored over her letters, though, I saw no mention at all of San
Francisco, the city that had drawn her west fifteen years earlier. Instead, she talked about our relatives in Portland. She

"dreamt of them" she wrote, and asked Mom to make contact with Dorothy. *June 11, 1980, . . . As I say, get ahold of Dorothy for me. . . . How are their four children? Do keep in contact, answer this letter, and we'll all try to do our best. When I was young I didn't know what I did, now I know more.* At first I thought she got the cousin count mixed up because Dorothy only had two children. But then I realized she was including Dorothy's two stepsons. Rachel rarely mixed up details about family. No, she wasn't headed for California, as my parents had said. She wanted to be in Portland near family.

However, Dorothy's family, Rachel soon learned, lived in Canada for the entire summer. Alone now in Portland, Rachel got herself arrested and admitted into the Oregon psychiatric system. *July 1. Dear Mort, Now since I have no family contacts, I want to tell you that I'm really in a hospital, brought here by the police after setting a fire. This place is called Dammasch, and being unhappy I want to return to Seattle (this is Portland) or else I would go start to Missouri soon. . . . I'm looking forward to a long life of happiness. . . . Yours, Rachel.* Two days later she wrote again, adding a curious detail about her arson escapade: she said she set that fire with "Indians." I'm not sure what her point was. But like the flurry of these letters, the fire she set sent up smoke signals, frantic SOS messages that she needed a place to live. In August she grasped her pencil tightly to underline the words that expressed her fury and frustration. *I'm locked up here and can't go to Work. In fact, I can't go anywhere as they have a big trap for runaways. And I am one since the day I've left [Michael's] house and never intend to go back.*

By October she sounded less desperate, even professed to

be enjoying her "network" at Dammasch. She noted that she had completed four of her six-month court-ordered stay and no longer wanted to live with "any of the siblings." She would rather go back to St. Louis State Hospital. Changing her mind from one letter to the next, she clearly couldn't decide what to do. I think she would have tried another plan with her family, but nobody proposed one. How desolate she sounded by year's end. *December 30, 1980. Dear Dad, I want to know how long I must stay here. Now I must take a shower every day. What the hell does that matter, for I am exceedingly unpopular, afraid of those near me, so I just enclose my misery. Yours, Rachel.*

How could I have thought the beauty of the West would make any difference when she was locked up inside for acting on impulses she couldn't control? How could it make up for the loneliness, neglect, and isolation she had to endure? Reading these letters, my chest ached—as though to put me through the grief my father must have felt as he watched his children's plan for Rachel go awry. I could almost feel the silent heart pain that he never acknowledged.

Reading these letters, I felt ashamed that I had never thought through the consequences of leaving Rachel on her own. All those months she was sending out smoke signals, I just wanted my parents to make the decisions, as they had for so many years. I had my priorities. My school-age children for one. My new job for another.

And then the accident.

Barry bought a moped to get to his office two miles from our house. A bright yellow Honda. Smaller than a motorcycle. Bigger than a bicycle. We won't need a second car, he said. I told him what I had heard about the dangers of city traffic.

He attached a flexible pole with a flag on the back fender. "I'll be OK," he insisted.

Two days before Thanksgiving I got the call at my office. A fireman on the line was trying to tell me Barry had been hit in front of the fire station on the Post Road. A broken leg, he said, trying to keep me calm. Somehow I knew it was more than that. Have someone drive you to the hospital, the fireman added after hearing my sounds of panic. Barry was in surgery when I got there. His spleen had burst and had to be removed. Then his lower leg had to be reconstructed. During the months of recovery Dad cheered Barry on with letters studded with corny jokes and whimsical sketches. How gratifying it was to me to see how much the two most important men in my life loved each other.

The following August, just when Barry graduated to a splint and a cane, my father had a fatal heart attack. If he had felt the silent one preceding it (as we learned later from the autopsy report), he never mentioned it to anyone. He was sixty-four, only a few months into his early retirement.

I helped Mom with funeral arrangements while Julie arranged for Rachel to fly to St. Louis. Rachel's behavior was stunningly appropriate. Her subdued presence in the packed funeral hall seemed like a miracle. And more magical still, Julie got Rachel on a flight back to Portland without any drama. I was grateful Julie managed all that. I knew I couldn't have done it.

Back home in Norwalk, a black hole opened up in my chest. It buzzed and yawned there until one afternoon, alone in the car, I rolled up the windows and drove through rush-hour traffic bawling at the top of my lungs. Weeks later the throbbing subsided, but my jaws locked up. They clicked and creaked when I opened and closed them. TMJ, said the dentist. During lunch breaks at work, I sat in a bathroom stall whispering conscious relaxation mantras. I needed to send warmth to all the tiny muscles in my cheeks and jaws, through my back and belly, my legs and toes. If I could get my insides warmed up with sessions morning, noon and night, I could make it through the day. I couldn't worry too much anymore about Rachel's life in Oregon.

WHAT JULIE KNEW

"Why didn't you say anything?" I asked Julie over the phone as she helped me reconstruct the events of this story—me in my Connecticut home, she in the easternmost reaches of the Atlantic coastline. Recently resettled, Julie found Halifax a hospitable city, so laid back compared to booming Boulder, where she had lived with her husband and twin children for the past fifteen years.

Julie had been our consolation prize for having to move to Indianapolis in 1953. She appeared that summer, a tiny bundle in Mom's arms, the day Rachel, Michael, and I came home from summer camp. Oh, the wonder of her as she grew the big brown eyes in her tiny porcelain face. I was transfixed. The curly hair that sprang from her scalp before she could walk. Wiry, like Mom, who held both tiny feet in her hands while infant Julie arched up tall and erect without support. We gasped, but Mom balanced her. She didn't fall. She became a petite bundle of energy, who never seemed to catch up in size with the kids her own age, let alone with her siblings.

When she was little, Julie took long afternoon naps, and once a week, while she was sleeping and the others were busy elsewhere, Mom gave me piano lessons and I learned to play "Muss I Denn" from the *Fireside Book of Folk Songs* with two hands. C major, no sharps or flats. Julie told me later that it was hearing me practicing that made her want to play piano. And she did. Julie poured out her heart on children's classics, legs dangling from the bench. By her teens, her piano accomplishments far surpassed mine.

Julie knew a lot more than I did about life with the Goodmans after Rachel became so ill. She had to put up with Rachel's bizarre behavior during her whole adolescence. I was away at school when Rachel was first hospitalized. I quickly got married and moved away. Michael did the same. Julie, on the other hand, was always there when Rachel came home on weekends. She was there when the neighbors complained about the sight of Rachel stretched out naked in the backyard. Julie was there when Dad dashed off to New Orleans or Kansas City or wherever to bring Rachel home from a police station.

While I ensconced myself in my family and suburban life, Julie decided to leave a job as a chemist at Bell Labs and live in New York City to study music. With catering gigs to support herself, she lived in a spacious, rent-controlled apartment opposite the medieval Cloisters Museum at the north end of the city. There, she saw firsthand Michael's post-divorce lifestyle and his relationship with Keith.

Now, surrounded by my files of family letters as I connected with Julie long distance, I learned she had known early on about Keith. "Sure, I met him. He was nice. Young." In New York, Michael and Keith had dropped in on her occasionally. "I knew Michael would need someone to help with Rachel," she says, "but I was wondering how the plan could possibly work out with Keith in the house." Anticipating my next question, Julie adds, "I didn't mention it when we were meeting with Peggy Papp, because nobody else was talking about it. I knew nobody would listen to me."

She was right. Even at twenty-five, living independently in New York, Julie was still considered the baby. I was seven years older, Michael five, and we had always been too quick to dismiss whatever she had to say when she tried to join our conversations.

"Michael was brave and valiant in volunteering to take Rachel, but I thought he would need someone there to help him. I thought it should be you or me," she answered. "That's why I suggested that Michael and Rachel live on the East Coast, so we could help. But Michael wanted to be near his daughter, and you weren't about to move to Seattle. And of course, neither was I."

Julie explained to me she kept waiting for Michael to mention Keith at our planning meetings, and when he didn't, she didn't feel comfortable being the one to bring him into the discussion. It pained her that her older siblings still thought of her as the baby of the family.

Julie reminded me that at some point in our discussions she asked, "What's Plan B?" and nobody answered. When the plan failed a few months later, we defaulted to helplessness: there was nothing more we could do for Rachel and, as Michael now said, she would have to work things out on her own. Call it tough love. Call it benign neglect. To Rachel it felt like abandonment. Sometimes it felt that way to me as well.

What bothered me most, as I looked back, wasn't my failure to ask the right questions, draw Julie out, or make suggestions that could conceivably have put a brake on the rapidly evolving situation; rather it's that I was so absorbed in my own life that I just didn't give my attention to what was happening. Even then I knew I was using the needs of my family to shield me from the needs of my fractured Goodman clan. And it wasn't just Rachel who suffered when I averted my attention. Julie did too. Two years after the Seattle rescue, she let me know how much I let her down when she needed support in other areas of her life. I felt she was being unfair when she told me that, but I understand now how distant I seemed to her.

You would think Julie and I would have comforted each other. Shared our fears about Rachel. Reassured each other that everyone, she and I, Mom and Dad, and Michael, too, were all doing our best. But we hardly talked about all that. We both wanted to move forward with our lives. She wanted to become a professional pianist. I wanted to keep my family safe and I wanted to explore new worlds through work.

Just after Rachel moved to Seattle with Michael, a Danish brewery offered a press junket. "Go," Barry insisted. "It'll be good for your career. Enjoy your time there." Everything at home went fine while I was away and while Rachel was settling into her new home with Michael and Keith. I got to see Hans Christian Andersen's home, where he conjured up his fairy tales, on an overland flight to a new brewery in Jutland. I added a weekend to the trip, all expenses paid, to see the harbor mermaid and explore Copenhagen's main square. I knew how lucky I was to have a husband who shared childcare and housework responsibilities fifty-fifty. Barry loved me. He loved my whole Goodman family.

Once Rachel left Seattle, my waking nightmare recurred: my sister standing with accusing eyes on the other side of our front door—stringy hair and slack belly under a stained shirt, pushing forward, persistent. "It didn't work out with Michael," she would say, gruff and impatient. "Can't you let me stay?" Sometimes I sobbed and turned to Barry to hold me. Sometimes the fear and grief persisted, and I felt drained the next day.

"Could we bring her to live here?" I finally asked Barry—because he was a social worker who helped families in crisis. Because he never flinched when I shared the shame of Rachel's illness that summer I met him at camp. Because Rachel stood up with us under the chuppah by the fireplace in my parents' living room, decorous and quiet in her knee-length dress of crisp blue silk, a clutch of white flowers in her hand. But now she was out West. Living wild. Cut loose by her family. Why couldn't I help her?

"She would need a very special place," Barry answered. "Stabilization in a hospital, and then we would have to see." He talked about halfway homes. Day programs. I knew Rachel would stand for none of that for very long. Michael had tried and failed. I didn't want to be next.

Julie bought an airline ticket to visit Rachel in Dammasch. She wanted to see for herself how Rachel was. But before she could go, Julie became ill with a mysterious infection that required weeks of hospitalization. Doctors thought something was wrong with a kidney, but none of the tests were definitive. Years later a doctor, checking a scan, told her she had scars from a burst appendix. "I guess the stress of what we went through made me susceptible too," she mused when we finally were able to compare our memories. "It built up in me and burst. Like it did for Dad."

So after a year of meetings, discussions, and complicated cross-country moves, the entire plan was upended. The entire project was dead. I wasn't surprised, but I was disappointed. I was angry at Rachel. *She just wants to live like a bum*, I wrote to my mother when I heard she took off. I directed my anger at our failed plan toward her. I knew that she could be impossible to live with. Manipulative and childish. I couldn't give up the idea that she could get better if she only tried.

Writing to our parents, Michael confessed that the depth of Rachel's problems surprised him. He admitted he had been naive to think he could help her. She was unreachable, he said. His experiences with her revealed to him the depth of her problems but also her extraordinary powers. She knew how to survive. Let her be a gypsy, a bum, an outlaw, he said. Let her be a seer or a poet. Only she could decide what was next.

I believed from what I heard from others, without doing direct investigation, that Rachel would get better care in Washington and Oregon than Missouri. And I didn't argue with Michael's advice that Mom and Dad leave Rachel to her own devices and enjoy their own lives. They seemed ready to do that now. They had tried their best for fifteen years. Wasn't it time for them to free themselves of the daily burden she had become? With Rachel out West, they had a chance for a well-deserved respite. Who wanted a life of frustration and hopelessness? Not my parents, not Michael, and not Julie or me. We all had our dreams, our pleasures, our commitments and responsibilities. So I agreed that Rachel might as well stay where she was. Michael, Julie, and I—we had no plan B.

We kept in touch with Rachel mainly through letters,

phone calls and packages in the years that followed. Rachel divided up the responsibilities. She asked Mom and Dad, then just Mom after Dad died, to send packages of clothing and cash. She asked me for books and sometimes a little cash too; from Julie, who was single for many years, she came to expect—and receive—annual visits. She knew what each of us could do.

Soon after Rachel left him, Michael was admitted to a PhD program on the East Coast, where he lived for several years. Subsequent teaching jobs kept him away from the West Coast for years at a time. Eventually he settled back in Seattle, just a few hundred miles from Oregon, where Rachel remained for the rest of her life. He didn't get involved with her again. I was puzzled by the way he distanced himself after going to such great lengths to help her. He went to such extraordinary lengths to free her from the straitjacket of psychiatric medications. From conversations we had later, I finally realized that the pain he experienced living with Rachel in Seattle ran so deep that he couldn't bear the emotional turmoil that would come with seeing her again. I understand why that would be, but it still saddens me that they never reconciled.

Rachel's move west sent shock waves that hollowed out lonely spaces in our Goodman family. They rang in my ears at first, but after that I could hardly even feel the reverberations. They just settled numbly in my soul and stayed there for decades to come. For years I knew very little of what she was going through. Sometimes I didn't even know where to write her.

Would Rachel's life have been better had she returned to St. Louis, where she had family? I know that question will never have an answer. I just wish that someone had been able to help us, Rachel's family, show her love in a way she could accept. I wish I had understood how terrible it must have been for her to know we wanted her to be the way she used to be. I wish someone had explained to her parents and siblings that it was the illness, not lack of will power, or character, that made her run off and behave so terribly. And I wish someone had been able to help Rachel make peace with the terrors that kept her on the run.

Rachel knew she could never again be the beautiful, vibrant person she had been. She turned to that place inside herself that nobody understood, and we turned to our own lives, away from her pain. We did what we thought was right by leaving her out West on her own. I told myself and anyone who asked about her that her quality of life would be better there. I didn't like to admit the decision was a triage call, a way to preserve my own way of life. Only later, when my children were grown and I was near retirement, did I allow myself to think about it as an act of abandonment. Only then did I feel the awfulness of the decision I joined. Of what I did.

A few years later, Michael received his degree. I didn't read the thesis he dedicated to our father. I didn't go to his commencement ceremony either. It seemed inconvenient to make a seventy-five-mile trip in the middle of the week. I didn't want to use up any of my ten vacation days. And I wasn't ready to stop being angry with him for a plan that didn't work, for cutting himself off from Rachel. I wasn't ready to stop being angry with myself either.

RESPITE FOR DAD

When I was a child and Dad was driving the car during a family trip, I would ask him a question, like what's the name of the next town, and he wouldn't answer. He just kept driving. After what seemed a long time, he would blurt out random information about some place called Belleville, startling me. I would burst out laughing because by then we were already miles from the town I'd asked about and I was now busy playing a license plate game with Michael, so whatever Dad answered had become a non sequitur. Why was it that he always seemed preoccupied and a little removed?

Then, when Michael and I were in high school and Dad tried to talk to us about something he deemed important, we didn't want to listen anymore. We tried to ignore him. "Stop *gumping*, Dad!" I don't know the origins of this verb; we made it up long before Tom Hanks's movie character was created. My brother and I guffawed through our bubble of teenage irony; gumping had something to do with the throat-clearing Dad always did when trying to get our attention. We didn't believe our father had anything serious to impart to us; we even made fun of his profession: why in the world would anyone want to be a Jewish Community Center social worker, we asked each other, while collapsing in giggles.

Growing up, I saw him get respect at work that he didn't

get at home. When I went with him to his office, people rushed up to him with greetings and questions, I saw how they admired him and how he cared about them and how he wasn't talking in non sequiturs because he was no longer preoccupied. His work was where he was needed and where he needed to be. And then I fell in love with Barry and married my own Jewish Center social worker. Barry became Dad's colleague for three years. "Your father has such a great reputation because his thinking is so creative, so far ahead of everyone else's," he told me. He did things like get grants to bring kids from the special education schools into regular camp programs and then published research results in academic journals. That was way back in the 1960s, before anybody talked about mainstreaming.

I wonder whether that's the kind of thing Dad was thinking about when we drove through Belleville when I was a little kid and he talked in those non sequiturs. Was he thinking, thinking, thinking about ways to help the marginalized, the outcasts, those who would otherwise be doomed?

The last time I saw my father, he surprised me with a question I never expected to hear from him: "How would you feel if it were your daughter we were talking about?" He wasn't talking about Rachel. We didn't talk about Rachel anymore. Not since she left Seattle. Rachel was somewhere in Oregon now, housed in a psychiatric hospital where I liked to imagine her on outings enjoying the rugged beauty of the West, collecting all the gifts of nature she loved.

The day of my father's probing question, he and my mother were visiting their East Coast daughters. He and I were walking past the book shops, boutiques, and bodegas on Broadway near Columbia University. Mom and Julie walked ahead of us. Dad seemed to be having trouble keeping up, and I had dropped back to talk with him. He was huffing and puffing, and I couldn't help being impatient. "You're still exercising, aren't you?" I asked. He assured me he was. He must be coming down with a cold, he said. Spring was around the corner; it was too soon for allergies.

No, we weren't talking about Rachel on that walk. We were talking about Julie. "How would you like it if it was your daughter who worked at a bar all hours of the night?"

"It's not just a bar, Dad; it's a jazz club. Dizzy Gillespie comes here to play. Working in restaurants is what musicians and artists do in the city." I never thought of Dad as a snob before, and now I was puzzled that he was so upset that his Barnard-educated daughter was working nights for tips. He wasn't happy about her decision to quit her job at Bell Labs in New Jersey and move back to the city. But she wanted to go back to college, to Hunter, to study piano performance. I tried to stand up for her: "She's twenty-eight, Dad. She loves the piano. She doesn't like doing chemistry anymore. She'll be fine studying music. It's what she wants to do."

Being from the Midwest, my father couldn't have understood how the restaurant industry supported New York City's gig economy. His third daughter was still single, so she needed a real career to support herself. Waiting tables was surely not what he envisioned for her. I couldn't tell him everything she had done to stay unattached and free to pursue her dreams. I couldn't talk about the boyfriend or the abortion. But I did tell him to stop worrying: "Julie can take care of herself."

That's when he let loose his plea to put myself in his

place. To imagine a daughter of mine running into the street to wrest tips from drunken diners. Or taking late-night subways home to an apartment in the remote northern reaches of the city. But I couldn't imagine having an adult daughter in a vulnerable situation. When I think about this conversation now, I wonder if maybe my father was redirecting concerns about Rachel that he couldn't admit to himself, let alone to me. We should have been talking about Rachel. Hers was the lifestyle to dread, not Julie's.

But at the time I just knew I couldn't feel what my father felt at all. I couldn't even imagine my daughters grown up, let alone living alone in the city. I felt only the magic sway of a golden cord looped loose and lovingly around my own family— two healthy young girls, Barry, and me. I could feel our space expanding as we knocked down walls, made new rooms, and bought shoes for growing feet. No matter the night wails, the red, roaring eardrums. No matter the ear infections, the insistent strep bugs, the toddler's skin split and stitched above the eye. No matter their father's burst spleen and crushed leg. All of that eventually healed. Wouldn't my daughters always be okay in our special circle that leached away doubt and pain? No, I couldn't imagine my father's worry. I couldn't put myself in his place.

Even so, his plea for empathy, one parent to another, pierced me. My glib assurances began to feel hollow. Walking down Broadway to Julie's restaurant, I couldn't really answer my father's challenge. Were we even talking about Julie? Because we never talked about Rachel. We chatted, pursuing less painful topics, with the gray wind bouncing off our backs, until we caught up with Mom and Julie. Inside the restaurant, we entered Julie's world. "Great to meet your family," said her bartender friend with the bright black curls. A waitress, gauzy purple blouse billowing over her bell bottoms, put down her tray and gave Julie a hug.

We sat by the window and Dad had a beer. Julie told us how much she enjoyed working with singers, the challenge of joining two musical minds, soloist and accompanist. She told us her plans for her spacious, pre-war apartment that looked out over Fort Tryon Park: new linoleum for the kitchen, new shelving for her hi-fi and albums.

As Julie talked, I could sense that my mother was impatient. She couldn't wait for Julie to finish. She turned to me with an urgent question of her own. "How about sending the kids to us for a week this summer?" She and my father, it seemed, had come up with a plan to fly in Michael's daughter from Seattle and my two from Connecticut. Grandparents and grandchildren would enjoy each other in St. Louis. No middle generation needed.

"I don't know if they're ready to take an airplane by themselves," I answered. "But I'll talk to Barry about it."

"They'll love it," my father added, joining in. "We'll take them to Forest Park and the zoo. And I want to take them to the new children's museum, Magic House, farther out in the County."

I could see how excited my parents were. But I didn't fully understand just why. I didn't understand then how much it would mean to have all your grandchildren in your home, cousins giggling and plotting together. I didn't know what it was like to hear their laughter rising like spray from the tides.

We let our children make the trip without us. Michael's daughter was allowed to fly by herself from Seattle. Air travel had little friction then, and we all knew it would be a happy adventure. Still, when I saw my girls, eight and eleven years old, walk down the TWA jetway at LaGuardia to meet their grandparents at St. Louis Lambert Airport, my heart stuttered and my stomach surged. When their two brave backs receded from view, Barry and I clutched hands. We told each other what we needed to hear: they'll be all right; the stewardesses will watch them. Two and a half hours later we got the call. They had landed safely. My parents were overjoyed.

MY FATHER'S BROKEN HEART

I lob a tennis ball across the net. It taps the court and bounces softly toward the two girls. They giggle, they laugh, they jump away and then toward it.

"This one's for you," I shout to one. "Dad will send you the next one," I shout to the other. I cheer them on. First Barry alternates his serves. Then he fakes them out, making them guess who will get the next one.

I'm no tennis player, but I'm glad to be outside on a court in this Catskills resort before school starts next month. It's our first vacation since the accident. "Throw it to me now, Daddy, to me," I hear. Barry leans toward the net. He can't run yet. He still wears a leg brace but he stands and walks. He's had plates bolted into crushed bone, and skin grafted from his thigh and then his rear to seal it all up. He's got more surgery to go, at the end of the year, but now he stays on his feet. The more he stands, the faster the bone grows back. The doctor says it's a miracle, but it looks like his legs will be the same length.

Our game sends a symphony into the surrounding pines: the boing boing of one yellow ball after the next, Barry's clear tenor announcing the plays, the girl's staccato shouts of anticipation and glee.

Suddenly a loudspeaker calls my name. I have a call inside the lodge. The back door leads into a long hallway to the office. The dark interior feels ominous after the sunny tennis court. Someone meets me and points to a telephone on the wall. A few footfalls pierce the silence.

The phone is one of many in a row against the wall separated by small plastic dividers that define personal space without giving privacy. I pick up the handset, my mind blank with anticipation. I couldn't imagine who was calling me here. For some reason, I hadn't told anyone in the family where we were going. Just a local friend.

My sister didn't prepare me. Nobody did. Nobody could. "Debby, it's me, Julie. Dad died."

Syllables tumble through my ears but make no sense. I can't process her words. "You're kidding," I say reflexively.

She repeats herself. "He had a heart attack. He's dead." I fall to the floor, screaming. A resort employee nudges me into an office where I can wail without disturbing the other vacationers. The four of us gather in our room. Barry makes a reservation and arranges for me to meet Julie in New York for a flight to St. Louis that day. We explain to the girls why our vacation is ending.

"We just got here," wails our little one. It is only the third day of our vacation week. She doesn't understand what is happening. Neither do I.

Barry says he will take the girls home and follow me out in time for the funeral. Zipping my suitcase shut, I feel a quaking in my gut. I run to the bathroom. Three days of vacation shit shoot down the toilet. I tremble with the force of it, and the feeling of utter emptiness. Now, I tell myself, I can fly.

I meet Julie at LaGuardia. "Rachel should come to the funeral," she says to me on the flight to St. Louis. I can feel her frame, slight as it is, buzzing with energy. I can't think, I can't move; my hands and feet don't even feel like they belong to me. How can I make arrangements?

"Yes, she should. But I'm not sure how to reach Rachel. Where is she now?"

"I'll take care of it," Julie says. "You know I'm not a child." Later she would tell me how hurt she was at my first words when she called, my expression of disbelief: "You're kidding," I had said. Why would she joke about such a thing, she would later ask me. Why didn't her older siblings ever take her seriously? But those recriminations came later, as they do in families that go through a tragic death, or illness. Now, she keeps me together on that flight to a funeral we can't fathom. How can our father be gone? I clutch her hand, as though I'm the younger sister.

Julie and I open the front door of my mother's house, the red brick house with the Mediterranean roof tiles on the Midwestern street lined with sycamore trees. As Mom runs to greet us, I hear voices in the dining room. Her friends have come to wait with her, to protect her from her grief. Mom insists we sit down to dinner. Why is she acting like a hostess at a dinner party, I wonder.

I watch my hand hold a fork. Move pieces of chicken to my mouth. My mouth chews. Mom keeps talking. Her words don't stop. I sit mesmerized by the way she keeps reciting her story.

"He just saw the cardiologist for his blood pressure. The doctor said he was fine." She whines. She blames. She doesn't cry.

Yesterday, he took his usual bike ride, she says. He came home and filled the bottom of the Italian espresso pot with water and put it on the stove. She heard a thud from her room upstairs. She ran downstairs. He was on the floor, flat on his back, motionless.

"The water from the coffee pot hadn't even steamed," she exclaims, wide-eyed. "I called the ambulance. I breathed in his mouth. They couldn't revive him."

And then she starts the story over. She is furious with the cardiologist. She had asked him questions, but he wouldn't talk to her about his patient, her own husband. She is so angry she wants to sue him. I don't understand then that her verbosity is the way she is dealing with her shock.

I don't try to stop her. I can't. I stay silent. She keeps passing food. She keeps talking. I watch the platter move around the table.

The funeral hall is packed. The rabbi talks. Everyone loved Mort Goodman, people say in words and with their silent presence. A leader in the Jewish community. An innovator. A mensch. Too young. Too young. For some reason the casket, contrary to Jewish custom, is open. I see how dead he is.

Rachel sits with the rest of the family in the front row. Her face hardly moves, but I can see the grief in her eyes. She is clean and neatly dressed in a white blouse and blue skirt. I don't know how Julie arranged her trip, but she did it.

Back in the house, I never see Rachel talking to Mom or Michael. What could they have said? I reach out for words that will make sense to Rachel, and to me. I must have found something to say, but I have no memory of what it was.

Rachel leaves the day after the funeral. I give her a hug. I tell her how glad I am that she came. I think about how glad I am she is still alive. Rachel murmurs back, her blue eyes blinking a message that was inscrutable to me then. Only now do I understand it: without my father, any hope Rachel had of returning to St. Louis is also gone. He was the one who advocated for her. He was the one who had once rescued her from her scrapes and escapes. Now she is really on her own.

I never got to ask my father how he felt about what happened to Rachel, but I found some clues in the hospital records, which included correspondence between him and a Dammasch social worker. I don't fully understand why Dad told the social worker it was best for Rachel that he stay in the background—best for Rachel or best for him?—but I'm grateful he forbade the use of electroshock and lobotomy.

I suspect he wanted to wait and see how Rachel did. That he felt his advocacy work with NAMI might help Rachel someday. His lawsuit against the state hospital had been settled by the federal appeals court: a consent decree now mandated specific improvements. Maybe these changes would benefit Rachel in the future. But for now, during all of 1980 and half of the next year, Dad needed respite from his fifteen years of tumult trying to get her care. He had begun exploring new opportunities, even applying for positions in the New York area in the hopes of living near me in Connecticut and Julie in New York. He printed up business cards and began counseling families with adult children experiencing serious mental illness.

The social worker's last note to my father said: *Rachel will be discharged from Dammasch Hospital July 31, 1981.* What a bombshell that news must have been. Rachel had been there a year and now another revolving door was swinging into motion, releasing Rachel into a dubious situation. I know how upset my mother got whenever this happened and can imagine how stressful this news was for my father. Three weeks later my father was dead.

I never saw Dad again after we had dinner in New York and he shared his fears with me about Julie. He didn't tell me about all the letters Rachel sent him asking to come home, and I didn't ask what he felt about her situation now. I didn't ask because I feared the conversation might involve me. What help could I provide? And who would be her guardian when he and Mom were gone? Julie? Me?

Dad continued to send funny notes illustrated with his drawings and doodles. Cartoon clips for my young Garfield fan. I have photos of him with his three granddaughters at the St. Louis Zoo. Horsing around in the backyard not even two months before he died. I look at those photos and am haunted by the question I couldn't answer when I was a young mother: how would you feel if it were your daughter? But the photos also console me. I remember how my two young daughters and their cousin spent that one last week with him. How they sweetened the end of his noble life.

Many years later I began wondering what it was like for Rachel going back to Portland the day after the funeral. I finally found some clues in the hospital records. Dammasch had just released her to a boarding house, as Dad had learned in that note from the social worker. As calm as Rachel appeared at the funeral, she must have been reeling when she got to Portland.

I got to fly home to loved ones who consoled me. Friends who came to my house for shiva calls and embraced me. Who hugged Rachel when she was grieving?

Is it any wonder that Rachel fell apart and misbehaved? Was kicked out of one boarding house and sent to another? Sought refuge at a Salvation Army shelter for two weeks before she finally exploded and pushed a police officer? That she walked into the side of a building because what could hurt any worse than losing the man who rescued her? As far as I can see from the hospital notes, nobody knew what set her off. Not the police, not the psychiatrists, not the judge who recommitted her. They didn't know she was grieving when they sent her back to Dammasch. They had no idea how much Rachel loved her father.

I Found My Freedom at a Price

I found my freedom at a price
I regret; only the present wind in the jungle
Calls me home.
Whispering trees in a phantasmagoria,
Years I have followed this service,
Only now, awake, do I know my own.
Nights I lay on beds to whispering hums,
Sounds oppressing as they called me home,
in the St. Louis cemetery.

—Rachel Goodman

PART V

Road to Freedom

REUNION IN PENDLETON

Brilliant orange rays blanketed the cloud-tipped peaks of the Cascade Range, engulfing the puddle hopper that was flying me from Portland to Pendleton. For the entire hour of that trip, I kept my face pressed against the window, to soak up the view of sunset across the mountains. I was so immersed in the sky that I almost forgot I was on my way to see my sister, a long-term patient at Eastern Oregon Psychiatric Center.

My visit began as a business trip to Redmond, outside of Seattle. I was manager of a conference program my company was hosting with Microsoft. The year was 1986, when CD-ROMs were the shiny new thing. Our discussions—imagine being able to access an entire encyclopedia or an interactive game on a single disc!—were welcome distractions from worrying about my long-delayed meeting with Rachel.

Rachel had been living in the northwest since 1980, and except for the quick trip she made to St. Louis for my father's funeral, I hadn't once seen her face to face. Not for seven years. I talked to her often on the phone and sent her packages, but I had never gotten myself on an airplane and flown out to see her. In those seven years I had mothered two girls through adolescence while launching a career promoting and writing about various industries.

I had liked learning how the business world worked; most

everyone I ever knew was in a professional, creative, or academic career. But despite my achievements, I sometimes felt disconnected from it. In my mind, earnings, market share, and other benchmarks executives worried about paled in comparison to what my family faced, dealing with Rachel. I was happy to stick with writing articles and brochures. What's more, I hadn't ever been able to manage Rachel's situation and never felt, outside of my own household and family, that I was a take-charge kind of person.

Before being transferred to Pendleton in eastern Oregon, Rachel had cycled back and forth between Dammasch in the Portland area and Oregon State Hospital in Salem, both near the western coast. These cycles included boarding houses and group homes, where she was always too disruptive to stay. She often went off on her own, camped out, and drank wine with homeless friends, until eventually she would get in trouble or ask to be readmitted when she needed a place to live.

I hadn't managed to visit Rachel in Portland or Salem—I never found a good time to go and I felt uneasy making plans not knowing where she would be. From what I heard now, however, Rachel was staying put. No running away, no discharges. Maybe she was too worn down to live like the footloose poet she always dreamed of being. As soon as I learned about the Redmond meeting, I knew it was finally time to see her. I booked a side trip to Pendleton.

I didn't expect Rachel to get much in the way of treatment or protection from hospital systems. I knew my sister well enough to know she was too proud and stubborn to submit to their programs. But I also knew she needed a place to go when the outside world became too difficult for her. And I knew that I wasn't able—or willing—to offer my own home as a refuge.

Visiting her meant I would have to look her in the eye and admit that no matter how much I loved her I was helpless to set
her free. Maybe that's the real reason it was so hard for me to
go. Finally, however, I had found the strength I needed. Maybe
this special assignment gave me confidence. If I could manage
to put together a conference program to introduce an obscure
new technology, I could manage to see my sister.

Now, during the plane ride from Portland, a new feeling
of excitement chased away my apprehension as I flew over
the snow-peaked mountains. In Pendleton, I checked into a
motel on a high plateau nestled within the dome of the sky. It
glowed over a dusty earth covered with tundra and wild
grasses as far as I could see. The sky seemed to hug me, infuse
me with its glow, and I felt reassured that I could now do
what I had put off for so many years.

Below, near town, loomed the hospital: Eastern Oregon
Psychiatric Center. Later that day as I waited for Rachel to
meet me in the front hall, I felt chills chasing away all that
warmth of the big sky. I must have been too frozen by dread
to put down many memory traces. I mainly remember my
longstanding fear: that rage and humiliation hidden behind
her unyielding eyes would rain down on me, condemning me
for brutal acts of abandonment. But that didn't happen. Her
affect was flat, from medication or the illness or both. I do
think Rachel was happy to see me. I know she was glad for
me to check her out of the hospital for day trips.

"We went to the rodeo," she told me as we drove downtown. With whom and when, I wanted to know. But she
mumbled sentences that were unintelligible, and I couldn't get
any more details from her. Pendleton, I knew, was famous for
its wool blankets, but I hadn't yet heard about its rodeo

roundup shows. Eventually I got the picture: groups of hospital patients were taken there on outings. One small bright spot in this dreary existence.

As I looked for a parking spot in town, Rachel pointed to an intersection with run-down stores and a bar. "The Indians come here," she said, her speech thick and slurred. It took me a while to accept her words as fact, not delusion. I finally realized Pendleton did indeed have a visible Native American population, many of them indigent. I felt foolish for doubting what she told me.

She led me briskly through the local streets. "I need to buy cigarettes," she said and directed me to a variety store. I bought her Camels. Unfiltered. She lit up and blew off a fleck of tobacco from her lip.

In downtown Pendleton, with its faded Old West storefronts and streets, the reality of Rachel lifted the film of fear that clouded my senses. Yes, she had strands of gray in her hair. Missing teeth. But she still stood straight, taller than me. Her shoulders, always so reminiscent of our Cleveland grandmother, presided over her imposing belly.

We walked into a small, dimly lit store filled with jewelry, wooden carvings, and small appliances. "Can I buy you something?" I asked her, hoping for any demand I could satisfy. "Do you need a portable radio?" I asked, remembering her frequent requests from her hospital days in St. Louis. She shook her head no.

The clerk busied herself in the back of the store while Rachel and I examined the jewelry stand. A strand of beads, with wood and colored glass and twisted threads, caught her attention. I watched her touch them, her fingertips so much more tapered than mine. These were the fingers I had watched as a child dancing across our piano keyboard, turning the pages of her books, holding her pen, or lifting a fork in the air as she argued her points at the dinner table.

I paid for the beads, expecting her to wear them now. But she put them away in her drawstring purse. I hoped she wouldn't trade the beads or give them away; I wanted her to keep them as a souvenir of my visit.

On the drive back to the hospital, Rachel lit up a cigarette. Before I could object, she exhaled out the window. "They don't let us smoke anymore," she told me glumly. She shoved the rest of the pack deep into a pocket. "I can't smoke and they won't let me eat sweets because of diabetes." I struggled for words to respond and then she blurted out, "I can't stand it anymore."

Nothing could be done about the cigarette ban. I remembered my mother's concern when she learned Rachel was being transferred to a non-smoking facility. She wrote to the authorities about how much Rachel needed to have her cigarettes, but of course no exceptions could be made. Like all the other patients, Rachel had to make do with the nicotine gum dispensed by nurses and occasional forays into town, sometimes authorized, sometimes not.

The next morning, instead of taking Rachel out first thing, I met with a psychiatrist who asked to speak with me. I suspect it was the same one who had asked Julie about childhood sexual abuse. In his gray windowless office, he told me that Rachel kept climbing into women's beds at night, molesting them. I had an uncomfortable feeling he expected me to do something about it. Talk to her, maybe, and tell her this behavior had to stop? That was ridiculous; she would shoo me away in a minute. Or was he asking me what to do about this frustrating situation? Equally bizarre. What could I possibly tell him about how to manage his patient, even if she was my sister? I left as quickly as I could, too distraught to remember anything else he said.

My third and last day in Pendleton, I took Rachel to a diner for lunch. She consumed a sandwich and Pepsi with vigor; I was glad to see her happy there. But when she stood up from the red vinyl bench to leave, I saw a big wet spot on the seat of her brown pants. Now I understood why the nurse at the hospital mentioned that Rachel refused to wear paper underwear. She'd become incontinent. While I cringed in embarrassment, Rachel acted oblivious. With her back and shoulders set square, her head held high, she marched out of the diner, wet bottom and all. She seemed to be far beyond caring what anyone thought about the way she looked or smelled.

Only in her writing did Rachel expose her desolation and pain:

I fly, I scream, I gnash, I cry out in pain and bewilderment. I want out!

I see the skies and dream like a rodent does in the slick of the night.

I eat lonely in the daytime, lonely at night, and I walk out with my nose up in the Aire, and cry and scream in pathetique.

Before her transfer to Pendleton, Rachel had sent me manuscripts on ruled yellow paper for safekeeping. Her handwriting was hard to make out, and the confessional stories I was able to decipher were disturbing. She was clearly off her meds and in hobo mode, camping in the woods, with occasional refuge in the Salvation Army shelter.

In a note accompanying her stories, Rachel had asked me

about my own writing. "Send me something of yours," she said. "I want to read it." But I had always written for commerce—trade publications and trade shows. How could I explain I never wrote from my heart the way she did? I didn't believe I could even if I wanted to. Rachel was the poet in the family. And for all the years she was alive, I needed to keep our spheres distinct and separate. While she took flight, all lyrical and fantastical, I stuck to business. She wouldn't have been interested in what I wrote, I told myself. I absorbed myself in it, but even I wasn't passionate about it. My work occupied only my head. Though I knew the idea made no sense, part of me feared that writing about the feelings in my heart might make me crazy. Crazy like Rachel.

I eventually learned how Rachel left Pendleton and got out of the hospital system for good. How she herself lobbied for her freedom and established personal agency after so many years in a system that made all the rules. A notice I found online explained how to obtain hospital records from Oregon's mental health department. After I sent in her death certificate and proof of our relationship, the records arrived in two large cartons filled with reams and reams of papers.

At first all I could do was shuffle through them while my eyes glazed over and my mind shut down. Typed admission and discharge reports. Handwritten nursing logs. Authorizations and physician's orders. Findings from medical exams. Assessments from social workers and therapists—occupational, musical, and recreational. And—the documents that most made me weep—inventories of Rachel's personal belongings upon admission: *Dresses—white long sleeve, red corduroy, green long sleeve, beige dress with tie; Personal items—1 auburn wig, 1 pr white gloves; Underwear—2 pr panty hose, 1 pr white undies, 1 beige bra.*

I was appalled by the violations of her dignity, the blanks or glaring mistakes in her history, and the prevailing sense of futility. I skimmed the contents, but it was hard to keep digging. I attached some sticky notes and put the documents back in their cartons and into the closet.

Months later, one sun-filled day in a summer house by the ocean, I set the two cartons of records on the dining room table and pulled out the reams divided by rubber bands. I wanted to know where Rachel was when, especially during those years I didn't see her. I was able to create a spreadsheet listing her hospital admissions, departures, and readmissions. This analytical task stanched the pain of agonizing updates about my sister's transgressions and intermittent progress. From this chart, I created the timeline I needed, and a solid second draft of this story. But I still sensed gaps in my understanding. How did Rachel survive all this? How did she end up in the college town of Eugene?

Two years later, as summer turned to autumn, I took the cartons from my closet and dove back into them. I pored over the records, again overcome by the tedium of hospital protocols. Then, at the bottom of the last stack, I glimpsed Rachel's familiar handwriting: a letter on ruled paper to her Pendleton doctors—Dr. Miller, her psychiatrist, and Dr. Condon, her psychologist. I could see from the very first line this was different from others I had read. Her purpose was clear. She was writing to gain admission to a newly established program back West at Dammasch: *Just a note to tell you I've heard about the move to Dammasch being planned and I'd like* to be part of this program. . . . I hear it's a work program . . . that's 4–5 hours a day. When I was younger I worked a lot, many years in various programs [that] worked out for the best and I think this program would too. She was aware that the psychiatric wards in Pendleton were slated to be closed in the near future, she noted, so now was a good time for her to make a change.

Like any petitioner, Rachel knew how to butter up the authorities: *However I go, it will be hard to say goodbye to you two people who've done so much for me these past months. But I have recovered and I do think this trip for the work program in Western Oregon is just the thing to edge into now.* But I also felt the deep sincerity of her closing words: *I do believe in the values of work, that it's best for the human soul.* They reminded me of the aerogrammes she sent from Israel about work she loved to do—outside in the fields and even in the kitchen, laundry, and children's unit. I wanted to reach back through the years and tell Rachel how proud I was of her: You took a chance. You took responsibility for your future. You made the system work for you.

Rachel's request was approved. She went back to Dammasch and three months later she left the hospital for good and moved into the "outside" world. Rachel kept in touch with Drs. Miller and Condon for years. She always asked to be remembered to people she knew at the Pendleton facility. She reminded the doctors to *keep them supplied with sufficient clothes and food and, when they're ready, a place in the community for them too. For they were good friends of mine and deserve the best.* She signed off with great optimism: *Well, I'm doing my best and improving and intend to continue. Life is fascinating and interesting, don't you think so?*

"YOU COULD HEAR A PIN DROP"

My next reunion with Rachel took place several years later on the other side of the state. From Dammasch Rachel was released to independent living under the auspices of Laurel Hill Center, a well-respected rehabilitation agency in Eugene that arranged housing and jobs for its clients. We met at the agency's building on the north side of the Willamette River, which skirts the University of Oregon on its south side.

Again, I struggle to get past the fog of sorrow that clouded my memory of our reunion. Did we embrace? Did I plant a kiss on her cheek, so scarred then with chronic skin infection? I do remember that after we greeted each other she led me from the lobby into a kitchen. That she took out a ceramic cup from the cupboard and a jar of instant coffee, poured hot water from the kettle into the cup, and added a spoonful of dry creamer. I remember the clank of the spoon, the sharp crystalline aroma from the can, the drops of brown and white liquid clinging to her spoon after she stirred it and placed it on the countertop. The movements of her hands were easier to watch than the fear and suspicion in her eyes. I don't remember if she offered me a cup, but I know I would have declined. I didn't drink instant coffee.

Later that day I sat with her in town, in a diner on Franklin Boulevard, with my hands encircling a cup of freshly brewed coffee. The waitress who came to our table didn't seem alarmed by Rachel's slurred speech or her stained clothing, not even by her sunken jaw, which terrified me with its naked toothlessness. Perhaps she'd seen Rachel before, maybe when Rachel's social worker, Steve Williamson, had taken her there. That's who we were waiting for—the man I had heard so many good things about from Julie.

Sitting nervously, I made small talk with Rachel until I saw her gaze turn toward the door. Steve had arrived. He was a burly man and, surprisingly for his age, walked with a cane. His beaming smile traveled faster than his body as he made a wry comment about his bad knees. I could see in his face he was excited to see me. "I met your sister, Julie," he said. "It's great that you made it out here too."

Rachel had a contented smile on her face, and nobody was staring at us. Eugene was a special place, I thought, as Steve bent his frame into a seat at the table. "Here's the booklet of Rachel's poems," he said. He pulled a copy out of his backpack and handed it to me. I had received a copy already in the mail, probably from Julie, but I thanked him profusely. He had worked with Rachel to compile recent poems, add clip art, and create stapled copies. The clip art didn't seem to me like illustrations Rachel would have selected, but that didn't matter. It was a remarkable project, I said to them.

Rachel didn't warm to compliments. I sensed she found them condescending, or maybe that was my own sense of smallness as her younger sister. As we sat in the diner, Rachel remained silent while Steve and I chatted. My fear of offending her compounded my awkwardness. She could get up and disappear in a minute. Steve was between client appointments, and I knew I wouldn't have a lot of time to speak with him. I wished I could ask him how Rachel was "doing." Was she staying put instead of disappearing into the woods? Was she staying out of trouble? Was she accepting the help she needed? I couldn't ask him while she was there, but that's all I could think of. Maybe that's why I couldn't focus on the poems in front of me. Looking back, I realize that talking about them would have been a good way to communicate with Rachel, to share at least some of my feelings about her. Maybe she would have answered in sentences instead of nods and mono-syllables. But I couldn't. To have read them with any care I would have had to absorb the despair and anger she expressed in them, and I was too consumed by guilt and anxiety to do that.

After Steve left us, Rachel took me on a walk across the University of Oregon campus. She pointed at a building and told me she sat in on classes there. I wasn't sure whether to believe that, but I could see how happy she was to be walking there. The campus was green, lush with vegetation. Nobody looked twice at her on the campus, or in the diner we had come from. I was struck by the way people in this laid-back college town seemed so accepting of Rachel—a woman with stringy hair, pocked face, ill-fitting clothes, a protruding belly, and a far-away look in her eyes. I was glad to be able to be with her in public without any sense that people were judging her.

Afterward she came back to my motel with me for a while, and we sat on a bench in the garden outside. She didn't need a ride back to her apartment, she said. She wanted to take the bus. "In a while," she told me. She rummaged in her handbag and took out a small tin. I watched her open it and carefully sprinkle loose tobacco into paper rectangles, lick the paper and seal a roll. She lit up, flicking loose strands of the tobacco from her fingers. A little while later she said goodbye. I stopped to see her in her apartment the next morning. It was clean, airy, and close to a bus stop. I felt deeply grateful that Rachel, through the help of people at Laurel Hill, had a place of her own to live.

Steve was no longer working at Laurel Hill when Rachel died ten years later. But when he heard about her death, he sent an e-mail to his former colleagues sharing his memories— and admiration—of her. His note made its way to me. After I read it, I knew I needed to contact him for more information, something I had never done while Rachel was alive. When Steve and I had met at the diner, I'd been concerned about intruding on their relationship. I'd also secretly (and incorrectly) believed that a social worker with such compassion would naturally expect a sister to be more directly involved with Rachel than I had been. Now I felt free to pepper him with questions about my sister.

Steve said that Rachel came to his attention in 1992 after Laurel Hill Center, a private, non-profit mental health agency, agreed to take a dozen or so people considered chronically mentally ill out of the back wards of Dammasch State Hospital and into their program. This was part of the work release program Rachel had applied for from Pendleton, on the other side of the state. For placement in its particular program, Laurel Hill requested trial visits and an assessment.

For its two hundred or so clients, Steve believed Laurel Hill was the best opportunity available for community-based mental health services—supervised housing and work programs—that could keep them out of the hospital. Clients knew it, he said, and Rachel did, too. By the time she applied for the program she was middle-aged, he pointed out, and ready to accept the agency's help.

"For the past ten years," Steve told me when I phoned him, "Rachel had been transferred from one state hospital to another as populations were reduced and rebalanced." At that time, before I obtained Rachel's voluminous records from the state, Steve knew more about her history in the system than I did. To me, her life in Oregon was an unending blur of revolving doors in and out of the hospital system. Which is why I'd often lost track of her for periods of time.

"I could see that Rachel didn't have a chance to keep a job outside. She wouldn't make it in the vocational program Laurel Hill was offering. But I liked her. I thought she deserved a chance." He wanted her out of Dammasch, and he figured out a way to get her released.

On a trial basis Rachel was assigned janitorial duties at the Laurel Hill office. Steve went to check her work there and found a poem lying on the reception desk. Rachel, he realized, had sat down and typed it up. Steve was stunned. "I wasn't a poet so I gave it to Linnea, a senior colleague, who was one. She was as impressed as I was."

Rachel, Steve said, reminded him of Opal Whiteley, a local literary legend. Her unusual life had inspired him to research and make public her story of early genius followed by tragic decline. Born in 1897, Opal grew up in Cottage Grove, a lumber town not far from Eugene, where she collected specimens from the natural world, documented her findings, and became a self-taught expert in botany, biology, and related sciences. Widely hailed as a child prodigy, she conducted courses for children in religious schools. From the age of twelve she traveled across the state giving lectures that combined science with religion and mystic philosophy. She was already a celebrity when she arrived at the University of Oregon in Eugene, her early admission secured because of the extraordinary breadth of her knowledge. Her behavior was also extraordinary. She danced across campus with a long braid trailing her tiny body. One account describes how she bent low over the ground, singing a hymn to an earthworm. Bright as she was, her mind was far away from the classroom and she had trouble keeping up with her studies. She left college and went to Los Angeles. There, she taught the children of Hollywood moguls who helped her publish her first book. From Los Angeles she went to Boston to secure a place in the literary world.

A story published in the *Atlantic Monthly* when Opal was in her early twenties made the young writer a sensation. Her second book hit number two on the bestseller list. But the diary she published next, which she claimed to have written at the age of six, defied credulity. It was filled with obscure literary allusions and a preposterous claim to be a French princess who was kidnapped, adopted, and abused. Her career abruptly ended. Estranged from her family, she traveled throughout Europe and stayed with friends. She was committed involuntarily to a psychiatric hospital in England, where she lived the last forty-four years of her life.

Here I sat at home, a decade after Rachel's death, pressing the phone to my ear. I was riveted by Steve's words. "I started writing about Opal as PR for mental health. She was somebody that people in Cottage Grove could relate to," Steve told me. He set up Opal Whiteley database at the University of Oregon. He created the Opal Whitely Memorial to help people understand the complex issues of mental health. Opal would likely be labeled autistic today, Steve said, but the diagnostic label didn't matter to him. He admired Opal's power as a poet. And he was determined to fan that ember in Rachel too.

As I listened to Steve talk about his literary project, I understood how it had galvanized him to try to achieve better outcomes for his clients, and to use Opal as a symbol of the talent that can be nurtured in many people whose abilities are discounted because they're considered mentally ill.

Steve enlisted the support of Tom Wheeler, the housing director, in hiding Rachel's real condition from the assistant director, who wasn't likely to approve their plan. "Maybe the reason I liked Rachel so much is that she said things I wished I could say to management. She just let it rip—bam bam bam." I knew what he meant. I could just imagine Rachel telling the administration that their rules were ridiculous. Rachel had a blunt staccato way of speaking that conveyed an unmistakable attitude: Don't tell me what to do. I'm smarter than you.

"We wrote up glowing work reports to get her discharged to our work program," he said, laughing conspiratorially as he confessed his ruse. His implicit justification: writing poetry *was* her work, not sitting in a sheltered workshop assembling eyeglasses or mopping floors.

Laurel Hill staff met several times to select candidates to admit to their program. By the final meeting, Rachel still wasn't on the list. But then Linnea read Rachel's poem, "Water." "You could hear a pin drop," Steve said. "Total silence. I knew she was in. It was a unanimous vote."

When Rachel moved into the first apartment Laurel Hill obtained for her, Steve visited her every day to help her with the transition. He made sure she had help with the skills she needed to survive in the real world. Shopping. Money. Medications. Help with her diabetes. These were the skills that would keep her away from prostitution, shoplifting, and camping out with winos. Steve was determined to anticipate her needs before a crisis could develop. His approach worked. After a few months he could see she would never have to go back to the locked wards of Dammasch. He continued to encourage her to work on her poetry, which he eventually put into the booklet he brought to the diner where he had met Rachel and me for lunch. Just as he had with Opal Whiteley, Steve listened to the voice that emerged from the poetry, and he found it eloquent.

Steve saw humor in behavior that would have made me, or any family member who tried caring for her, despair. "When Rachel wanted a pet," he told me, chuckling, "our housing worker got her a guinea pig. Boy, what I had to do for that guinea pig. Later she moved to another apartment, and the landlord ended up charging us fifteen hundred dollars because its droppings were everywhere. Laurel Hill had to cough up the money. That was hard to explain." As Steve said, Rachel "could be stubborn and cantankerous."

Still, Steve admired Rachel, just as he admired Opal Whiteley. None of Rachel's problems negated her gift for survival and fierce independence, nor her literary gifts. "I'm very proud of the work I did with Rachel," Steve said. "She had a reputation as a very 'difficult' client—which she was. But she was also very rewarding to work with. Your sister was the most tragic case of lost youth and promise I have ever known. She was struck by one of the worst cases of schizophrenia that I ever saw. I'm very glad that she was able to build a life here."

I was glad too. So much more than glad. I was relieved. I

was comforted. And I carried gratitude inside me from my head to my toes. Steve, who put his job on the line to free Rachel, was much more than Rachel's first case worker in Eugene. He was her fan and her savior. Nobody could give Rachel back her intact mind, but Steve helped restore her dignity. The fact of her freedom, that gift of compassion from Steve, consoled me. Without it, I doubt I could ever have forgiven myself for abandoning her.

Water

An ellipse adjoins the river
Water that shushes by;
Narrow thin stream of water
silt carried with the gentle
murmurs of life exhumed.
Flashes of lightning and bright rapids
of slow treacherous instincts.
White tails of fish rapidly charging
down stream, down currents with
foam on crests of waves and love
in my treacherous heart for these
mute gods of Neptune haunting
the great abyss of longing.
For as each sailor ties a knot
I go down deep till bright waters
roll over and over
the sinking hulk of my body
covered by each wave one by one.
Still the water's placid.
Each ripple of river-water
flowing along
very unaware of the piece of humanity
it has eaten, floss on the waves.

—Rachel Goodman

REGENERATION

I almost didn't recognize her. Only her eyes looked familiar. Underneath her cheekbones, her mouth was askew. Puckered cheeks collapsed into her jaw, like my Bubbe Anna when she was in her nineties. When I last saw her, three years earlier, Rachel had missing teeth. Now she had none.

It was the summer of 1995, three years after my first visit to Eugene. Steve was no longer working at Laurel Hill, and Nick was now her social worker. Before I went to meet her in the lunchroom, Barry and I met in his office. "Rachel's deteriorated," he told us glumly. "She's been refusing medication for the past week. She's suspicious of everyone." Worse, the previous night she had been kicked out of her apartment. She banged on neighbors' doors, forced her way into one of them and got into a fight, Nick told us. "We put her up in a motel temporarily. We need to find another apartment for her." I turned my back to Nick to grab some Kleenex and wipe the tears smeared across my cheeks. Nick stopped his litany of Rachel's transgressions. "Are you okay?" he asked.

"I'm just so sad," I murmured. He nodded sympathetically. His pause was merciful but temporary. He resumed his update. Even if Rachel did well during the day, everything came apart at night, he explained, when she walked and she wandered. She had Thorazine to help her sleep, but either she wasn't taking it or it wasn't working. She also needed four daily doses of insulin and wasn't always around to receive them. "I'm worried I'll walk into her room and find her in a coma," he said.

"Did anything like that ever happen?" I asked.

"No, but it could."

My throat was throbbing. Barry squeezed my hand. He knew I had more questions, and since I couldn't speak, he asked them for me: How often did Jason see her? Did she participate in any group programs? From Nick's answers I knew Rachel had basic care, and that she wasn't very sociable.

Finally, Nick pointed me toward the lunchroom. After taking in her altered appearance, I called her name from the doorway. She turned around and I made my way toward her. When I reached out to hug her, she waved me away; maybe she was self-conscious about the fresh scratches on her face, from last night's fight. We said our hellos from opposite sides of a lunch table. "Are you going to be here tomorrow?" she asked.

My heart stopped racing when her voice, with its familiar cadences, began to reach me.

Jason, her aide, had brought her here from her motel. I could see he prepared her for my visit: her clothes and back-pack were clean. But the strain on Rachel was palpable, our conversation slow and halting. She asked me to give her fifteen dollars for food and cigarettes. I told her maybe later—I didn't want her rushing off for cigarettes. Rachel asked me again. I changed the subject and asked her to join Barry and me for lunch.

We went to the Japanese restaurant right next door so we could easily get her back in time for her insulin check. Sitting next to her, I couldn't understand much of what she said. She mumbled. Her tongue slid loosely over her gums. But she pointed at the menu so I would know which noodle dish to order for her. She managed to make important desires understood.

Rachel returned with me to my motel again. From the cozy back garden, I showed her a freshly cleared trail. But she was too tired to walk, and we returned to my room. I offered her coffee from the drip machine, but she preferred the instant kind she carried in her backpack. Even with the caffeine, she could hardly keep her eyes open. I suggested she lie down on my bed, but she shook her head and went outside to smoke. Once inside, she leaned back in the upholstered chair against the wall. Her chin sank to her chest and her eyelids faltered. When I repeated my offer for her to use my bed, she yelled, "NO, DEBBY, I DON'T WANT TO LIE DOWN." She wasn't mumbling anymore. Every word rang out like a shot, reminding me I was just a younger sister with no right to condescend. I struggled to find the right way to express my concern.

I tried talking about those issues Nick had brought up with me. Did she get drugs from the street? She shook her head and looked at me angrily. Did she wear Depends? "Why are you asking?" she demanded. I dissembled, saying I also have bladder problems (true) and might need them someday (God, I hoped not).

Maybe this was too condescending. These were Nick's issues, not mine. I just wanted to build on our past together and share a bit of our lives in the present. But how could we? My sister had no place to live now. She needed help and I didn't know how to give it. My throat filled with shame and helplessness. I pushed back the sobs until after I dropped her back off at the agency.

The next day Rachel seemed to appreciate my concern about her eyesight. Like me, she had worn eyeglasses since childhood—without them she couldn't read a word. She had shed her eyeglasses just as she had shed her dentures, but this bothered me even more. Rachel always loved books, and during all those years she spent in hospitals, she assigned me the job of selecting and shipping them to her. I hated the idea that she was giving up reading, a pleasure we shared for so many years.

Now I offered her a pair of my old glasses to try out. She squealed, "These are neat!" I gave her some material to read. Not a book but letters she had written long ago. I brought them to use them as a springboard for conversation.

Her delight soon faded—it must have been difficult to use my bifocals—and she took them off. But she continued to squint at the words in front of her. As she leafed through the letters, she kept glancing at me to see what I was doing (a crossword puzzle). She pointed to a portion of her letter saying she was dropping out of school in San Francisco and said, "Someone else wrote that." She couldn't explain who she meant by "someone else," which frustrated me. Maybe she was disavowing her youthful decision. (Rachel had always longed for another chance at college.) Or was it her illness, the "cognitive impairment" characteristic of schizophrenia, that severed her connection with her youthful self?

After another night in Eugene, Barry and I packed up to begin our vacation. Before we left, I met Rachel at Laurel Hill to say goodbye. I wanted to leave her the money she said she needed, but Nick asked me not to. He said she would spend it on beer and speed and get in trouble. I bowed to his judgment and left her just a dollar in change, three packs of Marlboros, and a bag of food she had picked out at the 7-Eleven. I also left her the long-ago letters she had written to me. I hoped they would prolong our connection.

We drove north, found a camping site, and spent the next day at Mount St. Helens driving through miles of blown out forests. The visitor center ran a continuous loop of video clips showing the 1980 eruption. Collapsed mountains. Forest remains covered by ash and debris. Lakes dammed up with trees that rolled down the mountains like pickup sticks. The rescue pilots couldn't recognize the landscape. And even though these first responders knew the area intimately from years of camping and exploring, the entire mountain was so transformed they struggled to get their bearings. The narrator's voice was incredulous: how could something so lush, so productive be utterly transformed in a moment? The ranger marveled at the way nature rebuilt the mountain landscape; how life emerged in dead trees, recovered from devastation. How scientists tracked the return of native fish and birds and even discovered new species, never before seen here. I couldn't share his amazement at nature's destruction. I wished Rachel could experience its powers of recovery.

After touring Mount St. Helens, Barry and I camped at the base of Mount Rainier. We hiked among thousand-year-old trees on our way to see the twenty-six glaciers eroding the mountain. We puzzled out the twists and turns of ancient branches thickened into braided trunks. I was fascinated: "Why did it turn this way?" "Look how those two trees grew together. They've intertwined, like us!" Barry even got me to hug a tree. Its gnarly bark pressed into my hands and my cheek, and I pondered the survival of these towering trees through storm and fire and pestilence. Somehow, they did their magic. I breathed the air of the forests and the mountains. This was no place for sobbing.

I got an update from Nick a month later when I talked to him by phone during my lunch break. Unwrapping a sandwich at my desk, I listened while he told me his current concerns. Rachel was still unable to keep an apartment, and the agency might get her a trailer—so she couldn't be evicted for wandering halls and bothering neighbors. The plan sounded drastic. I didn't know what to say.

That winter Rachel wrote me from her new address. It wasn't a trailer after all:

February 17, 1995: Dear Debby, I'm all right now, Debs. Have an apartment by myself and wash and clean and all. . . . I saw a doctor today. Had a friendly talk with him. Then I visited at the community center in the smoking room, waiting there to come home. Last two days was a blizzard in the city. It was beautiful. . . . One day, when the buses didn't run, I walked home all the way, a few miles. Had no trouble. Am watching the TV now as I often do when there is nothing else. Write me soon. Love, Ray.

It would be another three years before I returned to Eugene to see her. By then she had yet another address. Not a trailer, not an apartment. Miraculously, it seemed, Rachel lived in a house of her own in the woods. She was happy there and wrote me frequently.

A HOME OF ONE'S OWN

"Are you sure we're going the right way?" my mother asked. She craned her neck to peer out the car window.

I nodded and showed her the note paper with directions I had taken down from Rachel's case manager at Laurel Hill. From our motel in Eugene, we had driven a mile down the main road, Franklin Avenue, away from the university section of town and toward the border with Springfield, Eugene's sister city. Lining the road were auto parts and repair shops, warehouses and bleached-out signs. When I reached the used auto dealer, I looked for Brooklyn Street. There was no street sign in sight, but I turned at the car dealership, as instructed. After a few feet the street turned into a dirt road covered by a wooded canopy.

Despite its familiar name, Brooklyn Street felt like another country. Rachel's home was in an unincorporated, unzoned community in a no-man zone between Eugene and Springfield. It was known to the locals as Glenwood, and had become a refuge for trailers, meth users, the homeless, and people on the margins. Laurel Hill was able to rent out a number of these residences for clients who wouldn't have been accepted as tenants elsewhere. Rachel had never been able to tolerate housemates or house rules and, to my mind, this little bunga- low in the woods seemed perfect for her.

The road ended amid a circle of little homes, about six hundred square feet each. I saw the number I was looking for on a mailbox: 269. "Here we are, Mom. This must be Rachel's place." I was nervous and excited at the same time. I hoped my mother was too. But she felt something else entirely. From her seat in our rented car, she let out a wail that emanated from her belly and filled her throat. "This isn't a house, it's a shack!" I should have squeezed her hand to reassure her. But her cry overwhelmed me, like a lightning storm moving toward me. Oh God! Why does she have to carry on like this? What was she expecting to see? I tightened my grip on the steering wheel and looked straight out the window. To me the view—a quiet grove of cottages—was charming. I didn't understand why Mom was so disappointed.

"It's not so bad, Mom," I managed to say, edging the car on a bare spot by the grass. I groped for the handbrake and clicked it into the lock position. "Oh, come on, Mom. It's nice here. Let's go see her." She quieted down and unsnapped her seatbelt.

Cats greeted us at the front door, then Rachel. She returned our embraces cautiously. I knew she needed time to trust us not to judge or criticize or take her away. Her cheeks had filled out somehow, with or without dentures. The scabs were gone, but scars of her long battle with a staph infection remained on her face.

As we stepped inside, I felt my mother stiffen. The kitchen was littered with remains of cat food tins, unwashed dishes, pamphlets, opened bottles of milk, and cracker crumbs. It was a shocking sight. For the most part, though, the smells of stale coffee, milk, and cat food had escaped through the half-open kitchen window and screened front door. Those that were left mingled with the damp and mold native to these Western woods.

Tension seemed to crackle back and forth between Mom and Rachel—the static of expectations, resentments, and disappointments. My gut, my shoulders, my jaw ached. Every darting glance, every grimace, and every awkward silence brought back to me my childhood feelings of impotence in the face of conflict. I saw my mother's anger and bewilderment when she looked at Rachel, who commanded her surroundings with a sense of regal decrepitude. Why couldn't Mom just be glad that Rachel had a place of her own? I felt as though I was crouched on the cone of a volcano just before it vented. It made me furious. I wanted to grab my mother and take her home on the next plane out of town. But duty and determination held me back.

Visits with Rachel had been hard for my mother ever since Rachel got ill and allowed only Dad to see her in the hospital. Now I was glad she was pushing herself past her comfort zone—phone calls, sending checks and packages. Two years earlier she had flown from St. Louis to Portland and her sister, Dorothy, had driven her the hundred miles to Eugene. But my mother was disappointed when her sister decided to get home before dark, cutting the visit short, and didn't want to ask her again.

So I was the logical one to accompany Mom now that Julie was pregnant with twins. It was three years since my last trip to Eugene, with Barry, and time for me to visit again. But I had known it wouldn't be easy with Mom. My stomach always clenched when I watched her and Rachel together. I knew I would have to rely on my sense of duty to get through the trip.

We managed a short visit, and then I took my mother

back to the motel. "How can they let her live here like this," she kept wailing as I drove. I felt Mom's despair spill into me. I was a mother, too. What if Rachel were my child? How could I possibly have endured what Mom was going through? Here I was watching our mother watch Rachel—and all the grief, Rachel's and Mom's and mine, got tangled up together. I needed to extricate myself, to stop feeling our mother's sorrow as though it were my own.

Overnight, something changed. The next day the three of us went to a park and a sense of calm descended. Mom was quiet. I watched the two of them walking ahead of me, holding hands: Rachel with her broad shoulders and sure-footed walk, her hair now grayer than our mother's. Every gesture, every word between them seemed to reach for acceptance and affection. Mom, as sturdy a walker as her daughter, had to look up a good six inches to catch Rachel's eyes. When she talked, Rachel nodded. Then Rachel patted a spot on a bench where she wanted Mom to sit down with her, and the two of them continued their conversation.

As I hung back so they could have time alone, I glimpsed something crawling out of the stream that ran along the park. Something that radiated strangeness. I turned to face a long, plump creature with a rat's tail, high beady eyes, and sweeping whiskers. And then another such creature behind it. I stepped back but kept staring, frightened but mesmerized. They were nutrias, I learned later, South American rodents brought to the Northwest for their fur and now an invasive species. Their faces and movements made me shiver. But neither Rachel nor my mother was fazed. Rachel just laughed and shrugged when I pointed to them. Mom was unconcerned. Only I seemed unnerved by these strange creatures.

That walk in the park turned out to be the first time since Rachel became ill that I saw my mother and my older sister at peace with each other. I prayed it would last and no stray remark from Mom would cause Rachel to bolt. None did.

Afterward Mom seemed satisfied with the visit. She didn't talk a lot and she didn't complain. She seemed to have accepted what she couldn't change. Her concerns about Rachel's housing faded away and the tension in my jaw and shoulders subsided.

"I'm tired," my mother said the next morning as I got dressed. I knew she must be emotionally exhausted.

"Why don't you stay here and relax. I'll visit Rachel now and come back for you later," I said. I left her in the garden along the river behind the motel.

When I saw Rachel, I explained Mom would visit later. Rachel then asked me to come with her to meet her friends next door. She pointed to a bungalow of similar but not identical design as hers, about thirty yards away. A thin, wan-looking man in jeans and a faded green T-shirt greeted us at the door and then his wife appeared. Sturdier, in darker clothes, she invited us into the living room. Rachel and I sat down on the bed that served as a couch. Our hosts took the Salvation Army chairs. No cats jumped up. No garbage was in sight. The room was threadbare but clean. If only, I thought, Rachel could keep her house like this.

At first I felt as though I were performing on a stage, just going through the motions of a social call. In a few minutes, though, my presence seemed real, and I felt drawn to this couple. They were open about their psychiatric histories and told me about the difficulties they faced making ends meet. I judged the lines in their faces to reflect those hardships, not years; they must have been fifteen years younger than my sister, then in her mid-fifties. Rachel watched us in conversation, her impassive face giving no clues to her emotions. I don't know how long we visited—maybe half an hour, maybe fifteen minutes. Time seemed suspended in this quiet grove of bungalows.

Responding to some internal signal, Rachel stood up and said it was time to go. "I need to get some cigarettes," she told me outside. The food mart, she indicated, was across the main road, opposite the car dealer at the corner of Brooklyn Street. She asked me for money, and I gave her a twenty. We walked the quiet path that smelled of earth and air; I followed her gaze as she lifted her chin to the sky. "I like the birds," she confided softly, shyly. That's when I heard cawing and wings beating their way toward the crown of the tree ahead of us. "They're my friends," she said. She seemed to be talking about the birds as well as the couple next door.

Suddenly she veered off the path toward the car dealer's showroom. She opened the glass door and made a beeline for the coffee urn against the far wall, took a cup and filled it. A salesman approached her on our way out. "You shouldn't be here. You know you're supposed to get your coffee somewhere else." I sucked in my breath and waited for a browbeating that would shame me as well as my sister, but no, the man seemed more exasperated than angry, like the worn-down parent of an adolescent.

And just like a teenager, Rachel ignored him and marched outside into the brisk spring air with the steaming cup in her hand. Her composure took my breath away. She seemed so damned competent in executing her flight plan.

Rachel bought cigarettes, cat food, cheese, diet soda, and sliced bread. "You know I can't have sweets. They say I have diabetes." I nodded and complimented her on her will power. I knew a restrictive diet couldn't have been easy for her. When Rachel had been in hospitals, she had no control of her food. She complained bitterly about the restrictions, and the shots too. But she never admitted to symptoms. Looking back, I wonder whether her mood swings were tied into the diabetes. At the time, though, it wasn't her diet I worried about; it was the chain smoking. She was constantly coughing and clearing her throat. But I couldn't urge her to quit or withhold money for smokes. It would have been futile. Cruel.

Thanks to Laurel Hill, Rachel lived the rest of her life, four more years, in this house in the woods. Mom didn't visit again, but she seemed to accept Rachel's situation: that Rachel had people to bring her medications and make sure she had food. She was safe and protected, just as our mother had always wanted. I had my own reason to be happy for Rachel. She had a home, her very own, where she was free to come and go as she pleased. Exactly what I had most wanted for her. And when people asked how Rachel was doing, I had an answer I wasn't ashamed to give.

A LOVE THAT
BLOSSOMED LATE

During that tumultuous visit with my mother and Rachel together, I tended to underestimate the strength of their relationship. A clearer picture of it would emerge years later—
from the letters I extracted from my mother's St. Louis
basement. After an initial rough sort, I shoved a stack of them
in a folder that I marked, "Rachel to Mom, 1990s." Most of
them, I saw after skimming quickly, began and ended with
appeals for money. That was reason enough, I believed then,
to dismiss the rest of the content as filler.

The folder lay in my office closet for years. For a long
time, I had just moved the folder around like unwanted food
on a dinner plate. But whenever I picked it up, a small, beige
postcard with an unnerving picture dropped out, as though
demanding I take some action. Finally I examined the pen and
ink rendition of a bear rearing up on its hind legs. With the
drawing's top-down perspective, the mountain creature was
taller than the birch trees in the background. It bared its teeth
and raised its claws. The printed caption provided the relevant
warning: "Grizzly—one of the most feared animals the
mountain men and pioneers encountered. . . . Known for his
strength and power, he is also very unpredictable." Barely
two inches of space remained for Rachel's personal note:
Mom, Hi. I'm fine. Can you send me the money right away. I

didn't want Debby's. Expecting yours. Love, Rachel. I chuckled at my sister's choice of postcard for this request. Was the bear a half-joking threat? It was certainly meant to get Mom's attention—along with a speedy check from her.

Suddenly, I was eager to absorb the trove of letters that started with Rachel's move to Eugene, where she had come to work and live independently. As I began reading, I sensed more and more that Rachel wanted reassurance that she could make it on "the outside." And my mother, who had always wanted her safe in hospitals, gave her that support. Through all Rachel's ups and downs, she never tried to get her committed again.

After several starts and stops, I read the letters slowly. Slowly enough to read what lay unsaid between the lines. I let go of my long-held suspicion that Mom didn't love Rachel enough. I saw how Rachel began a new kind of relationship with Mom after Dad's death. I saw how she approached and retreated. How she confided and questioned. How she shared her fears and her dreams about living on her own. Yes, the feelings between them were complicated. But they were loving. I saw the bond between them was as deep and as mysterious as any human connection can be.

January 1992. A jubilant postcard home announced her newfound independence from the hospital system: *Am now living in Eugene and have a home and a job. Connected with Laurel Hill Work Center. Scenery here is great! Could you get in contact with me soon?* The postcard showed Mount St. Helens, the volcano located halfway between Seattle and Eugene—its undamaged majesty on the left and its cataclysmic eruption of 1980 on the right.

July 1992. *Dear Mom, I'm having a lot of trouble lately—*

especially with the doctors. I've got diabetes and so must take finger-prick (drawing blood) two times a day, a shot of insulin daily, a special diet free of sugar, and now trips to the doctor. . . . She wants to examine my feet. They just have been saying diabetes leads sometimes to blindness and leg amputation. The idea of it scares me, Mom, and I want to know how I can protect myself so I'll never get an operation again. And too, how to get away from all this treatment. Such vulnerability. I don't think I had ever seen Rachel drop her bravado to expose her fears—like a child showing wounds to her mother. She then describes her work on the Laurel Hill cleaning crew, confiding like an uneasy adolescent, *Does Doug really like me I wonder?* She reflected on her past and future: *For a long time I was lonely. Now I'm a little unhappy but still manage to plod along and think I can stay here in Eugene a long time.* She is disappointed in demand for her paintings: *No one around here thinks my art is very good! Hah. Maybe another time.* Her sign-off is especially affectionate: *Mom, take care and remember I love you.*

August 26, 1992. Rachel reported a recent reunion: *Julie and I had a nice visit. We hiked up a high mountain, drove around the countryside, and visited at home. She will be back later this year.* She writes about excursions and picnics with her work group, how much she enjoyed a Scandinavian festival in a town nearby. *Will you send me Debby's address? . . . I'm not sure of it.* Rachel and I did correspond, more frequently once she came to Eugene. During one visit I told her I sometimes struggled with depression, and she followed up with a letter giving me advice on medications. Every once in a while, she asked if she could live with me. How I dreaded those requests, which I avoided answering.

March 30, 1993. In this letter, using the typewriter Steve Williamson found her, Rachel intermittently forgoes capital letters. She addresses Mom by name and writes as though to a dear friend: *dear sophie, just a letter to tell you how i am and a little of my life. Well, I still work five days a week, and though it's hard i'm keeping on with it. usually have some fun with it, we were just transferred to a new crew, and it's taking me a while to get used to their intensity. . . . I do some art, mainly ceramics. it's lots of fun. i'm so glad you liked the little booklet I sent you that steve helped me put out. it's the ones we liked best. steve is very good to me, comes over a lot and helps me. so do some other people, and another man who I date sometimes. he just divorced his wife and is very lonely.* She is listening to classical music on the radio, she says, and in the evening will watch *Star Trek* on television. She seems happy: *when i'm outside i get a feeling about the immensity of oregon. it's a feeling i've had for some time. i love to roam around the country, collecting, camping, etc, I do love the west. i hate being cooped up at home, so get out as much as i'm able. we're in a valley surrounded by mountains here, and it's lovely and tempting.* She says she'll call when Julie arrives. *julie's visits have been going on for some time. . . . we go hiking too you know. write me back, mom, thanks.*

March 19, 1994. *Thanks for your many phone calls. Do send me the money when you can.* Rachel is enjoying the approach of spring and watching people of every age on her way to the store. She writes about Gerry. *He's really a clever little guinea pig and is surely handsome with his coat of white and black fur. He eats a lot of lettuce too for an animal his size.* She says she is sitting in on classes at the university. *My poetry will come to you in a few weeks. . . . Take care and don't forget to write back. And call.* She is proud of her writing. And is glad she can share it with her mother.

May 29, 1994. Rachel reveled in her freedom to come and go at will. *One morning I came upon my bicycle standing against a wall and took the idea to ride it outside. It's been sitting there a year and an age. . . . One street took me down to the Church, another up through a small business district to the street lined with wooden plank houses on a few blocks. . . . I remembered the turn signals and used them. I sped up and slowed down. . . . I still today have ideas of taking trips out to the edge of the city and to the country spots, where I could relive life as I've always wanted it to be.* And then, a response to an invitation I never before knew Mom had made: *As far as visiting you in St. Louis in the fall, I must decline. I think it's too much distraction now and I don't want to take all that time out.* Rachel did seem to genuinely appreciate the offer but deferred further discussion to their next phone call.

March 14, 1995. Rachel has been moved to the outskirts of the city. No more walks to the coffee shop; she has to take the bus everywhere. Maybe it's the disruption of the move that prevented her from writing for so many months. But it seems she and Mom have been talking by phone about a possible visit. *Dear Mom, You still could visit me, but you know, things aren't stacking up well here. I barely have enough food for myself here, so that is out. Then, the other day, I found the bed wasn't working right (it's a stowaway) so I don't know how we could manage the sleeping over. I mean it's broken and would be very hard to bear. Then, there's no transportation around here that can be used at all. I barely manage a bus back and forth from work. Taxis and other buses don't come this way. I don't know how you could afford a hotel. They're very* expensive. . . . *Your friend, Rachel.* How transparent and flimsy her excuses are. Couldn't she see that? Then I remembered something I learned in a NAMI workshop I had taken not long before and went back to check the manual: *Those who remain severely ill instinctively sense how badly damaged their human faculties are, and they greatly fear encounters that might expose the devastated self to the world.* Maybe this fear is why she resists a visit. I had never imagined what it felt like for Rachel to know she was a burden. An embarrassment. A monumental disappointment. She couldn't face her mother yet, but she still held fast to their relationship.

March 29, 1995. Rachel has advice for Mom, who seems to have confided something of her own concerns as she faced retirement: *Let's hope you'll get to NY to settle down, as long as you believe it's practical, and find a new life for yourself to edge into. The girls are there too. I can get along in Oregon, but I think you need something new. . . . You'll get a new kick out of life.* In a veiled reference to her romantic life, she confides to Mom details of her current friendships: *Don't be scared if I have a few friends or need a friend to visit or talk with. Usually they're girls now: I haven't had a male friend for ever so long. No, I'm not a whore; haven't been so for many long years. Dropped all that you see.* She continued nostalgically about friends from her past—Janet in Boston and Anita in Indianapolis—before signing off: *Mom, take care and do well with yourself. I'm hoping we and our family unit will work out. Julie and Debby are amazingly well. . . . Yours, Rachel.* I remember the journal Rachel had sent me for safekeeping and the pledge she wrote in it to stop "whoring around." I realize she has resisted the temptation to make easy money on the streets. Regular checks from Mom have helped her to keep her vow. No wonder she sent that post-card with a hulking, hungry bear as an emphatic reminder.

October 23, 1995. Rachel has been moved to Veneta, a small town north of Eugene and almost an hour away by bus. She must have lost her typewriter in the transition; this and all her subsequent letters are written by hand. Now she writes home describing her trips to Eugene and the long ride back. She stops short of complaints, but I realize this remote town must be difficult for her. I find that among the letters to Drs. Condon and Miller, there is one from Veneta. It is a desperate plea for help: *I can't live this way.* She mentions demons and asks if she can be readmitted to the hospital in Pendleton.

July 22, 1997. Rachel did not go back to the hospital. Laurel Hill found her an apartment in Springfield, across the river from Eugene, and her crisis passed. *I go downtown or to the university every few days. It's nice to be back. . . . I still have Julie's flowers here at my doorstep and keep them in the health and beauty they need.* With four malls in the area and multiple coffee shops, she has places to explore.

Spring 1998. A printed notecard with a cartoon shows a cow dressed in a blue dress walking upright across a field, her arms loaded down with a lamp, toaster, and assorted belong-ings. The caption: *I've moo-ved,* with a road sign pointing to Greener Pastures. It's easy to miss the pun, based on just one extra letter, so Rachel points it out. *You get it? Mooved.* The appropriate blanks are filled in with her new address: 269 Brooklyn Street, which was precisely where my mother and I would find her that summer when we went there together.

October 1998. Maybe the visit from Mom and me revived Rachel's desire to be near family: *Could you help me move out to Debby's in Conn? I want to find a place to live there, either with her and family or nearby.* Two paragraphs down, in a pen that looks like it was added later, she changed her mind: *Mom, instead of living at Debby's, I think I need a hospital. I can't live in this real world anymore. I feel weak and upside-down, just hanging there, wallowing, screaming. . . . Help me find my place.* She then mentioned a recent hospitalization (medical, not psychiatric) where she wasn't allowed to smoke. *I'm not so much unhappy as giving up. I can't live like this here anymore. Or anywhere else unless I find my sort of peace and tranquility.* I don't know how Mom responded, but I do know Rachel didn't give up.

January 3, 2000. In Oregon, Rachel's experiences with Native Americans had sparked a belief in their spiritual system. *That's what I believe in,* she once told me during a visit. On psychiatric admission forms she sometimes identified herself as a Protestant or a Baptist, maybe because of the refuge she found at the Salvation Army mission. Now, as part of her evolving spiritual quest, she asks Mom about her beliefs: *Have been thinking of Judaism lately. I'd like to get to Temple again. Like to worship in the old traditions. Part of knowing yourself better. What is prayer to you? What could you tell me about what your older relatives felt about the Jewish faith? What do you know in prayer and its application on life?* Did a sense of mortality from her recent hospital stay (physical not psychiatric) nudge her toward the religion of her birth? It's not surprising her thoughts turned to the man in her life who wrapped his life around its values and its culture: *Remember Dad? He was a good person and I miss him immensely.* As it turned out, Dad would have been so proud of her return to her roots. Only after her death, three years to the month after writing this letter, would I learn the length to which she went to practice her religion.

THE PIPE ORGAN FACTORY

I returned to Eugene three years after I went there with my mother. This time Barry came with me. As sometimes happened when I planned a visit, Rachel sent messages right up to the last minute saying she had changed her mind. "Don't come here. I don't want to see you." Her case manager told me that Rachel was understandably anxious about seeing family. "But come anyway; she'll be here." She seemed confident. And sure enough, when Barry and I drove up the dirt road and parked in front of her house, Rachel came outside and stood on the porch to greet us.

I was startled by the mass of gray and black fur slinking around the porch railing and into the kitchen, still encrusted with dirty dishes and half-empty milk containers. The cats must have birthed several litters since my last visit. What alarmed me more than the feline mass was the acrid, shapeless pile of clothes that now commanded the center of her bedroom. It seemed denser than the mounds of clothing I had seen in her St. Louis apartment when her life first began to fall apart. This pile looked as though someone had upended several cartons of Goodwill boxes to be sorted and washed. When I eventually asked Rachel about doing something to clean up the pile, her eyes narrowed and she shook her head. "It's okay," she muttered. These were treasured belongings. Nothing was to be touched.

Alone with Barry later, I awaited his reaction to Rachel's

living conditions and his professional insights. He was now director of an agency that provided housing for people like Rachel, though few, I knew, were as severely disabled as she was. "We would be shut down by the health department if one of our clients had a place like this," he told me. But he wasn't irate or indignant, like Mom had been. He was sad, like me, and nonjudgmental. I was years past expecting any big changes in her behavior. But at least here in this no-man's land between two cities, she had her own space, pets to care for, and the songs of the birds around her.

On the second day of our visit, Rachel took Barry and me for a walk in her neighborhood. That's when I discovered she lived by the Willamette, the same river Barry and I had walked along behind the motel where we were staying a mile down Franklin Boulevard. During this walk with Rachel, and still very close to her home, we came to a large red building, as big as a warehouse, with a loading dock facing the path. I stopped at the sign that said private property, but Rachel urged me on. "It's okay, it's okay; they let me go here." We followed her and sat quietly on the grass lawn between the riverbank and the big red building.

On our way back from the river, Rachel walked ahead to her house, and a man came out of the building to talk to me and Barry. "Yes, it's fine for Rachel to walk here," he assured us. He told us the building was a pipe organ factory, owned by John Brombaugh, whose instruments, he told us proudly, were played in churches all over the world. It was stunning to discover that a world-renowned organ workshop stood next to bungalows for the chronically mentally ill. This really was a no-man's land of no zoning, I thought. "We're really worried about her," said the pipe organ craftsman, bringing my focus back to the task ahead. "The agency doesn't seem to be taking care of her very well."

His comment was a gut punch to me. I could hardly breathe. When your sister walks around with a face scarred from years of skin infections that she didn't want to cleanse, toothless because psychotropic meds have dried the teeth out of her mouth and she won't wear her dentures, squinting because she won't use her glasses, and coughing because nicotine is the only thing that can counteract the fog of medication in her brain, you tell yourself that you have to accept what can't be changed. But here was someone who seemed to think that something should be done. I wasn't sure what alarmed him about her circumstances. Was it her odor? Her toothless jaw? Had he seen the cats and food and filth spilling from her cabin? Even though I knew his concern was genuine, I didn't have the composure to ask him exactly what deficiencies in her care most alarmed him or what he thought Laurel Hill should be doing better.

"We'll be meeting with the staff this afternoon," I told him. "We'll talk to them about what's happening with Rachel." I didn't want to barrage them with requests and demands. I didn't want to be a pushy advocate for her. I knew from all those years of not being able to help her how hard it was to do anything that would make a difference.

During the meeting I did, however, try to tactfully express some reservations about the care she was receiving. The case worker we met with told me how the agency staff brought her the insulin and psychiatric medication she needed, but she was often away from home, and they couldn't just leave it for her. They set up appointments with doctors, but sometimes she refused to go. They went food shopping with her to make sure she complied with her diabetic diet, and she had made progress in her ability to make the right choices buying food at the store. But if she wanted to use the money from her disability check for tobacco, they couldn't prevent her. Nobody could. I myself sent her money whenever she wrote saying she needed to buy cigarettes.

As for the squalor inside her home, the encrusted kitchen, and the mountain of cast-off shit, they said that was a really tough problem for them to solve. Sometimes, they said, they sent cleaning crews in when she was out of the house. But if she was home, she denied them permission, and they couldn't override her wishes without a legal process that would jeopardize her eligibility for independent housing.

I didn't probe then for deeper answers or demand a higher level of accountability. I was too overcome by a whirlwind of emotions, a mix of shame and fatigue, but mainly of gratitude. I appreciated what Laurel Hill made possible, the home they found her after her problems living in an apartment complex. So what if she piled the clothing she shed into a monument right in the middle of her bedroom? Rachel was smart and gifted. She was stubborn. She needed to live her life as she saw fit.

"Do you need anything?" Barry asked Rachel before we left after our first day visiting her. We had already walked and talked together. I just expected to mark off the time spent with her. He looked for other ways to be useful.

Rachel coughed, nodded, and cleared her throat. "A sleeping bag," she answered.

I was relieved when she declined my offer to come shopping with us. I needed time with Barry to decompress. "We'll bring it tomorrow," I said.

We found a Walmart and a sleeping bag and then went

back to our hotel. We explored the trail behind it, a walking path along the Willamette, which passed university buildings and ended before it got to the bend near the organ factory. The moist air and lush vegetation of the riverbank gave me the oxygen I needed to breathe after being around Rachel. "God, she smokes so much," I said to Barry.

"It's one of the biggest problems with the chronic population," Barry said, using professional shorthand. He wasn't distancing himself; he just wanted me to know Rachel wasn't the only one. "It's hard taking away smoking privileges," he explained. "There's always a big backlash." But he did feel strongly about enforcing a ban at the outpatient center he directed.

I understood the backlash. I couldn't withhold from my sister money for the one pleasure that got her through her day. It wouldn't make a difference anyway. If she couldn't buy them, she would roll them. How many times had I watched her seal and smoke her cigarettes?

We returned the next morning with the shiny blue sleeping bag. Rachel thanked us with quick nods between flicks of her cigarette. I was glad she liked it but didn't quite understand what she planned to do with it. It was futile to ask her directly; she wouldn't answer. Maybe she planned to sleep in her side yard while there was still a little warmth in the night air. I imagined her kicking aside the Coke bottles and food wrappings before unrolling it under the trees. Or maybe she would carry it inside to the back of her bedroom, shove aside the frightening pile of T-shirts, blouses, and elastic-waisted bottoms she hoarded there, and clear an extra sleeping spot for a fellow wanderer.

The following year, the fall of 2002, Barry signed up for a professional conference in Portland. I decided to accompany him. Together we would take a side trip to visit Rachel—I needed his emotional support to go there again. It was the fall of 2002, a little more than a year since our last visit. It was my third visit to Eugene and the last time I would see Rachel.

I had always felt awkward talking about my children with Rachel and usually held back because of the baby boy she claimed to have given up. Many years earlier, in St. Louis, I often brought my first infant daughter to my parents' house, where Rachel would sometimes be visiting on weekend passes. Holding the baby in her arms, she turned her face to me and said, "You know, I have a son." Rachel looked me directly in the eye. Not a glare exactly but the look, unblinking and emphatic, sent unspoken words to me: I'm your older sister, and I had a baby first.

I assumed Rachel's son was a delusion, as no news of him had ever reached me, and never did. Later, as I thought about her statement, I figured it was more than a way to put me in my place. It was also her way of making sense of a new scar across her abdomen.

Some months before I gave birth, Rachel had undergone emergency abdominal surgery. I heard about it from my parents. They were told it was necessary to remove an acute pelvic infection, presumably from STDs. The surgery took place in a municipal hospital that took in indigents. It was during the period when she was released to inner city boarding houses and sometimes ended up in the streets.

To my mind, major surgery seemed like such an extreme treatment—couldn't she have been treated with a D&C and antibiotic drip?—that I suspected Rachel was the victim of involuntary sterilization, a procedure that was sometimes performed on women deemed mentally incompetent. I had a lurking fear that she was a practice case for a third-year intern on ob-gyn rotation. I imagined a resident at City Hospital handing a scalpel to an intern and instructing him on a hysterectomy, or tubal ligation. I was angry when I thought Rachel might have been violated by medical doctors, but pursuing the issue seemed futile. One federal case in the family was enough, and the damage was done.

Rachel mentioned this son to me several times over the years, and I came to understand she believed he had been taken for adoption. As I saw later in her hospital admission documents, she sometimes told intake staff she had a child. It was hard to know what to believe from her medical records. The information Rachel provided even about herself had wild variations. Sometimes she called herself Steve. Sometimes she was Protestant. Sometimes she had a son.

I feared that talking about my daughters, their talents and careers, their lives and loves, would bring her pangs of remorse for the son she believed she lost, for children she couldn't have. Then too, she never saw my girls again after that visit twenty-three years earlier when she came to stay with us before the family meeting with Peggy Papp. I never let myself think about Rachel's involuntary isolation from family—even though, unlike sterilization, it was something I could have done something about.

Over the years Rachel frequently asked after my children in her letters. I wrote her about them, but when I visited, the subject of children became too painful to discuss. Still, I always tried to overcome the feelings that choked my words and keep her reasonably up to date.

Visiting her that last time in Eugene, I managed to share some good news. I told her my younger daughter was engaged to be married. We were sitting in chairs on the slab outside her house watching her cats play. Rachel's face lit up and she asked, her voice high with excitement, "Can I go to the wedding?" I was stunned. I had never heard her respond so quickly, and with such vulnerability. Her words seemed to pierce right through her usual armor of sulky distance.

I should have anticipated her request, but I didn't. I had never even discussed the possibility with my family. I couldn't even begin to think about it. It would be so much more complicated than bringing her out to Dad's funeral, a somber and small gathering. This was a joyful celebration, and I already had more arrangements than I could handle. Rachel was twenty years older now; she looked more frightening. How could I bring her across the country to a gathering of more than a hundred friends and family members?

"I don't know. It's going to be in Brooklyn. Let me see . . ." I said, my voice trailing off. I felt nauseous looking at her kittens tumbling over the front step.

"It's okay. Never mind." Rachel knew I meant no. She regained her reserve and dignity.

I felt horrible. Rachel had once stood next to me as my maid of honor, in those first years of her illness. And now I couldn't invite her to her niece's wedding.

As it turned out Rachel died a year before the wedding took place. She never would have made it there. But I know how happy she would have been to be invited. It was only after her death that I learned how motivated she could be when she wanted to be included.

Out in the Hills Is a Treasured Spot

out in the hills is a
treasured spot, that only you
and I can find. I took a walk
there the other day and found it
glistening well as usual.

a long road and another, and
then the enjoyment of it.
walk and walk and you'll get
there too; see the animals
and plants along the way,
hear a wolf howl to the
north, and you see you have it made.

so instead of working yourself to
death, just lean back and dream;
dream of a day in the country;
cause babe you ain't at home anymore.

—Rachel Goodman

PART VI

Rachel at Rest

NOW I COULD MOURN

The oystermen used ice breaking boats to keep the channel open in Norwalk Harbor that January. There hadn't been a freeze like this one for years. Despite the bitter cold, life went on as usual. Barry and I did our twenty-mile commutes, in opposite directions, on I-95, where road salt and the heat of traffic kept the highway clear. It was just the two of us coming home now. Our adult daughters lived on their own. There were no grandchildren yet and our house, an empty nest, had settled into stillness.

The phone rang while I was reading the newspaper. I searched for the handset and managed to find it, before the ringing stopped, under a discarded section at the other end of the couch. I expected to hear from one of my daughters in Brooklyn. But it wasn't either of them. It was my sister, Julie, who now lived in Boulder.

"I have sad news," she said. I folded the paper and laid it on the couch.

I thought something had happened to Mom, who was staying with Julie for a week. She was at Julie's on one of her quarterly visits to see the eight-year-old twins. Perhaps Mom was sick and had been taken to the hospital. Or maybe she'd had another blowout fight with Julie's husband and had dashed off to the airport in a huff vowing never to return. But no, it wasn't about Mom.

"Rachel died," Julie said. "They think it was pneumonia." I felt a clanging inside me. Like metal doors swinging in and out in the wind.

Twenty years earlier it was Julie who had called to tell me Dad had dropped dead on the kitchen floor. This time, I didn't fend off disaster with the reflexive words of denial I'd used then—"You're kidding." I gasped. I shuddered. Breathing slowly, I felt decades of worry slide off my back. But I didn't sink to the floor keening. I was able to let the news sink in.

Shocked as I was, I instantly remembered the groan and rattle of Rachel's cough two months earlier when I visited her. I could almost visualize then how the cigarettes were hollowing out her lungs. I'd felt a jolt every time her ominous cough exploded through her chest.

"She died in her sleep," Julie added. That was something to be grateful for. She didn't die in a psychiatric ward, or alone in the streets. She died in her own home, her bungalow in the woods.

So this is it, I thought to myself. This is the end. She had her freedom. She had her cigarettes, for better or worse.

It was January 20, 2003, just three months before Rachel's sixtieth birthday. I was well aware that mental illness takes at least ten years off an afflicted person's life span and quickly calculated that it took another ten years from Rachel's. The tragic shortfall resulted from many causes, including physical, emotional, and societal. As every admission form in her revolving-door hospital career noted, "Rachel is unable to care for herself." Who could?

"How's Mom?" I asked.

"She's quiet," Julie answered. "She was the one who opened the door to the policewoman." The Eugene police had called Boulder to send an officer out to break the news in person. "She seems sad in a subdued sort of way. You know Mom." I did. I knew how Mom didn't like to let down her guard. I knew she was always a street kid at heart. But still, her armor had plenty of gaps, and I was grateful that she wasn't alone in her St. Louis house when she heard the news that her firstborn, her beautiful, talented, difficult daughter, had died. I knew how awful and confused Mom felt that she had been unable to help Rachel. I also knew how hard it was for her to deal with those feelings.

"Let me talk to her," I said. Then I heard Mom's voice, the forlorn sound of a helpless child. She recounted everything Julie had just told me, but all I could hear was a wordless plea not to be blamed for something she didn't cause and couldn't understand. Hearing the pathos in that voice, I wanted my bossy, take-charge mother back.

Julie's twins were making noise in the background, and Mom was glad to go attend to them. She put Julie back on the phone before I could say goodbye to her. Julie and I talked about funeral arrangements, and she suggested a memorial service in the spring, when we could all meet in Boulder and scatter ashes from the mountains.

"But she never even visited the Rockies," I objected. I couldn't quite articulate the deeper reason—that I shuddered at the very thought of cremation. The sudden change of state, from solid to gas in just a few minutes, was too drastic, too terrifying to me. What's more, I didn't believe that fire could set Rachel's spirit free.

Rachel's mind, through endless rounds of sorrow and futile therapies, had taken decades to decay. But her body, scarred and abused as it was, had stayed strong until the end. Why not keep her body intact for a while? Why not transport what was left of her, bury her in the St. Louis cemetery near her father and grandmother? Why not say prayers there that honored her existence? Maybe then her life and death would make a little sense.

Julie seemed to understand what I couldn't put in words. "That's just what I would do, but if you and Mom and Michael all want a burial, it's okay with me."

"Let's think about it. Then I'll make the arrangements. You've got the kids and Mom to deal with," I said.

I had lost the older sister I knew as a child, but I had never mourned her. I had never said goodbye to my older sister, who loved to travel and write, who made music and art, who talked to me about poets and philosophers. I couldn't mourn her because she was still alive.

The losses my sister endured were continuous, cumulative. All those years I had stood by helplessly as illness stole her away. I shuddered at the acrid smell of fear and neglect that dogged her endless pacing. I winced to see her squinting because she wouldn't wear her glasses or gumming her food because she wouldn't wear her dentures. I trembled when she came to me in dreams, reciting her anguished poetry.

To mourn the sister I knew as a child I would have had to give up all hope. I would have had to disown the part of her that was left. As diminished as she became, Rachel never forgot who she was, who she had been. How could I?

I couldn't mourn her and I couldn't comfort her. It was easy to send the books and clothing she wanted, but it took all the courage I could muster to visit her. I didn't know how to talk to her about what happened, so I depended on small talk. I felt like a traitor if I acknowledged her mental illness or asked her about her years in the hospital. When I was with her, words froze in my throat. Or tinkled like ice filled with air bubbles. When I sat face to face with her, I struggled to share news of my life, so far away from hers.

What could I ever say to Rachel from my heart? It seemed cruel to tell her about my children and husband, even my career. It seemed even crueler to tell her how much I missed the older sister she had been, the sister she could never be again.

Now, everything had changed. At last I could help, and at last I could mourn.

When the county medical examiner returned my call, he told me the circumstances of Rachel's death based on the police report and his physical examination. A man had flagged down the police on the main road in the middle of the night, he told me. "We figured he was homeless. He said he was frantic to get help. We interviewed him and let him go. There was no foul play. We made sure of that. He said he had been in Rachel's bed when she stopped breathing. He said he was her boyfriend." The examiner's voice sounded gentle and calm.

My own breath was tight as I waited for the official to continue. I felt a flash of embarrassment that a homeless man was with my sister during that intimate moment of death. Shouldn't one of us, her family, have been with her? But in an instant, I let my shoulders drop and my breathing resume. This wasn't one of the men who raped her, who traded wine or shelter or cigarettes for sex. "I have a boyfriend," she had said when I visited her two months earlier. She wouldn't tell me anymore, but I knew enough about him now. The frantic man who ran out to Franklin Boulevard to find help had been intimate with Rachel in life, as well as death. She hadn't been alone. She hadn't been with a stranger.

"There were no signs of foul play," the medical examiner repeated. "The police questioned the man and released him. I examined her body and found no signs of struggle." I figured he meant there would be no criminal investigation. The thought of one hadn't even occurred to me. I had no inclination to lay blame. I pictured my sister expiring peacefully in her sleep underneath a faded blanket, pilled and green, though later when I got the full, written report, I saw a different picture. And I realize now that the boyfriend, had he been fully competent, would have called an ambulance when he saw her writhing on the floor.

At the time, though, I felt only relief that the boyfriend was with her. The county official gave me just the information I needed and promised to send me the full report when he completed it. He told me what funeral home to contact. I put down the handset and picked up my coffee mug, pebbly gray with a blue circle around it, one of the squat, wide-mouthed Dansk set I found in perfect shape at a neighbor's tag sale. I leaned my head back to swallow the last half-ounce of black coffee. I looked at the few soggy grounds huddled at the bottom. I had gotten through this conversation, and it wasn't as hard as I expected. I didn't have to explain anything about Rachel. I didn't have to make excuses for her lifestyle. I had spent my entire adult life haunted by forebodings of rejection and ridicule washing against Rachel, splashing against me. How could I help but feel that Rachel's life was a stain on my decency? She couldn't help herself, she didn't choose to lose her sanity, but I agreed to leave her in Oregon. No, the medical examiner didn't care about any of that. He talked to family survivors all the time. He knew they had stories, but he didn't need to hear them. His voice told me there was no need for shame.

All of the conversations—with my mother and my siblings, with the social worker, with the medical examiner—swirled in my head as I went to bed that night. Barry held me, comforted me, and took in my pain. "You visited Rachel before she died. That meant a lot to her," he whispered. "It'll be okay." His breath in my ear made more than words; his presence made sense of the pain. Five years earlier, Barry had lost his older brother, a brilliant, troubled man who, like Rachel, couldn't help creating havoc for his family. Barry's arms contained the heaves of my chest. They reeled me back to love, and everything we shared.

I woke up refreshed, knowing what I had to do next. I needed to bury Rachel in St. Louis. I obtained a plot in the Jewish cemetery near our father and grandmother. Mom and Julie and Michael agreed to the arrangements. We had gone through so much agonized second-guessing about Rachel's life. By comparison, this decision was easy.

The graveside service took place a few days later on a day so cold that a shelter with a heater had been erected for the family gathered outside. I warmed myself under the canvas for a while, then walked over to the hill of freshly dug soil. A ceremonial shovel stood upright in the dirt, filled with filaments of roots and invisible microbes that clung to them. I breathed in the soil's velvet smell and listened to the silence of its pebbles, paused in their tumbles through the ground.

Somehow that dark earth, so self-organized, so quiet, and as patient as skin, consoled me. When the prayers were over, I caught my breath and scooped up a handful of the dirt. It slid under my fingernails and stuck in the folds of my palm. I brought the dirt to one cheek and pressed it there, salting it with my tears. Finally I reached for the shovel and dug out a clump of earth that yielded to the cold metal blade, then burst apart as I tossed it on the bright, polished wood below. Looking down into the darkness, I whispered the one thing I had to say, "Goodbye Rachel, I love you." I passed the shovel to Julie. And with that I felt free—free like Rachel—to go on with my life and to shed that sense of guilt that kept shadowing me.

PRAYERS

He will cover you with his feathers, and under his wings you
will find refuge; his faithfulness will be your shield and
rampart. You will not fear.

I saw floating feathers illustrating the words from Psalm 91:4,
but I didn't pause to read them. The loopy font and stock
artwork looked so cheesy to me that the card's spiritual sen-
timents flew right over my head, carried off by the angel
wings. I knew from the return address that the card was from
Laurel Hill, the agency that provided housing, medication,
and counseling for Rachel.

I was back home in Norwalk following the funeral in St.
Louis almost two weeks earlier. My throat felt scratchy. I
hoped I hadn't caught a bug on the airplane trip home. I
needed to clear my head now. After the funeral, Mom had
surrounded herself with her friends from the Methodist con-
gregation who had welcomed a little Jewish lady to sing with
them and play piano during their services. They sat in our
living room, read Rachel's poetry, and looked at photos of her
when she was beautiful. They knew nothing of Rachel's illness
and they listened raptly when my mother told them her story
of her eldest daughter. "She went to Israel and contracted
meningitis. She became brain damaged and never recovered."

My mother never used the word "schizophrenia," and the self-control I had to muster to let her live with her version of Rachel's story exhausted me.

I took the card to the living room sofa, pulled my feet up, leaned into the corner of the armrest, and began to read. Written on the inside of the card were eight personal notes with signatures in as many shades of blue and black ink. I was too tired to make out the handwriting just then. I put the card back in the envelope, extracted myself from the sofa, and threw away the junk mail. I took the bills and the Laurel Hill card upstairs to my desk and started to read again.

"Rachel touched so many lives," one said. I rolled the wheeled chair back and forth. She was "special," another said, "memorable," "admirable and independent." She was "appreciative of small favors and returned some of the joy of being alive." Did Rachel have friends at Laurel Hill? Friends who actually thought these things? Maybe they were staff members, whose job it was to say the right things at such a time. I had seen how aloof Rachel was when I had met her at the agency. How she headed for the kitchenette to mix instant coffee and had turned to leave before the black liquid even stopped sloshing in the cup. "Let's stay here for a few minutes to visit," I said to her then, motioning to the chairs in the room where people walked through now and again. She shook her head. We had to go right away.

"Of course people at Laurel Hill got to know Rachel," Barry said when I showed him the condolence card. As director of an outpatient center, my husband had acquired a freestanding building for clients who lived with chronic mental illness. It was a social club where they could meet, make meals, and eat together. "You don't know how she was with them when you weren't there with her." My husband believed in people. Given enough time and the staff, he trusted that people who were hospitalized could rejoin communities. Barry doused my skepticism with pools of conviction, making it easier for me to resume my grieving. Okay, yes. The people who knew Rachel at Laurel Hill were important to her, and she to them.

Steve Williamson, the mental health worker who got Rachel out of the hospital system for good, had left Laurel Hill years earlier. His name wasn't on the condolence card I now held in my hands, with the ninety-first psalm and the feathers and angel wings. But I felt his legacy all over it. *He will cover you with his feathers . . . you will find refuge.* It was Steve who first covered for Rachel. He made sure she always had a home. He made sure that the people whose job it was to help her understood she was someone worthy of respect.

When I saw Steve's name on the e-mail he sent to his former colleagues, I couldn't help thinking about my meeting with him and Rachel at the diner on Franklin Boulevard by that no-man's land between Eugene and Springfield. How eagerly Steve had pulled Rachel's booklet of poems from his backpack to give to me. What lengths he had gone to in sponsoring her and sharing her work.

Within a week of Rachel's death, Laurel Hill held a memorial service. I wished I could go, but with our own family gathering in St. Louis having taken place so recently, a trip to Oregon seemed impractical. Still, it would have been gratifying to speak with more of the people who knew her in Eugene.

A few weeks after the e-mail chain and Laurel Hill condolence note, I received another card from Eugene in a smaller, crisper envelope. This time I didn't recognize the return address, or the name engraved on the outside of the card: Elaine Barrer. My fingers tightened on the paper as I read her words: "I attended services with your sister the week before she died."

IT TAKES A MINYAN

I suspect Rachel walked to synagogue that first time. It was a good three miles away from her home, not too daunting a walk for her if it wasn't raining. Her legs were strong, and besides, she didn't have to be hassled by bus drivers. "Sometimes they won't let me on the bus," she had once told me. She seemed only mildly aggrieved at the injustice of her situation. Resigned.

She probably just grabbed a shirt and sweatpants from the sweaty and soiled clothing marinating in a hill by her bed. She wouldn't have noticed the smell of stale urine clinging to them. She would have just put them on—in a fog, in a funk. Was her lack of hygiene a "fuck you" to society? To the world that rejected her? Maybe. But sometimes I think her brain just didn't register the acrid smells that so offended people, that her olfactory center, like so much of her brain, just failed to compute that input.

I can picture her outside, on her way to the synagogue, her shoulders broad and square as she shut the front door without bothering to lock it. How she left food for her cats and dropped some cigarettes in her bag. How she walked along the bus route, found the building, and fixed her eyes ahead of her as she approached the front door and a woman stepped forward to greet her. "Welcome to Temple Beth Israel. Have you been here before?" Rachel would have walked straight on by. She didn't like to answer questions; she interpreted them as threats. Paranoia. Yes, she had plenty of that. But maybe she was too self-conscious to answer, despite all those years of flagrant apathy toward her body when she didn't seem to care that her jaw had sunk in against her gums because she stopped wearing dentures, that she had to squint to see because she discarded her eyeglasses. She just flicked things like that away, like tobacco flakes on her fingers.

Inside the building, Rachel would have quickly found her way to the women's service. She may have accepted guidance from an usher, or she may have just followed the strains of chatter and chanting that drifted into the hallways from the small meeting room where ten women were gathered for their service.

When Elaine agreed to speak with me, she said she had only a few minutes to talk. But I had many questions, and she had vivid memories to share. As it turned out we were still deep in conversation after forty-five minutes.

"When she came in, I thought she was a homeless person who just wanted a place to rest," Elaine told me. "With her blonde hair and blue eyes, I wouldn't have known she was Jewish." (Blonde hair? Not really. It was gray hair that had yellowed from lack of care.) But Rachel's actions convinced Elaine otherwise. "I knew she was Jewish as soon as I saw her mouthing the Hebrew prayer," she said.

I could hear Elaine taking an extra breath before continuing. "You know your sister didn't smell good. And the women's minyan, our little group, met in a very small classroom. So her odor was a problem. Yona, one of the leaders, asked her if she wouldn't mind joining the main service instead of the women's minyan. Rachel would be okay in a larger room. The odor wouldn't be so bad."

What a tactful solution to a delicate predicament, I thought. Air and space would dilute her smell. By inviting her to a service in a larger room, these women had found a work-around. They didn't have to offend her by telling her she would have to shower and shampoo.

Elaine told me she didn't really expect Rachel would come back the next week. But she did. Though not to the larger sanctuary they had suggested. "Rachel left after Yona talked to her. But she came back the next week. All washed. Hair clean and combed. Wearing a dress." She rejoined the small women's group. She understood what she needed to do to join them.

I wish I could have been there on the bus with her when she returned to the synagogue, showered and shampooed. Seen how she briskly showed her pass to the driver. Took her seat without incident. I wish I could have seen her as she walked into the small, cozy classroom, blue eyes blazing, to claim her rightful place among the women of Temple Beth Israel.

I've never been able to understand why Rachel opposed personal hygiene so vehemently during most of her adult life. In the hospital records I obtained long after her death, I learned cleanliness was often the primary object of her reha-bilitation plan. She was hard to persuade. Once, when a nurse handed her shampoo and soap in the shower, Rachel rebuffed her, saying, "Water is just fine." Another time, upon hospital readmission after time spent with transients down by the river, she herself reported that she had been kicked out of the tent because of her smell. Why, I kept wondering, was she so stubborn? Why did she refuse to wash herself?

But now, here in Eugene, she was ready to bend. As Steve Williamson told me, she had mellowed; he believed she came to understand that what she had in Eugene was as good as it was going to get. In addition to the help she could take or leave, she was free to make choices about where she wanted to go. She chose to comply with Yona's request.

It couldn't have been easy for her. I think about all the courage it took for Rachel to shower, dress neatly, and return to the synagogue. She had to trust that when she got there, she would be admitted into the private prayer room. Trust! What a leap that took. That was even harder for her than cleanliness. But she found a way to cross the moat separating her from a frightening world.

Finally Elaine said something that amazed me. "After Rachel arrived, Yona invited her to perform an aliyah, to lead the prayer before the Torah portion. I never heard your sister talk until then," Elaine told me. I heard a note of wonder in her voice. "The women's minyan was the right group for Rachel. She must have sensed our sympathy." Sympathy? At the other end of the phone line, almost three thousand miles away, I winced. Rachel had always seemed to me too proud to accept sympathy, and I had never found a way to express mine. But somehow the women in the minyan did. All it took was a simple gesture of inclusion. Yes, the women's minyan had been the right group for Rachel.

On that January day, hair soft and fragrant, her dress intact and unspotted, my sister got up from her metal folding chair when the Torah was opened. She walked to the front of the small makeshift prayer room. She had put aside her fear and cleansed herself. She accepted the honor they extended and joined the women's community.

Rachel, the loner, let down her guard. In the Oregon valley, where winter is mild and earth doesn't freeze, she accepted the warmth of these women. Rachel listened. She responded. She dug deep into her past to revive a taproot to sustain her.

I wish I could have been there to see her reciting the prayer at the bimah in the front of the room. I wish I could have heard the ancient syllables rising and falling in well-worn rhythms through her throat, her tongue, her lips. How she stood at the lectern wrapped in dignity and remembrance.

Sometimes I yearn to see my sister whole again. I don't mean childhood images from old photos and ingrained memories. I want to see the finished Rachel, complete in herself, grown into her sixth decade. Then I remember my conversation with Elaine. I close my eyes and imagine Rachel rising to be honored by the women of the synagogue. Seeing her there, I feel as though she never left me. We've been separated by thousands of miles and by the paths we followed on our life journeys. We've been separated by illness and by death. And yet, despite everything, we will always be sisters.

In Delicate Aroma

In delicate aroma
I walked the beach at night
Where the moon
Joined sand into sea
And the waves rolled back the world.

Here shattered night
Makes clean each grain it meets
Where yesterday
A sand-crab walked
And found its mate for safety.

Roll back the world
For so I have been free
With a crab
And the sea
And my shadow on the moonlit beach.

—Rachel Goodman

EPILOGUE

In the Jewish tradition, we say, "May her memory be for a blessing." The memory of Rachel is just that. She gave me what I needed to finish her story. Not forgiveness—I can't ask her for that—but her blessing. Forgiveness, like my story, had to come from me.

This writing journey has taken me through forgotten layers of time, space, and memory. And it has brought me to where I wanted to be. Knowing Rachel never blamed me, I found a way to forgive myself for being largely absent during Rachel's adult years—and to thank her for breathing life into my words.

Rachel's poems, stapled into well-worn booklets, now sit on a bookshelf next to my office window. The three-ring binder with the mottled blue cover holds typed pages—a journal of memories, and of stories about characters struggling to make sense of their lives. I try to see Rachel's tapered fingers picking up these flat, crisp pages, interrupting their blank white stares with the dips and rises of her pen and pencil. I listen for the creak of the typewriter platen as she pulls out another fresh page. Lined and unlined, punched and bound, these papers have soaked up her soul and her life, resisting judgment, assuaging pain. They are leaves that have endured for fifteen, thirty, fifty years. Sometimes I forget where I left them and then I panic. I can't let them fly away.

Rachel is buried next to her father and maternal grandmother in a St. Louis cemetery. On her headstone is an engraving: a hand holding an old-fashioned feather pen. Mom and I picked out the design together because we wanted to honor Rachel's expressive talent. Her words, her music, her art never flourished the way they would have had she not been felled by mental illness. But I am glad she left us what she was able to complete, the poems and letters that speak to both desolation and dreams. And while I regret not being more available to her, I am glad she shared so much of herself with me.

Rachel never gave up on life; she lived it with a passion that inspired me.

I began this journey feeling she wanted to pass her pen to me. I finished it grateful for the courage she gave me to write this story, the story of Rachel, my family, and me.

ACKNOWLEDGMENTS

Two mentors made it possible for me to write this book. Christine Pakkala at the Westport Writers' Workshop gave me tools to "dig deeper" and persuaded me to make Rachel's story my writing priority. When my emotions about the past became painful and confusing, Stephanie Carrow helped me sort them out in therapy. Her warmth and wisdom sustained me.

I'm grateful for the support of my surviving siblings. Julie Post deepened my understanding of our family dynamics, corrected dates and details—and most importantly, enthusiastically encouraged me. My brother gave me his blessings. Rachel's dear friend and mine, Judith Leff, revived her memories of Rachel as a young adult, as did Holit Bat-Edit and Rosalyn Boxer, who knew her in Israel and New York City. Steve Williamson answered all my questions about Rachel's life in Eugene with his characteristic generosity.

Writing pals at many stages of this project provided welcome fellowship and valuable feedback. Among them: Jen Sage-Robison, Francis Doherty, Katherine Ryden, Lesley Téllez, Gabriela Kruschewsky, B.L Crook, Alfred G. Vanderbilt, Rebecca Martin and Holly Mensching. I am thankful for the input and encouragement of family and friends who read and improved my manuscript, including Barbara Schutt, Jane Lerner, Sharon Cohen, Susan Boyar and Susan Epstein.

I was incredibly lucky to have an accomplished editor as a dear friend. Beth Rashbaum pruned and shaped my first rough manuscript, and gave me confidence to send it out to the world, including to Linda Dyett, who published a version of my Pendleton chapter in NYCWoman.com

From the dedicated parents at NAMI Southwest Connecticut, I learned firsthand how families today can be helped to cope with serious mental health issues. I applaud and support NAMI's advocacy for housing and community services. From Jenny Logan's course at Brooklyn Institute for Social Research I learned why those who have experienced overmedication and unnecessary hospitalization advocate for autonomy, inclusion and civil rights. Rachel would want to be counted among them.

My gratitude to my family has no bounds. My husband's love is in every breath I take and his understanding of life's challenges in every word I write. His achievements in the field of community mental health have filled me with pride and given me hope that solutions to our mental health crisis are possible. I cherish the miracle of our years together. Our grandchildren have been a source of unending delight. Marlayna Kasdan grew up watching me write this book—and keeping tabs on my progress. The Kasdan-Grollo siblings—Quinn, Benjamin, and Dahlia—shared their passions: from baseball and hockey to environmental stewardship to graphic novels and novel haircuts. As I delved into the past, they showed me the future. May they always—to echo the words of Eleanor Roosevelt—believe in the beauty of their dreams.

ABOUT THE AUTHOR

Deborah Kasdan had a thirty-five-year career writing about business and technology before retiring and joining Westport Writers' Workshop to make her personal stories come alive. She has served on the board of directors of an intergenerational housing organization and the National Organization on Mental Illness (NAMI)for Southwest CT. She is a passionate swimmer and yoga practitioner, and a grandmother of four. During the summer she and her husband vacation near the great Nauset Marsh of Cape Cod and live the rest of the year in Norwalk, Connecticut. She is currently writing a novel based on her mother's stories about growing up in 1930s Chicago.

She Writes Press is an independent publishing company
founded to serve women writers everywhere.
Visit us at www.shewritespress.com.

The S Word by Paolina Milana. $16.95, 978-1-63152-927-6. An insider's account of growing up with a schizophrenic mother, and the disastrous toll the illness—and her Sicilian Catholic family's code of secrecy—takes upon her young life.

Committed: A Memoir of Madness in The Family by Paolina Milana. $16.95, 978-1-64742-042-0. After more than a decade of keeping her mother's mental illness a secret from the outside world, Paolina Milana longs for freedom from the madness of her home—but when her father suddenly dies, she becomes the sole caregiver for her unstable mother and sister, shattering her hope for escape.

Edna's Gift: How My Broken Sister Taught Me to Be Whole by Susan Rudnick. $16.95, 978-1-63152-515-5. When they were young, Susan and Edna, children of Holocaust refugee parents, were inseparable. But as they grew up and Edna's physical and mental challenges altered the ways she could develop, a gulf formed between them. Here, Rudnick shares how her maddening—yet endearing—sister became her greatest life teacher.

Newcomers in an Ancient Land: Adventures, Love, and Seeking Myself in 1960s Israel by Paula Wagner. $16.95, 978-1-63152-529-2. After leaving home at eighteen in search of her Jewish roots in Israel and France, Paula learns far more than two new languages. To navigate her new life, she must also separate from her twin sister and forge her own identity.

Jumping Over Shadows: A Memoir by Annette Gendler. $16.95, 978-1-63152-170-6. Like her great-aunt Resi, Annette Gendler, a German, fell in love with a Jewish man—but unlike her aunt, whose marriage was destroyed by "the Nazi times," Gendler found a way to make her impossible love survive.